PROFESSIONAL CHILD AND YOUTH CARE

DATE

PROFESSIONAL
CHILD AND YOUTH CARE

The Canadian Perspective

edited by Carey Denholm, Roy Ferguson,
and Alan Pence

UNIVERSITY OF BRITISH COLUMBIA PRESS
VANCOUVER 1987

PROFESSIONAL CHILD AND YOUTH CARE
The Canadian Perspective

© The University of British Columbia Press 1987

Canadian Cataloguing in Publication Data

Main entry under title:

Professional child and youth care

   Includes bibliographical references.

   ISBN 0-7748-0244-8 (PBK)
   ISBN 0-7748-0273-1 (Bound)

   1. Child care - Canada.   2. Child care services
- Canada.   I. Denholm, Carey J., 1951-. II.
Ferguson, Roy, 1942-.   III. Pence, Alan R., 1948-
HV861.C2P73 1987   362.7'12'0971   C86-091598-0

Printed in Canada

ISBN 0-7748-0244-8 (PBK)
ISBN 0-7748-0273-1 (Bound)

To our children,
Justin, Andrea, Alexander, Leah
and Eliot.

Contents

Contributors

Preface

In this book, the first of its kind, the contributors illustrate the broad scope of child care in Canada and note some of the similarities, differences, and critical issues within selected practice areas. Child care is portrayed as an extensive concept and a diverse field. Where child care was once primarily defined within the context of residential care or day care, it is now being seen in Canada from a wider perspective, as will be outlined in the subsequent chapters. However broad child care service might now be, it is the essence of child and youth care practice, with its unique blend of caring and professionalism, that binds it together.

We also identify some of the key persons and programs upon which an expanded child care service network is built. In acknowledging the history of the child care field, as well as its current state, it is our intention for the text to serve as a transition to the future. The future embodies change which can, in turn, be viewed as creating either threat or opportunity. It is hoped that this text will be useful in facilitating adaptation within the field, so that the future of child care across this country will continue to be filled with opportunity.

This book represents the joint efforts of many contributors; we believe this is one of its greatest assets. We have thoroughly enjoyed the collaboration with our colleagues from across the country in producing this book and we would like to offer it as a tribute to the Canadian child and youth care field.

Roy Ferguson
Carey Denholm
Alan Pence

Acknowledgements

The editors wish to acknowledge the dedication of those child and youth care workers within these many areas of child care practice who have labored for years with high commitment and low social and financial reward in order that the children and youth in their care would have a brighter and stronger future. Without them we would be a less caring society and without them the foundation stones of the child care profession, upon which this book is based, would not have developed. We would also acknowledge the insights and strengths of those families and children who have participated with child care workers in defining the roles and responsibilities of professional child and youth care work. Finally, we would like to acknowledge the support and participation of the editorial board members who shared their expertise and enthusiasm for the energies of the child care profession to make this book possible.

1

An Overview of the Scope of Child Care in Canada

ROY FERGUSON, CAREY DENHOLM AND ALAN PENCE

INTRODUCTION TO THE TEXT

It was with an odd mixture of excitement and consternation that, two years ago, we began working on this book. On one hand we felt, particularly from our perspective as educators, that the child care field desperately needed a text.[1] On the other hand, we were faced with a number of difficult issues. Foremost among these was whether the text should reflect a North American or a Canadian view of child care. After considerable discussion, we decided to adopt a Canadian perspective in the book. This was a hard decision to make, because it could be interpreted as a form of isolationism by our colleagues south of the 49th parallel, at a time when we were actively developing closer child care links between Canada and the United States. Obviously, there were also significant concerns about the potential market for the book once it was published. We felt, however, that the scope of the child care field in Canada was somewhat different from the U.S., and that it was vitally important to capture the unique Canadian perspective. Fortunately, in subsequent discussions with our American colleagues, we were strongly supported and encouraged in the directions that we had taken. In fact, the first and last chapters of this text contain material which first appeared in an article by Ferguson and Anglin (1985) in *Child Care Quarterly*. Now that the Canadian perspective has been addressed in the present volume, we have already begun work on a second text on professional child care which will include contributions by authors throughout North America.

The next major planning issue to be confronted was that of representing the broad scope of child care functions and settings across Canada.

This was a harder problem to solve since, within the confines of one text, it was not possible to include chapters on all of the elements which constitute the child care mosaic in Canada. Consequently, we have included chapters on the following eight areas within the child care field: residential child care, the juvenile justice system, school-based child care, child life (medical settings), day care, early intervention programs, community-based child care, and parent education/support programs. These particular areas were selected to represent points along the child care service continuum because they illustrated the diversity of child care practice and were essential from a developmental or an historical perspective. Obviously, there are many other programs and settings, such as rehabilitation or recreation programs, for example, which could have been outlined. However, the intention of the text was not to present an exhaustive description of the entire child care field but to illustrate that, in spite of the tremendous diversity of functions and settings, the similarities across these areas were greater than the differences.

Another major issue in the planning of this text was that of achieving a geographical representation of authors from across Canada. In order to illustrate the extent of the Canadian child care network, authors and editorial board members were selected on the basis of both interest area and geographical location. Clearly, there are countless others who could have been included, but the resulting group represents many of the key figures in the child care field across Canada.

Of course, when compiling a text of invited chapters, it is hard to maintain continuity among the contributions of authors with different perspectives, experiences, and writing styles. One solution to this problem would have been to devise an extensive format for the authors to follow in writing their chapters. We decided against this option, however, because we felt that it might be too restricting and might, in fact, create more problems than it solved. We felt that the differences could be considered a strength as well as a weakness; if there really were common elements across the broad field of child care, the reader would recognize them in spite of this diversity. We hoped, also, that the lack of homogeneity across chapters will reflect the color and vitality existing within the child care field.

The last major planning problem we encountered was identifying the target audience for the text. Since this would be the first text of its type in the field, it was difficult to avoid the tendency to adopt a "shotgun" approach to the market. We decided on the generalist perspective and hoped that the material would be of interest to child care practitioners, university and college students, and members of allied professions such as psychology, social work, education, and nursing. There is always a danger in pitching a book at too broad a target audience, but we felt this decision was somewhat justified—our intention was to present an overview of the child care field rather than going into great depth in any of the areas.

Having outlined some of the formative decisions in the planning of the text, let us first turn our attention to the current state of the field and some of the forces which are impinging upon it. This will be followed by an outline of the scope of professional child care. The introductory chapter will conclude with an examination of the essence of child care practice which, it is suggested, is the mortar that holds the mosaic of the field together.

THE CURRENT STATUS OF THE FIELD

The delivery of child care services to children, to youth and their families throughout Canada is the result of an evolution that has been shaped by a combination of political, economic, historic, and social factors. Professional child care in this country has moved away from being defined essentially within the context of the two primary historical streams of residential child care and day care toward a broad scope of interrelated but clearly identifiable areas of practice. Child care professionals function in a variety of settings which, together, constitute a wide continuum of services to children, youth and families across Canada.

There are a number of factors within contemporary society which have had a direct influence upon the evolution of professional child care: the normalization principle, mainstreaming, the movement away from a psychopathological orientation, an emphasis on prevention and early intervention, and an emphasis on program accountability.

The emphasis on the normalization principle (Wolfensberger, 1972) emerged in human service delivery mechanisms during the early 1970s. Simply stated, the principle advocates that developmentally handicapped persons should experience conditions of everyday life which are as close as possible to the norms and patterns of the mainstream of society. This ideological position has had a significant impact upon treatment philosophies and standards of care within the human services. One of the more obvious effects of the normalization principle was the movement away from institutional care whenever possible. There was a reluctance on the part of governments to build new institutions; in fact, many existing ones were closed down and the residents returned to their local communities where alternate systems of care delivery were developed.

The effects of normalization were also felt within the education system. Mainstreaming, or integrating special needs children in regular community schools, began as an educational philosophy and continued to gain strength until it became a legislated position in many parts of the country. As more developmentally handicapped children moved out of special classes and into the regular school system, the need for professionals in the schools to attend to the non-educational needs of these children became increasingly evident.

Another philosophical shift within the delivery of human services has been the movement away from a psychopathological orientation. In programs for children, youth and families, more emphasis is being placed upon the promotion of competence with a focus on normal growth and development.

Early intervention and prevention is another force which has shaped professional child care. Service agencies are now attempting to identify children and families with special needs and provide them with a program at the earliest possible point. The emergence of infant development programs in various provinces is a good example of the focus on early intervention/prevention. These programs are usually structured so that the provision of care is done by an interdisciplinary team working directly with the child and family in their own natural environment. Similarly, resources are being built into existing service structures such as hospitals, schools, and day care systems aimed at prevention. Although the effectiveness of prevention programs is difficult to evaluate, governments seem more assured that prevention should be a priority within the human services.

The last major societal influence on professional child care is the current tightening economy and the resultant emphasis on program accountability on a cost-effective basis. As service demands are either maintained or increased while economic resources diminish, programs will be required to demonstrate their effectiveness or modify to be more efficient. Clinicians will need to be familiar with evaluation procedures in order to demonstrate the efficacy of their interventions. Program structures will change to include more care provided by professionals with a generalist orientation, while expensive specialists will be utilized primarily on a consultative basis.

THE SCOPE OF PROFESSIONAL CHILD CARE

Child care is seen as a field with a broad scope; it is reflected in a model which Denholm, Ferguson, and Pence (1983) have depicted as an umbrella (Figure 1). Each of the sections of the umbrella represents a dif-

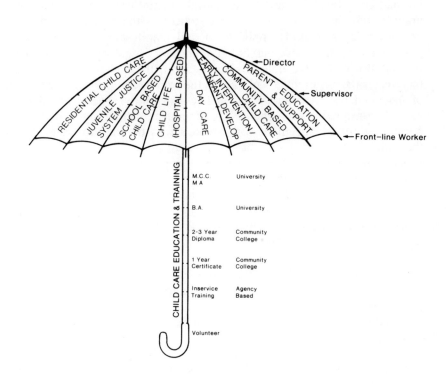

FIGURE 1. The Umbrella Model of Child Care

ferent specialized area of service, and the handle indicates the range of educational and training opportunities.

Just as the panels of the umbrella are interconnected, so are the various areas of child care practice they represent; all are necessary in order to provide a continuum of service to children and families. The generalist orientation and generic skills of the child care professional provide continuity in the system as children and families seek services from various segments of the model.

Child care education and training is seen as the handle in the umbrella model; the divisions indicate the levels available to the practitioner. The interval between each level of training is representative of field experience, so that education, training and practical experience interact within this sequential approach.

The handle on an umbrella is critical to its operation in the same manner that education and training is central to child care. Educational programs within this model must provide students with a broad, generic base of knowledge and skills applicable to all manifestations of child care practice so that they have maximum opportunity for vertical and horizontal mobility within the field. By implication, the higher up the handle, the greater the requirements placed on the standard of performance, level of independence, accountability, and responsibility. The model depicts the relationship between the levels of education/training and the opportunities for advancement within and across the various segments of the field.

The three divisions (frontline worker, supervisor, and director) indicated on the sections of the umbrella represent the major vertical levels of possible involvement in each of the eight major areas of practice identified throughout Canada today. The areas of practice demonstrate the broad scope of the child care field as well as the diverse range of employment opportunities available to graduates from the different training levels.

Of particular importance is the notion of horizontal mobility across the various segments of the umbrella. It is generally recognized that all child care employment areas have as their core a large number of similar knowledge and skill elements such as human development, interpersonal communications, problem-solving skills, counseling skills, program development, evaluation, and so forth. It is important, then, that education/training programs prepare students to function in the various employment settings with children, youth, and families who have a range of special needs. The encompassing nature of the umbrella model of child care represents a system of service delivery in which the preventive, primary, and tertiary levels of care for children, youth, and families are available regardless of setting or need.

The segments included in the umbrella model are not meant to indicate an exhaustive range of child care areas of practice but, rather, to represent some of the major areas at present. Certainly, other segments such as rehabilitation, early childhood education, therapeutic recreation, mental health, legal mediation, and work with gifted children, for example, could easily be included within this spectrum of child care services.

THE ESSENCE OF CHILD CARE PRACTICE

A commitment to addressing the needs of families within a context of caring might characterize the essence of the child care field and, perhaps, even distinguish it from other professions. Just as Maier (1979) sought to delineate the "core of care," child care professionals need to explore and attempt to set out the essence of child care practice. Ferguson and Anglin (1985) suggest four elements as being the essence of child care.

1) Child care is primarily focussed on *the growth and development of children and youth*. While families, communities, and organizations are important concerns for child care professionals, these are viewed largely as contexts for the care of children.

2) Child care is concerned with *the totality of child development and functioning*. The focus is on persons living through a certain portion of the human life cycle, rather than with one facet of functioning as is characteristic of most other human service disciplines. For example, physiotherapists are concerned primarily with physical health, psychiatrists with mental health, probation officers with criminal behavior, teachers with education, and so on. Only the emerging field of gerontology appears to share child care's concern with a portion of the life cycle as a totality.

3) Child care has developed within a *model of social competence* rather than in a pathology-based orientation to child development.

4) Child care is based on (but not restricted to) *direct, day to day work with children and youth in their environment*. Unlike many other professionals, child care practitioners do not operate in a single setting or on an interview or session-oriented basis.

Caring and professionalism are not mutually exclusive, and both need to be understood in terms of their essence to ensure that a suitable balance is maintained. The challenge to the child care field is that of evolving in a manner which acknowledges both the human and technical aspects of professionalism and maintains a good balance between them.

The next chapters will address different segments of the umbrella model of child care presented earlier. A variety of settings and functions representing the broad scope of the child care field will be outlined. The chapters are presented in a sequence, beginning with child care in institutional settings and progressing towards care which is community-based and emphasizes prevention and early intervention with the younger child. The chapters are ordered to begin with residential care, since it was one of the major historical roots of the child care field. The reader is encouraged to note how the above four elements reflecting the essence of child care are manifest in the areas of practice described in each of these chapters. The final chapter will look to the future and consider some of the implications of an expanded scope for the child care field.

NOTES

1. The reader should realise that the term "child care" as utilized in this text refers to both child and youth care.

REFERENCES

Denholm, C. J., Pence, A. R. & Ferguson, R. V. (1983). The scope of professional child care in British Columbia. In C. Denholm, A. Pence and R. Ferguson (Eds.) *The scope of professional child care in British Columbia.* Victoria, BC: University of Victoria.

Ferguson, R. V. & Anglin, J. P. (1985). The child care profession: A vision for the future. *Child Care Quarterly, 14,* 85–102.

Maier, H. W. (1979). The core of care: Essential ingredients for the development of children at home and away from home. *Child Care Quarterly, 8,* 161–173.

Wolfensberger, W. & Nirje, B. (1972). *The principles of normalization in human services.* Toronto: National Institute of Mental Retardation.

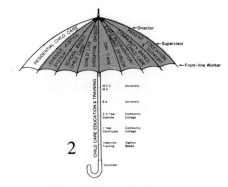

2

Residential Child Care

GERRY FEWSTER AND THOM GARFAT

INTRODUCTION

Whatever the future might hold for the profession of child care, its heritage has been firmly entrenched within the worlds of institutions, treatment centers, and group homes across Canada and throughout North America. In these settings, child care workers must deal with the social and developmental needs of children and adolescents twenty-four hours a day, seven days a week. Serving as the consistent human element between the child and a frequently confusing world, child care workers provide the essential mediating relationship through which the influences of parents, teachers, peers, siblings, and therapists take on meaning and relevance. No other profession has chosen to assume this breadth of perspective or level of personal and interpersonal responsibility. Beyond the time-tested theories and practices found in psychology, social work, education, or psychiatry, child care has been founded upon the accumulation of experience through involvement in the daily lives of children and young people. This experience has already done much to humanize and energize residential programs; indeed, the knowledge gained in these settings is now being increasingly applied to child care practices (see Hunter et al., 1982; Milner, 1982; Trieschman et al., 1969).

Since residential child care covers a broad range of facilities, programs, practices, and populations, it is necessary to restrict the scope of the discussion presented in this chapter. The focus is upon residential treatment for children broadly described as being "behaviorally and emotionally disturbed." This viewpoint reflects the particular interests and experiences of the authors, although it is acknowledged that residential child care workers are actively involved in hospitals, residential centers, and group homes serving physically and mentally handicapped, mentally ill, and learning disabled youngsters. Within the "behaviorally and emotionally disturbed" group, however, we would also include children considered to be chronically delinquent, depressed, anxious, aggressive, and developmentally delayed.

THE CONCEPT

Residential programs for "troubled" children and adolescents continue to struggle for acceptance within service delivery systems across North America. These programs are vulnerable to changing community attitudes, professional preferences, and economic considerations, but differential models of residential care and treatment have emerged and continue to develop. Proponents insist that, used appropriately, such programs can provide the most intensive and effective help for children and their families, while offering protection to both the resident and the community (Hoffman, 1974; O'Keefe et al., 1981). Opponents, on the other hand, argue that residential services provide intrusive, restrictive, and expensive environments reflecting society's general intolerance of deviant behavior.

An even more conclusive allegation is that residential programs simply "don't work." Conversely, proponents respond to this assertion by asking, "what doesn't work?," given that residential programs are infinitely varied in their philosophies, objectives, and practices. The debate is endless, since it involves matters of opinion, dogma, and polemics that have never been tested for differential outcome effects. In this sense, residential treatment is no better, or worse, than the field of psychotherapy in general (Deschner, 1982; Eysenck, 1965). Similarly, in the field of corrections, Martinson (1974), following an extensive review of programs throughout the United States, firmly concluded that "nothing works." A more cautious approach to the examination of residential care and treatment appears to call for carefully controlled research on the assumption that some things work, for some individuals, some of the time (D. W. Edwards et al., 1979; Hackler, 1978).

Research evidence relating to the treatment of troubled children and adolescents remains distinctly equivocal. And residential centers are generally the first component within the service spectrum to be challenged in terms of excessive costs, levels of intrusion, and humanitarian considerations. This situation is unlikely to change until such programs establish clear, attainable goals, expose their practices to analytic scrutiny, and demonstrate cost-effectiveness. Meanwhile, the widespread abolition of residential programs attempted in Massachusetts and California does not seem to enhance the overall quality of services to children and young people and appears to be influenced more by political considerations that service efficacy (Chafel & Charney, 1980; Miller et al., 1977).

Despite the lack of empirical evidence, the fact remains that child care practitioners and other professionals working in residential settings believe that they definitely help the young people entrusted to their care. This belief appears to be maintained whether such practitioners work in large multi-faceted interdisciplinary centers (see Herstein and Simon, 1977) or small community-based group homes (see Maloney et al., 1983). Hopefully, such beliefs will find increasing empirical support as child care and its related professions become more systematic and research-oriented.

RESIDENTIAL SERVICES FOR CHILDREN

Residential institutions, of one form or another, have flourished throughout history. Despite the varied nature of their activities, they can be characterized more by their similarities than by their differences (Wollins & Wozner, 1982). From the monastic retreats and English public schools on the one hand, to the maximum security prisons and mental asylums on the other, residential institutions have served to remove particular individuals and groups from the mainstream of society in order to bring about control, enlightenment, change, and protection. Admission has frequently been involuntary, based upon coercion or forcible removal, and "success" has been determined by the operating authority. More often than not, institutions of all types generate controversy, speculation, suspicion and, at times, open hostility about what really goes on inside. Yet society continues to tolerate and develop institutional settings for a variety of purposes.

Residential environments for children and adolescents have generally received an "institutional" label and have been subjected to the associated ambivalence, despite tremendous variations in programs, activities, and facilities. The harsh reality is that the residential setting is the only alternative for individuals who, for one reason or another, cannot or will not function within the established norms of social and familial environments. As Wollins and Wozner (1982) suggest, the ultimate value of such settings is determined by whether, in the final analysis, they expand or restrict opportunities for their residents. From a societal perspective, the question is: are residential programs for children intended to expand opportunities, or do they restrict such freedom in the interests of social control? As Thomas and Poole (1975) have suggested, this continues to be the most fundamental dilemma in establishing compatible goal structures within residential settings.

THE HISTORY OF RESIDENTIAL CARE AND TREATMENT IN CANADA

In a recent review of the development of residential group care and treatment programs in Canada, Pawson (1983) identifies three overlapping periods of influence. "The Puritan Era" (1600–1800) was one in which the group care of children was primarily a regional responsibility. The regions, in turn, tended to pass this responsibility to either municipalities or religious and private charitable organizations. While the primary focus of residential programs at this time was on the provision of housing and basic care for homeless, orphaned, or impoverished children, the disturbed, or disturbing, were often housed with the insane, the socially deviant, the mentally handicapped, and other "rejects" from an intolerant society.

"The Refuge Manager Era" (1750–1890) saw the beginning of the development of facilities created specifically for children. This period also witnessed the evolution of the concept of protection for children as opposed to simply the provision of housing. Canadian legislation both reflected and led this change in orientation (such as the Act for the Prevention of Cruelty to and Better Protection of Children, 1893).

"The Child Saving Era" (1850–1925) brought an increased emphasis on foster care for disturbed or delinquent children. This move toward deinstitutionalization and specialization can be seen as the point from which differential treatment programs for children and youth slowly began to emerge.

Throughout these periods, sponsorship for residential programs has been generally provided by either penal or welfare interests, although medical and educational interests also promoted various forms of residential intervention. (In fact, the first Canadian hospital-school for retarded children was founded in Ontario in 1876.) For the most part, however, residential services in Canada from the turn of the century to the 1940s consisted of orphanages run by welfare organizations for the "needy" and correctional programs designed to encourage children to change their antisocial ways through discipline and the learning of a trade. Many of these facilities were operated by religious organizations or other community groups, although there was a growing tendency for such organizations to seek some form of public subsidization. At the same time, legislation designed to protect children from various forms of abuse was gradually introduced into most provinces. Systems of public guardianship or wardship also developed, as did societies and organizations committed to protecting the well-being of children.

During the 1930s and 1940s, there was a distinct swing away from institutional care for the "dependent" child in favor of the surrogate family. The residual children were those who, for one reason or another, challenged the resources and tolerance of the community. While some of these children, through their antisocial behavior, qualified for correctional programs, others were grouped according to specific problems such as physical handicap, functional retardation, or mental defectiveness. The classification and treatment of children in accordance with the traditional concepts of mental illness is a relatively recent phenomenon (see D.S.M.III).

As residential programs began to specialize in the provision of services to particular populations, it became increasingly apparent that communities were seeking the removal of many children who, because they could not be classified, were slipping through the institutional net. Such children, through their attitudes and behavior, failed to conform to social expectations, frustrating families and exhausting the range of available community services. Since this behavior appeared to be all they had in common, these children were given the generic label "emotionally disturbed." Assessed and "tagged" in this manner, they became candidates for various forms of social control, including residential treatment.

Since these children's problems were relatively undifferentiated, and nobody seemed to have a quick "cure," residential programs—looking for a sense of purpose, along with the necessary resources—sought to legitimize longterm residential treatment. This movement seemed more the product of an intolerant society than of any serious attempt to identify and meet the needs of these children. By 1971, 205,000 Canadian children under the age of 18 were not residing within the parental home. It was noted that 3.2 per cent of this group were in facilities for emotionally disturbed or delinquent youth. Although some organizations attempted to use the surrogate family model as the cornerstone of longterm developmental treatment, others began to refer to their frontline staff as "child care workers" and charged them with the responsibility of meeting the day to day needs of the resident. In developing a new sense of identity, residential programs began to align themselves with particular therapeutic approaches, ranging from broad psychoanalytic orientations (Bettleheim, 1949; Davids, 1975) to more specific concepts such as reality therapy (Glasser, 1966) and behavior modification (Patterson, 1975).

These efforts attempted to combine individual treatment with strategic group care (Herstein & Simon, 1977; Whittaker, 1983) within the context of a total therapeutic living environment (see Polsky, 1962). The mandates of these programs were clearly influenced by the jurisdictional boundaries of provincial service delivery systems. Since most programs were either operated or funded by provincial governments, the jurisdictions involved were most notably Hospitals and Medical Care, Mental Health, Child Welfare, Corrections and Education. Regardless of mandate, however, "treatment" had clearly become the name of the game from the psychiatric hospital to the Ontario Training School. The task was seen as providing a total environment for residents that incorporated, or replaced, the influences of home, school, and community. With the professionalization of child care, the use of family therapy, the swing toward "normalization" (Wolfensberger, 1972) and the growing concern for escalating costs, this movement began to moderate during the mid-1970s. In an effort to retain community ties for children in residential care, "progressive" agencies began to involve families, use community resources, and, wherever possible, move treatment practices beyond the residential milieu. In this regard, the residential centers had actively pursued a process of "deinstitutionalization" even before the term became popular in the late 1970s and 1980s.

THE DEVELOPMENT OF RESIDENTIAL CHILD CARE

The professionalization of child care emerged alongside the specialization in residential care and treatment. As the limitations of the surrogate family model became increasingly apparent, the responsibilities of child care workers increased, and the role of the primary treatment agent emerged. The therapeutic value of child care became increasingly apparent and, even in traditional psychiatric settings, the value of these practitioners was acknowledged.

It was in the larger residential treatment centers, however, that child care emerged as the fundamental staffing component. As Berube (1984) has demonstrated, professionalization could not occur without a stable work force with appropriate training. Many of the developmental and educational requirements were created through the resources of larger residential programs. Junior colleges across the country responded, as did the universities in Montreal and Victoria, in setting up programs designed specifically for child care practitioners. These opportunities, along with the emergence of provincial child care associations, reinforced a sense of professional identity and a platform for collective action.

In residential centers, some of these developments have created tensions within organizational and professional structures. With the movement toward more multimodal treatment designs, child care practitioners tended to find themselves standing between the child and a confusing array of stimuli. Seemingly unaware of their unique role, many practitioners adopted a protective stance, assuming ownership for the well-being of the child. In one large Canadian treatment facility, for example, the child care staff refused *en masse* to accept directions given by senior clinical staff. In another institution, child care workers were temporarily replaced by nursing staff and paramedics. Fortunately, many of these tensions are being ameliorated as child care practitioners become fully contributing participants in the multidisciplinary process. The gradual incorporation of child care into the therapeutic arena has contributed significantly to moving the focus of treatment from pathology to normalcy and competence (Durkin, 1983).

During the late 1970s, child care began to move out of its residential homestead into schools, communities, and homes. New models developed, based upon relationship concepts (Garfat, 1984; Burns, 1984), scientist-practitioner designs (Jung et al., 1984), family intervention (LeTulle, 1979), community involvement (Perry & Ricks, 1983), and school-based services (Krueger, 1977). Meanwhile, publications such as *Child Care Quarterly* and *The Journal of Child Care* moved the profession beyond oral tradition and into the area of systematic enquiry. The overall effect of these developments on residential care and treatment programs has already been profound; there is no reason to believe that the impact will diminish in the years ahead.

CONTEMPORARY APPROACHES

Moving into the 1980s, residential services have continued to emphasize the role of the family and the community in the process of care and treatment. In the larger centers, the movement has been toward shorter term treatment intervention (Hoffman, 1974) combined with intensive community support (Fewster, 1979; Nelson, 1973). While treatment populations have become increasingly specific (Clary, 1975; Garrels, 1983) approaches have become increasingly multimodel (Pawson, 1983; O'Keefe et al., 1981). A predominant trend has been toward small group settings in the community, serviced through a central resource organization (such as Thistletown in Ontario or Youth Horizons in Quebec). Other initiatives have moved away from more traditional psychotherapeutic approaches to focus upon educational designs (Kreuger, 1977; Lewis, 1980; Trieschman, 1976) and family-centered models (Barker et al., 1978; LeTulle, 1979). In other cases, residential centers such as Dellcrest in Ontario and the William Roper Hull Home in Alberta have chosen to focus on non-residential community initiatives such as home care and day treatment programs.

In Canada, most of the recent developments in residential treatment have occurred within child welfare rather than mental health jurisdictions. This somewhat incongruous state of affairs can be almost entirely attributed to the federal funding system that supports provincial welfare programs but offers no assistance whatsoever to "mental health" initiatives. In many provinces, this means that in order to have access to residential treatment a child must first acquire some form of child welfare status. This can, of course, be distressing to both the child and the family, and they may resist or refuse what otherwise would be an appropriate placement. By the same token, providers of residential treatment services find themselves involved more in welfare and protection than treatment.

In spite of these developments, residential care and treatment continues to maintain the traditional "institutional" image; it is considered by many observers and policy makers to be an undesirable form of intervention, to be used only when all else has failed. While this attitude may well have promoted a misuse of residential programs, it appears to satisfy the conflicting perspectives of both those who wish to remove disturbing individuals from society and those who believe that such programs are, by their very nature, restrictive and punitive (Martin et al., 1977). Similarly, residential programs also become useful pawns for politicians and policy makers who wish to demonstrate humanitarianism, hard line fundamentalism, or decisive cost control through symbolic gestures. The chances are that this state of affairs will continue to exist until residential programs demonstrate that they operate in the best interests of children and families through the enhancement of options and personal autonomy. For this to occur, such programs need to articulate clear operational models that can be understood and evaluated in accordance with the identified needs of clients, service delivery systems, and the community at large.

RESIDENTIAL MODELS

For the residential worker, a particular program model or design offers both opportunities and constraints. Hence, the professional practitioner would be well advised to seek out those programs that provide the greatest opportunities for personal and professional growth. In reality, this turns out to be a highly idiosyncratic exercise, since no two residential programs and no two practitioners are identical. Models are based upon assumptions and beliefs about the nature of humanity, the nature of the social context, the causes of psychological disturbance, and the process of change. These assumptions are then translated into action through general objectives, goals, strategies, and specific activities. The closer the program and the individual practitioner in these issues, the greater the probability of achieving the desired outcomes. The further apart the program and the individual, the greater the potential for conflict, confusion, dissatisfaction, and failure. Clearly, where this unhappy state of affairs exists, the ultimate losers are the child and the family.

For residential care and treatment programs to occupy a legitimate position within the spectrum of child and family services, they must be matched to the needs of particular clients and service delivery systems. In this way, programs become accountable for what they do, and users become accountable for the choices they make. While much work needs to be done in this area, it is clear from the literature that many individual models have been emerging over the past few years (such as Fewster, 1977; Harris, 1983; O'Keefe et al., 1981; Pawson, 1983; and Trieschman, 1976). From an information-evaluation perspective, the task is one of examining these models differentially in terms of populations served, procedures used, costs involved, outcomes expected, and so forth. The first step in this direction might be the development of a broad typology within which the various designs can be conveniently grouped.

The typology offered here is both speculative and tentative and is designed primarily to assist the reader in recognizing the various orientations toward residential care and treatment in North America.

The Mental Health Model

From this perspective, society is seen as a living organism requiring built-in mechanisms (or antibodies) to maintain optimal functioning. For individuals, the term mental health implies that the mind, like the body, may take on various states of well-being ranging from exemplary fitness to debilitating disease and sickness. Terms such as treatment and therapy have been coined to define the task of producing a cure for the debilitating condition that will restore the organism to its state of wholeness and well-being. The process is, then, an event in which the practitioner must identify the particular malady, prescribe and implement a course of action, and assess the results of the intervention. For child care workers, the question is whether they are treatment practitioners or just adjuncts to the process, dealing with the "other twenty-three hours" (Trieschman, 1969) of the client's life.

Advantages of this model include: social and professional respectability; prescribed assessment and intervention methods; the security of time-tested tradition; established diagnostic definitions. Disadvantages include: clients may perceive themselves to be "sick"; clients may become dependent upon the practitioner for the cure; labels may become self-fulfilling prophecies; change may be attributed to the practitioner and not the client.

The Social Behavioral Model

This design assumes that society is a socialization context in which individuals learn to adapt to environmental conditions. Problems arise when learning mechanisms break down through individual inadequacies or situational anomalies. The task of the program is, then, to establish a learning milieu in which individuals are taught to adapt behaviorally through interpersonal and environmental contingencies. From this perspective, behavior change is assumed to be a prerequisite for psychological development and personal growth. Child care workers in these settings must be prepared to attend primarily to the overt behavior of residents, applying the technology of behavior modification along with techniques such as cognitive behavior modification.

Advantages of this model include: clearly articulated theoretical paradigms; well-developed and time-tested technology; specified and measurable outcome data; high competency feedback potential for practitioners and residents. Disadvantages include: a controlled and controlling environment; the lack of concern for non-behavioral aspects of client functioning; the reduction of the practitioner's status to technician; the lack of generalization of behavioral gains following discharge.

The Psycho Education Model

In this model, learning is considered to be an active two-way process between the individual and the world. Individuals make choices based upon their interpretation of available information. When information is made available and understood, individuals can then be responsible for the choices they make. Problems arise when information is lacking or when the individual is unable to comprehend it. The task then becomes one of establishing an interactional treatment milieu that takes every event as a potential learning experience for both the client and the practitioner. Child care workers in this type of environment have primary teaching responsibilities, attending to both the potential of the environment to provide and the potential of the individual resident to comprehend.

Advantages of this model include: attention focussed upon the client in context; relative freedom for both resident and practitioner to interact; relatively clear teaching-practice models of education; de-emphasis of control functions. Disadvantages include: unclear outcome indicators; unpredictability of events; questionable professional and public legitimacy; lack of standardized criteria for either admission or discharge.

The Systems Model

The systems orientation has gained popularity in recent years, particularly in the area of family intervention. The basic assumption is that all events, including behavioral events, can be best understood in terms of the systems they represent. In physics, these systems are part of the physical universe. In the behavioral sciences, such systems are assumed to exist within individuals and in the social milieu. Hence, to understand the behavior of a child, a practitioner must understand the context in which the behavior occurs. This is not the same as responding simply to environmental cues, since the environment has an ongoing life of its own and this organization is internalized within individual perception and cognition. The treatment task involves understanding how the systems work and using intervention strategies to bring about changes or modifications. Where the family therapist must come to terms with the family system, the child care worker must understand all of the various systems that impinge upon the life of the child and how these various systems might interact.

Advantages of this model include: practitioners acknowledge the complexity of human behavior; residents are not detached from the social world of home, school and community; the child is not perceived as the ultimate cause of the problem; the system of the residential environment is subject to ongoing scrutiny and analysis. Disadvantages include: treatment models are complex and vague; operational models are weak and indicators ambiguous; individual responsibility may be transferred to the system; systems are never "known" but are assumed from individual behavior.

The Correctional Model

The classical correctional model is based upon one aspect of learning theory: the function of negative sanctions. The basic assumption is that society must effectively inhibit antisocial or deviant behavior, through punishment or the withholding of rewards. Hence, the correctionally oriented program attempts to teach the resident the error of his or her ways through the imposition of sanctions—particularly the restriction of personal liberty. Child care workers in these settings usually find themselves in a highly controlled environment, teaching moral and social values to a highly resistant population of youngsters.

Advantages of this model include: clearly defined expectations and procedures; emphasis upon personal responsibility; clear delegation of responsibility and authority; environmental predictability. Disadvantages include: limited opportunities for practitioners and residents; conflicts between treatment and control functions; routinized environments; inadequate attention to differential treatment.

The Diversionary Model

Diversionary models may contain a whole range of assumptions about the nature of society and humanity. Their basic premise, however, is that there are certain essential pursuits that will divert an individual from debilitating problems through the acquisition of particular values, the enhancement of esteem, and the building of competency. Such programs might focus upon religious teaching, survival in the wilderness, learning a trade, working on a farm, or contributing to a closed community. Child care workers in these programs must accept the underlying values and be prepared to exemplify their characteristics.

Advantages of these approaches include: commonality of staff commitment; uncomplicated expectations; rejection of pathology notions; focus upon individual responsibility. Disadvantages include: simplicity; propensity for cultism; restricted opportunities for staff and residents; inadequate identification and generalization of outcomes.

The above categories are not necessarily exhaustive or mutually exclusive. Many programs might contain aspects drawn from a number of the models identified here. In this case, we would encourage the designers to articulate their model clearly and perhaps add to or modify it. Nor is it suggested that the model types described here necessarily reflect particular service delivery jurisdictions. It is possible, for example, for a program operating within a mental health jurisdiction to adopt any of the identified orientations. What is being proposed is that residential programs need to articulate their model and make it available for professional and community scrutiny (Mordock, 1979). The development of typologies should enhance consumer discrimination and empirical evaluation (Witkin & Cannon, 1971). It is further suggested that such efforts also serve to promote a more appropriate use of residential programs within the service spectrum, since such strategies are being increasingly designed to perform specialized functions such as shortterm stabilization

(Cohen, 1984; Perry, 1985) and preparation for adoption (Powers & Powell, 1983).

In developing specific models for residential programs, it must be recognized that residential strategies differ from other forms of intervention in a variety of ways. Many issues are peculiar to this field. In this section, we have chosen to highlight a few of these issues based upon their perennial presence and the expressed concerns of service users, practitioners, and providers.

Withdrawal of Funding

The vulnerability of residential programs to financial cutbacks, political postures, and philosophical swings has already been identified in this chapter. It must be stressed, however, that this vulnerability is one of the most critical issues affecting service delivery. If, in fact, there are children and adolescents who require residential services in our communities, the closure of residential treatment programs can have a number of very undesirable consequences. By continuing to test the tolerance and understanding of families and communities, these young people may well be caught up in escalating patterns of rejection and alienation (Martin et al., 1976). Some children undoubtedly end up in other forms of institutional care, such as adult mental hospitals (Chafel & Charney, 1980). Others, in need of treatment, eventually find themselves in conflict with the law and incarcerated within the penal system. It is interesting to note that the province of Ontario has recently announced the development of a number of new correctional facilities for youth, following a lengthy purge of residential treatment facilities. From the perspective of the practitioner and the service provider, the effect of this pervasive vulnerability is the withholding of legitimation, security, and support. Caught in this situation, it is not surprising that residential programs frequently resort to secrecy, gimmickry, unattainable aspirations, and false claims. Such a climate is hardly conducive to systematic planning, evaluation, and development.

The Decision to Refer

Admission to a residential program may remove a child completely from a familiar living environment and place him or her in a totally foreign milieu in the company of other children who may demonstrate bizarre or disturbing behaviors. The program is staffed by strangers and infused with policies, procedures, and rules designed to affect the child's behavior, directly and indirectly. This change may induce the trauma of separation, the fear of loss, and the powerful spectre of the unknown. It provokes fear and uncertainty, creates confusion, and invokes in the child tremendous questions about self and society. For these reasons, the decision to place a child in a residential program must be taken with great care and consideration for the impact upon the individual, the family, and the community.

While it would be comforting to consider such decisions as being made "in the best interests of the child and family," our experience suggest that such decisions are more determined by the attitudes and values of the community, the tolerance of the family and the community to deviant behavior, and the particular beliefs held by the professional community about the desirability of particular intervention options. Hence, assessed needs and background information are frequently biased toward the preferred strategy. In communities that place high value upon the maintenance of the nuclear family, the intervention choice may well be community rather than residentially based. In communities such as those in northern Canada, removal is often seen as a form of banishment from the communal order and is considered only as a last resort.

The imposition of such values may or may not be in the best interest of the child and family. In Canada, for example, we are not particularly accepting of behaviors that differ from the community norm. For this reason, we tend to see residential placement as a means of removing a deviant person from society, rather than a way of providing the most effective form of treatment. In general, the greater the tolerance of the community for deviance, the less the use of residential treatment. For this reason, the planning for residential placement must consider the particular needs of the child and family and the availability of a residential environment capable of meeting those needs. Unfortunately, we continue to use residential treatment based upon the level of disturbance that a child is creating for the community rather than on the value of the residential environment. In many cases, the *status* of the child becomes a critical variable. Since residential centers are generally funded through child welfare programs, access to such services is limited to those children who have some formalized welfare status. This situation increases the likelihood that certain children will be placed in residential centers while other, perhaps more appropriate, candidates, will be denied access.

The racial status of a child may also be a significant determining factor. As Pawson (1983) has pointed out, native children comprise 39 per cent of the total number of children in care in British Columbia, 40 per cent in Alberta, 50 per cent in Saskatchewan, and 60 per cent in Manitoba. A high proportion of native children are placed in residential treatment programs operated by members of the dominant culture. Despite increasing attempts to respond to these cultural differences (Stuart, 1983) the problem continues to be monumental. Fortunately, with the development of new information and assessment techniques, residential centers are more able to make a clearer statement about the possibility of a child benefiting from placement in the residential center. Such developments have made it easier to match a child's needs with the characteristics of a particular treatment environment. Again, this requires that residential centers be more explicit in terms of their particular operational model.

The Focus of Intervention

The residential treatment environment provides program planning for a child on a twenty-four hour a day basis. While this affords a unique opportunity for involvement in a child's life, it also produces a very special set of concerns for child care practitioners. In their text *The Other Twenty Three Hours* (1969), Albert Trieschman and his colleagues dramatically highlight the importance of considering the total day in planning for the treatment of children in residential centers. Since children and practitioners interact at all points of the day, any event may become a significant entry point for treatment intervention. The focus, therefore, of intervention and residential treatment differs dramatically from the focus of intervention in more community-based forms of treatment. The child care team, operating within its own model of treatment, must determine how such comon activities as waking up, going to bed, eating meals, self-hygiene, interacting with peers, or even reading a book figure in the overall treatment of the individual. Consequently, the focus of treatment is extremely broad; planning must take into account all aspects of the child's daily life. With the development of multi-modal therapy approaches, the emergence of professional child care has done much to convert traditional linear treatment approaches into interactional designs that encourage the child, and the family, to become active participants in the treatment process (Fewster, 1981).

Group Work in Residential Care

The fact that children in residential care must live together in a group makes the group context one of the natural areas for intervention and treatment planning. Such groups can become powerful forces in the promotion of positive change, or they can become equally powerful forces in resisting change or even in promoting regression. Thus, planning for an individual in residential care must take into account both the impact of the group on the individual and the impact of the individual upon the group.

The potential for negative group influence is one of the most regular concerns expressed about residential care and treatment strategies (Schaefer, 1980). In an environment where other individuals exhibit disturbed behavior, a child might express disturbance more clearly or feel an obligation to be as disturbed as the rest of the individuals in the group. Additionally, group norms may be more powerful than adult expectations in situations where clearly developed treatment designs are lacking. It is also frequently the case that an increase in disturbance is a manifestation of a child's resistance to being in the environment in the first place. Behavioral deterioration or regression, however, cannot be simply attributed to group effects. In some cases, it may indicate that the child, perceiving himself to have found security and protection, finally displays signs of disturbance which had been successfully controlled or concealed in former, less secure environments.

On the positive side, natural groupings of children in residential centers can lead to therapeutically meaningful activities and outcomes. The development of such designs as "positive peer culture" (Herstein & Simon, 1977) establishes the climate for this type of approach. As Whittaker (1983) has indicated, however, such group work does not necessarily have to follow the traditional group therapy models. It may be tailored toward the specific needs of the individual participants and programs. The potential here probably reflects one of the most exciting challenges in residential child care: the challenge of working with a group that actually lives together on a daily basis. Because of this, groups develop more rapidly than the traditional therapy group since they are not necessarily paced by the group facilitator. In residential groups, the interaction of group members occurs continuously, as opposed to being restricted to a fixed period of group interaction.

Differential Treatment and the Group Context

While many people perceive residential treatment to be primarily a group process, children are placed in such programs because of individual needs for growth and development. As a result, a child residential care worker must become skilled in the provision of individual treatment within the group context. While maintaining, supporting, and leading the group with one hand, the worker must be supplying the individual analysis, treatment, and caring with the other.

Some residential centers have chosen to meet this need for individualized treatment through other professionals who support the child care team. In other situations, child care practitioners focus upon individual needs while other clinical staff emphasize group intervention. Still other models of treatment call for the individual needs of the child to be met within the context of a specialized group therapy conducted within the residential center (Van Scoy, 1976). Clearly, these options will be determined by the particular model adopted by the center in question. In the final analysis, the residential treatment program must attend to individual needs on a differential basis; this cannot be achieved merely through the introduction of periodic sessions of individual counseling or psychotherapy. Individual assessment, treatment planning, and intervention must be an integral part of the system through which the residential center mobilizes its wealth of resources.

Normalization

The apparent artificialty of residential environments has been the focal point of considerable concern (Wolfensberger, 1972). While there is considerable variation in the degree to which residential treatment environments approximate life in the community, the chances are that the more intensive the program design, the less "normal" the environment. For children requiring intensive treatment, this may not be such a tragedy, since their regular environments have apparently failed to encourage normal development. The real problems begin to emerge when a child spends an inordinate amount of time in a residential treatment milieu. Obviously, this type of setting is no place for a child to experience normal developmental processes or the influences of socialization. In this regard, residential treatment centers are faced with a dilemma. By attempting to expose a child to all of the normal social and environmental influences, treatment resources can become diffused, and the time spent in treatment can be extended. On the other hand, most centers are expected to accomplish specific treatment goals as quickly as possible and move the child back into the so-called normalized world. As Davids and Salvadore (1975) have shown, pressures to reduce the duration of treatment can have a detrimental effect on post-discharge adjustment. It is quite possible, however, for a residential setting to provide an enriching, nurturing environment (Goldberg, 1982). As a concept for child development, then, normalization represents a useful notion. But applied to intensive residential treatment, it requires considerable caution in terms of its intent and application.

Control Versus Treatment

Since most children in residential centers are involuntary participants, their perceptions and experiences of treatment are markedly different from those of the voluntary client (Oxley, 1977). They frequently perceive themselves to be controlled; in testing out this hypothesis, they effectively force the residential staff into establishing controlling structures and imposing authority (Dahms, 1978). Since many children in residential programs appear to have external locus of control orientation to begin with (Friedman et al., 1985; Nicholson, 1980) the inherent dangers of a controlled environment are self-evident. Experience suggests that programs that strive primarily to control behavior tend to induce the dreaded state known as institutionalization; they foster mechanistic child care approaches that leave little scope for personal development or autonomy. Additionally, the pressure to control the behavior of children is often imposed from external community sources (Mayer & Peterson, 1975), particularly where delinquency is assumed to be a primary area of concern.

Paradoxically, it is in this arena that child care has faced one of its greatest challenges and, perhaps, made one of its greatest contributions. The primary task of the residential worker is to create in each child a belief in personal efficacy and autonomy. More than any other single factor, this appears to be the key to successful treatment in a residential setting. In our experience, it has taken the growth of professional child care to help to realize that this can be accomplished within a residential environment, since the pathway to freedom is, in fact, a transition from control to autonomy.

The Termination of Treatment

The discharge of a young person from a residential center is markedly different from the termination of treatment from community-based programs (Hirschberg, 1970). Just as the entry into treatment is a traumatic experience, so the termination of treatment can be anxiety provoking. The individual emerging from the residential program typically has been living in a very self-contained, psychologically closed community where interaction with, and the demands of, the outside world have been greatly limited. Returning to the community, therefore, means renewing relationships with a world that was experienced as hostile, depreciating, and rejecting. Leaving residential care also involves the separation of relationships with a large number of individuals, both children and staff, some of whom may have become extremely close and significant. Acceptance and success within the program may well be measured against the possiblility of rejection and failure within the community.

Given all that is occurring at the point of discharge, it is hardly surprising that many children exhibit severe regression when they near the temination of treatment. Process and timing are critical treatment-discharge variables. In order for the discharge or transfer to be successful, the residential team, in conjunction with the child and family, must be preparing for termination of treatment long before it occurs. As the date for discharge comes closer, the treatment team must help the child to take small experiential steps toward living back with the family and in the community. In this process, the child must have the opportunity to experiment with newly learned behaviors and attitudes in an environment which previously held different expectations. Preparing the family, or the alternative placement, is a task that must be undertaken by the residential staff, since only they understand the experiences of the child and know what needs to be done. Fortunately, in most modern residential treatment centers, the family is actively involved in the entire treatment process throughout its duration, making it possible for discharge planning to begin almost from the point of admission.

The timing of discharge from residential treatment is generally considered to be a grey area demanding considerable expertise and clinical judgment. In this regard, the child's state of readiness must be related to that of the family, school, and community. Although the present trend is toward shorter term treatment (Hoffman, 1974), premature discharge can significantly undermine treatment effects in the long run (Davids & Salvadore, 1976). Along with the state of readiness of the child and family, decision makers must also consider the availability of support resources and follow-up services.

The Cost of Residential Treatment

During the times of economic constraint, the financial costs of residential care and treatment become particularly salient to those who wish to curtail social program expenditures. While it is true that residential treatment has become an increasingly costly proposition, so have other components within the service delivery system. One problem is that the costs of operating a residential facility cannot be hidden or disguised; all of the necessary resources are on site and are contained within a single budget. The modern residential program provides a wide range of highly specialized resources and services twenty-four hours a day. Providing such services at a community level, on a far less intensive basis, would undoubtedly cost far more in financial terms. The fact is that, from an economic perspective, residential child care can be a viable proposition. Total care is provided to the child with support and treatment for the family. The twenty-four hour a day operation means that resources are seldom left idle. Services are immediately available and resources redirected to meet the changing needs of clients. Economies of scale reduce significantly the overhead costs of service delivery. Efficiency can be maximized through the establishment of financial and administrative controls.

On the other hand, the only way of resolving the cost issue is to compare, over time, the real costs of not using residential treatment for children and families who actually require such a service. This means a differential analysis of career costs for disturbed children and dysfunctional families. What needs to be assessed is whether or not effective residential treatment does, or can, reduce the overall costs of service delivery. Until this occurs, residential centers will continue to be the target for those who wish to withdraw finances from the system.

Effectiveness of Residential Treatment

Considering that residential treatment centers tend to cater to the most disturbed youngsters, it is probably safe to say that they do not work miracles, but outcome research on all forms of psychotherapy with children has produced little that is either convincing or compelling (Abramowitz, 1976). Ultimately, this critical question will not be adequately addressed until residential programs clearly state their goals and define their treatment strategies. Meanwhile, there is growing evidence to suggest that differential treatment effects can be identified (Davids & Salvatore, 1976; Deschner, 1980; Matsushima, 1979). Despite the equivocal nature of the evidence, it is clear that residential programs can be analyzed and evaluated; adequate empirical designs for this purpose are increasingly becoming available (Brubakken, 1974; Millman, 1977; Mordock, 1979). However, there are still many conceptual problems to resolve. Knowledge of the goals of particular organizations must be related to populations, time frames, and specific indicators of success. As Nelson et al. (1973) have suggested, an adequate evaluation of residential care and treatment must involve analysis of the family, the community, and the service delivery system. Until the task of evaluation is taken seriously, outcome information regarding residential services will continue to be tailored to meet the particular needs of the information provider.

FUTURE DIRECTIONS

Despite the objections and challenges, residential treatment programs for "troubled" children and their families continue to adapt to changing conditions and contribute to service delivery systems across North America. Without widespread popularity or acclaim, they somehow manage to maintain a developmental pattern that stands in sharp contrast to many of the revolutionary alternatives that come and go with changing fads and fashions. If nothing else, they continue to provide some security to the service spectrum and, should they finally go the way of the dinosaur, some things will undoubtedly be lost in much the same way as health care systems would suffer with the abolition of intensive care units. In this final section, we have attempted to highlight those aspects of residential care and treatment that appear to represent the most significant recent developments and future challenges.

Deinstitutionalization

From our perspective, the term deinstitutionalization more appropriately describes the movement away from remote residential facilities that hover in the murky chasm somewhere between society and oblivion. It represents a process through which residential programs become increasingly responsive to the individual needs of their clients, as members of families and communities. This cannot take place, however, with restricted funds or mandates. On the contrary, it calls for a renewed commitment and a remobilization of resources that expand the scope of residential care and treatment within the community (Bachrach, 1976). It requires the support and encouragement of funding bodies looking for rational service development rather than the traditional "quick fix."

Despite insecurities and uncertainties, many residential agencies in the last decade have managed to set a rational developmental course toward deinstitutionalization. These efforts represent some of the most exciting prospects for the future. In Canada, agencies such as Thistletown in Ontario, Youth Horizons and Shawbridge in Quebec, and the Ranch Ehrlo Society in Saskatchewan have been able to decentralize their resources with the development of small community-based facilities catering to the particular needs of the client population. The critical administrative issue in these developments is that the specialized clinical, educational, and social expertise and resources have not been decimated but have been remobilized to promote independent living for the service recipients. Other agencies, such as the William Roper Hull Home in Alberta and Dellcrest in Ontario, have developed extensive community-based programs that serve as extensions of, and alternatives to, the primary residential facility. Again, the apparent success of these initiatives has been built upon the concentration of expertise and resources developed through the operation of the central residential facility.

Where they have been allowed to occur, these developments in deinstitutionalization have provided a vehicle for the diversification and specialization of professional child care. Practitioners are becoming increasingly capable of moving freely between the residential centers and the community, as needs and events occur. Hence, we find child care professionals operating in schools, homes, and local communities, bringing new knowledge and skills to the professional domain.

The primary restriction on all of these initiatives is financial: those who pay for residential services insist on getting residential services; those who do not are often predisposed simply to withdraw funding. An additional problem arises from current provincial trends to decentralize services. The smaller local regions are often unable to support the extensive multidisciplinary agencies required for effective residential strategies (O'Keefe et al., 1981). The solution for such dilemmas is for agencies and funding bodies to review carefully the mandates of effective residential agencies and develop creative funding mechanisms that permit resources to be mobilized efficiently in accordance with the needs of the target populations.

Privatization

The tendency for governments to privatize social and health services has been pervasive throughout North America for a number of years. Predicated upon a belief that this will inspire community initiatives, reduce service costs, and reduce direct government responsibilities, the popularity of privatization seems to be escalating across Canada. While it is too early to assess the overall effects of this movement on the provision of residential services, we would offer some cautionary words to its proponents. In the first place, community initiatives will not reflect community needs unless such needs are carefully assessed by some independent authority. Secondly, shortterm cost reductions may be quickly lost when private operators establish a firm hold on particular segments of the market. Thirdly, a reduction of direct government responsibility may be accompanied by an associated loss of control over the expenditure of public funds. Our greatest concern, however, is for the quality of care and treatment. Unless standards are carefully articulated and stringently monitored, the programs considered the most successful could well be the cheapest, rather than the best. In the quest to reduce costs, child care would probably be the first to suffer, since the profession is generally less protected and regulated than its counterparts. In the final analysis, the client would be the ultimate loser.

Legislative Changes

While many Canadian provinces are currently examining or changing their child welfare and mental health statutes, national trends are more likely to be influenced by changes in federal legislation. In this regard, the proclamation of the *Canadian Constitution* (1981) and the *Young Offenders Act* (1983) are probably the most critical.

The potential impact of the new Canadian constitution on residential services has yet to be fully examined. When a school principal in Alberta can be charged for giving a 14-year-old student a detention, however, the implications become apparent. Those who work in residential and treatment facilities are becoming increasingly aware that most events occurring on a daily basis contain elements that could be challenged in accordance with the constitutional rights of residents. The flood gates have yet to open, but it is possible that program operators and practitioners will be called into question as individual Canadians become more conscious of their legal rights. However, this does not necessarily spell doom and disaster. It should, at least, encourage professionals to examine their existing practices and develop creative ways of meeting the needs of children and families without using overly restrictive or coercive devices. In fact, it is probably true that most residential programs have less to fear than most other environments since they traditionally have been open to scrutiny and surveillance. In our view, the application of constitutional principles could be one more step in bringing residential care and treatment out of the proverbial closet.

Family Participation

The incorporation of family therapy into children's residential services across Canada dates back to the early 1960s. Even before this time, many residential facilities maintained ongoing contact with families, frequently involving them in the treatment process. Over the last decade, however, natural and surrogate families have become critical elements in the residential mosaic, serving to preserve the developmental integrity of the child while changing their own styles toward enhanced individual and collective growth (LeTulle, 1979).

Because most residential centers deal with poorly motivated or resistant families, the problem of engagement becomes a critical issue. Residential workers have had to become particularly adept in the art of restoring the faith of family members disenchanted with both the child and the service delivery. Traditional family therapy approaches have been modified to incorporate a range of specific interventions based upon the concepts of self-help, group support, and parent training.

These developments in the areas of residential-family approaches have made it necessary for child care practitioners to resolve one of their most fundamental dillemmas: that is, who is actually responsible for the parenting role? By incorporating the family into the treatment program, residential workers have come to see themselves as professionals rather than surrogate parents. The challenge for the future is for child care workers to extend their unique areas of knowledge and expertise into the family context, thereby creating one more link in the process of deinstitutionalization and the range of professional family-focussed services.

Accountability and Evaluation

With the emergence of clear operational models, the stage will be set for residential centers to become increasingly definitive about what they do, why they do it, and how well they achieve their stated objectives. With the advent of multimodal approaches, the task of systematic evaluation is necessarily complex, but as Feist et al. (1985) have suggested, residential environments can be analyzed and differential outcomes can be identified (Davids & Salvatore, 1976). Modern computerized methods of data collection and analysis are already well established in the technology of many residential centers. In this regard, behavior-oriented programs appear to have the initial advantage (Wilson & Lyman, 1983) but it can be confidently expected that the technology will be effectively applied across a wide range of settings and program designs. Hopefully this trend will not serve to transform human beings into "dependent variables," and that the humanization of residential care and treatment will continue to be a major emphasis in all future developments.

SUMMARY

In this chapter we have attempted to outline the past, present, and future of residential care and treatment, albeit from an idiosyncratic perspective. We have suggested that residential programs should continue to be viewed as an integral part of the continuum of services to troubled youngsters and their families. For this to occur, such programs must take the leap of faith by coming forward and letting their intentions, practices, and outcomes be known. Governments and other funding bodies must establish the necessary mechanisms to provide a secure base from which new initiatives and longterm development might occur. In all of this, we see the ongoing development of professional child care as a critical factor in the evolution of child-centered services across North America in general and in Canada in particular.

REFERENCES

Abramowitz, C. V. (1976). The effectiveness of group psychotherapy with children. *Archives of General Psychiatry, 33,* 320–326.

Bachrach, L. L. (1976). *Deinstitutionalization: An analytical review and sociological perspective.* Rockville, Maryland: National Institute of Mental Health (DHEW), Div. of Biometry and Epidemiology.

Barker, P., Buffe, C. and Zaretski, R. (1978). Providing a family alternative for the disturbed child. *Child Welfare, 57* (6), 373–379.

Berube, P. (1984). Professionalization of child care: A Canadian example. *Journal of Child Care, 2* (1), 1–11.

Bettleheim, B. (1949). A psychiatric school. *Quarterly Journal of Child Behaviour, 1* (1), 86–95.

Brubakken, D. (1974). *Assessing parent training utilizing a behavioural index of parent-child interactions.* Paper presented at the annual convention of the American Psychological Association, New Orleans.

Burns, M. (1984). Rapport and relationships: The basis of child care. *Journal of Child Care, 1* (2), 47–56.

Chafel, J. and Charney, J. (1980). *Deinstitutionalization: Dollars and sense.* Paper presented at conference of The Council for Exceptional Children, Minneapolis.

Clary, S. (1975). *Diagnosis and prescriptions for L.D.: Problems of E.D. adolescents in a residential treatment centre.* Paper presented at the International Federation of Learning Disabilities, Brussels.

Cohen, Y. (1984). Residential treatment as a holding environment. *Residential Group Care and Treatment, 2* (3) 33–44.

Dahms, W. R. (1978). Authority versus relationship. *Child Care Quarterly, 7* (4), 336–344.

Davids, A. (1975). Therapeutic approaches to children in residential treatment. *American Psychologist, 36,* 809–814.

Davids, A. and Salvadore, P. D. (1976). Treatment of disturbed children and adequacy of their subsequent adjustment: A follow-up study. *American Journal of Orthopsychiatry, 46* (1), 62–73.

Deschner, J. P. (1980). Critical aspects of institutional programs for youths. *Children & Youth Services Review, 2* (3), 271–286.

Durkin, R. (1983). The crisis in children's services: The dangers and opportunities for child care workers. *Journal of Child Care, 1* (5), 1–14.

Edwards, D. W., Zingale, H. C., Mueller, D. P., Yarvis, R. M. and Boverman, H. (1979). Child therapy outcomes in a community mental health centre. *Children & Youth Services Review, 1* (1), 215–224.

Eysenck, H. J. (1965). The effects of psychotherapy. *International Journal of Psychiatry, 1,* 97–144.

Feist, J. R., Slowiak, C. A. and Colligan, R. C. (1985). Beyond good intentions: Applying scientific methods to the art of milieu therapy. *Residential Group Care and Treatment, 3* (1), 13–31.

Fewster, G. D. (1977). *The Social Agency.* Alberta: W.R.H.H. Publication.

Fewster, G. D. (1979). Canada: Residential adolescent treatment. In C. Payne and K. White (Eds.) *Caring for Deprived Children.* 228–256. London: Croom Helm.

Freidman, R., Goodrich, W. and Fullerton, C. (1985). Locus of control and severity of psychiatric illness in the residential treatment of adolescents. *Residential Group Care & Treatment, 3* (2), 3–13.

Garfat, T. (1984). *Entre Nous: Between Us.* Introduction to Fourth National Child Care Workers Conference, Montreal.

Garrels, D. (1984). Autism, the ultimate learning disability: A case management approach. *Journal of Child Care, 1* (4), 23–36.

Glasser, W. (1965). *Reality therapy.* New York: Harper & Row.

Goldberg, B. (1982). Institutional care versus home care. *Journal of Child Care, 1* (1), 21–33.

Hackler, J. K. (1978). *The great stumble forward.* Toronto: Methuen.

Harris, N. (1983). Renaissance House summary report. *Journal of Child Care, 1* (5), 15–19.

Herstein, N. and Simon, N. (1977). A group model for residential treatment. *Child Welfare, 56* (9), 601–612.

Hirschberg, J. C. (1970). Termination of residential treatment of children. *Child Welfare, 49* (8), 443–447.

Hoffman, A. (1974). *Indicated undergirdings of mastery learning.* Unpublished study conducted at Adlar Center, Champaign, Illinois.

Hunter, D., Webster, C., Konstantareas, M. and Sloman, L. (1982). Children in day treatment. *Journal of Child Care, 1* (1), 45–59.

Jung, C. H., Bernfeld, G. A., Coneybeare, S. and Fernandes, L. V. (1984). Toward a scientist-practitioner model of child care. *Journal of Child Care, 2* (1), 13–26.

Krueger, M. A. (1977). The "program day" as school day in residential treatment. *Child Welfare, 51* (4), 271–278.

LeTulle, L. J. (1979). Family therapy in residential treatment of children. *Social Work, 24* (1), 49–51.

Lewis, W. W. (1980). *Tennessee Re Ed: From innovation to establishment.* Paper presented at C.E.C. Conference on the Severely Emotionally Disturbed.

Maloney, D. M., Fixsen, D. L., Surber, R. R., Thomas, D. L. and Phillips, E. L. (1983). A systems approach to professional child care. *Journal of Child Care, 1* (4), 55–71.

Martin, L. H., Pozdnjakoff, I. and Wilding, J. (1976). The use of residential care. *Child Welfare, 55* (4), 267–278.

Martinson, R. (1974). What works—Questions and answers about prison reform. *The Public Interest, 35,* 22.

Matsushima, J. (1979). Outcomes of residential treatment: Designing accountability protocols. *Child Welfare, 58* (5), 303–318.

Mayer, G. and Peterson, J. C. (1975). Social control in the treatment of adolescents in residential care. *Child Welfare, 54* (4), 246–256.

Millman, H. L. and Pancost, R. O. (1977).Program evaluation in a residential treatment centre. *Behavioural Disorders, 2* (2), 66–75.

Milner, R. (1982). If you need my help just say the word. *Journal of Child Care, 1* (2), 11–26.

Mordock, J. B. (1979). Evaluation in residential treatment: The conceptual dilemmas. *Child Welfare, 58* (5), 293–302.

Nelson, R. H. (1973). *Community considerations in the evaluation of a children's residential treatment centre.* Paper presented at the annual meeting of The American Psychological Association, Montreal, Quebec.

Nicholson, L. (1979). Locus of control in a residential treatment centre. Unpublished manuscript, William Roper Hull Home, Alberta.

O'Keefe, E. J. and Castaldo, C. J. (1981). A multimodal approach to treatment in a child care agency. *Child Care Quarterly, 10* (2), 103–112.

Oxley, G. B. (1977). Involuntary client's response to a treatment experience. *Social Casework, 58* (10), 607–614.

Patterson, G. (1975–82). *A social learning approach to family intervention.* Vols. 1–3, Eugene, Oregon: Castallia.

Pawson, G. L. (1983). Residential group-care and treatment programs. *Social Work Papers, 17,* University of Southern California.

Perry, P. (1985). *Woods Christian Homes stabilization unit.* Unpublished program design.

Perry, P. and Ricks, F. (1983). Hard to serve youths: A new way. *Journal of Child Care, 1* (4), 37–45.

Polsky, H. W. (1962). *Cottage 6: The social system of delinquent boys in residential treatment.* New York: Russell Sage.

Powers, D. and Powell, J. (1983). A role for residential treatment in preparation for adoption. *Residential Group Care and Treatment, 2* (1), 31–69.

Schaefer, C. (1980). The impact of the peer culture in the residential treatment of youth. *Adolescence, 15* (60), 831–845.

Stuart, R. B. (1970). *Trick or treatment.* Chicago: Research Press.

Thomas, C. W. and Poole, E. D. (1975). The consequences of incompatible goal structures in correctional settings. *International Journal of Criminology and Penology, 3,* 27–42.

Trieschman, A. E. (1976). The Walker School: An education-based model. *Child Care Quarterly, 5* (2), 123–135.

Trieschman, A. E., Whittaker, J. K. and Brendtro, L. K. (1969). *The other twenty three hours.* Chicago: Aldine.

Van Scoy, H. (1976). The child care worker as an activity group co-therapist. *Child Care Quarterly, 5* (3), 221–228.

Whittaker, J. K. and Garbarino, J. (1983). *Social Support Network.* New York: Aldine.

Wilson, D. R. and Lyman, R. D. (1983). Computer assisted behavioural assessment in residential treatment. *Residential Group Care & Treatment, 1* (4), 25–34.

Witkin, M. J. and Cannon, M. S. (1971). *Residential centres for emotionally disturbed children.* Washington, DC: National Institute of Mental Health Publications.

Wolfensberger, W. and Nirje, B. (1972). *The Principles of Normalization in Human Services.* Toronto: National Institute of Mental Retardation.

Wollins, M. and Wozner, Y. (1982). *Revitalizing residential settings.* San Francisco: Jossey-Bass.

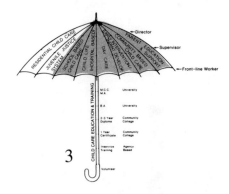

3

Child Care and the Canadian Youth Justice System

DEL PHILLIPS AND BARBARA MASLOWSKY

Child care professionals who work with young offenders need to know the law as it relates to youth, understand the way the youth justice system functions, and possess the necessary skill for working with adolescents. Statistics Canada estimates that during 1983, 49,130 young Canadians incurred 115,037 charges, including 90,032 offences for violations of federal statutes. Of those charged, 82.4 per cent were found guilty of at least one offence, and 74.2 per cent of all reported charges resulted in findings of delinquency (Statistics Canada, Juvenile Delinquents, 1983).[1]

The media is quick to bring more serious youth offences to the public's attention. The problem of youth crime is large and the public has acquired a strong perception of its importance. It has also recently captured the attention of Canadian legislators, who have passed the *Young Offenders Act* (Y.O.A.) (1984).

This chapter is primarily about the Y.O.A.; it is intended for child care workers who work with young persons who have come into conflict with the law. It is divided into three sections: the young offender and relevant aspects of the Y.O.A.; the operation of the law as bounded by provincial realities; and, finally, information about the job faced by youth workers when working with young offenders.

The Young Offender

Headlines in the neighborhood newspaper often contain lead stories such as, "Elderly Grocer in Hospital Following Robbery Attempt by Two Youths." The story might describe how the youths, aged 14 and 15,

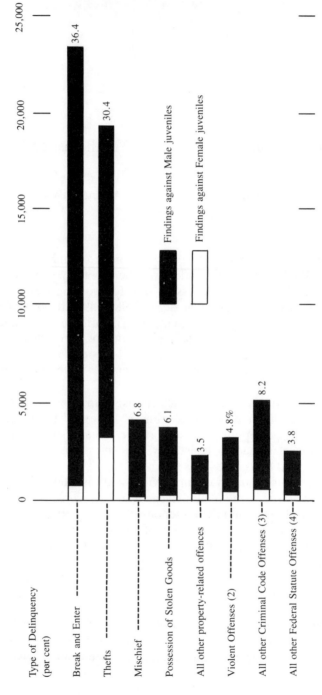

Number of Findings of Delinquency

FIGURE 1. Number of Offenses Committed by Canadian Young Offenders During 1983

(1) This chart is based on 64,301 federal statute charges which resulted in a finding of delinquency. Charges against adults (and companies) are excluded.

(2) Includes murder, attempted murder, manslaughter, assaults, robbery and sexual offenses.

(3) Includes 25 categories of offenses, including over 230 sections of the Criminal Code.

(4) Includes offenses against the Narcotic Control Act, the Food and Drugs Act, the Juvenile Delinquents Act (sections 2, 20 (3), 33, 34) and other federal statues.

entered a grocery store run by an elderly gentleman and demanded money. When he resisted, he was attacked and badly beaten. The youths were arrested several blocks away with the money, candy bars, and cigarettes stolen from the store.

The young offender comes into the youth justice system because of what he has done, not who he is. The youths in this vignette have become part of the youth justice system; although they are not representative of average offenders, they do attract the most publicity. According to Statistics Canada, violent offenses account for only 4.8 per cent of all criminal acts committed by youths (1983, p. 4). Figure 1 presents the number and per cent of youths found to be delinquent by type of offence.

The greatest number of delinquencies are committed by young persons 15 years of age. In 1983, only one offender in ten was female (1983, p. 4); male juveniles accounted for 89.1 per cent for the federal statute charges adjudicated. Given this information, the child care professional may well ask if the behavior of a young offender is substantially different from that of any other adolescent. Most adolescents test limits, conflict with adults, and face increasing societal expectations at a time when the struggle for independence, freedom, and recognition from both peers and adults is uppermost. Most live by the norms and laws of society, participating in institutions established by adults for children (such as schools, organized sports, community activities, and family activities). Although many so-called "normal kids" break the law at one time or another, few are ever arrested; of those arrested, most are "diverted" from the youth justice system by the police or court. Thus, repeat offenders or youths having committed serious crimes are the individuals most likely to become the clients of child care professionals.

Juvenile Delinquency

Although this chapter focusses on systemic issues related to the involvement of child care professionals with young offenders, theories about why youths become offenders deserve some consideration. Much has been written to attempt to explain why young persons come into conflict with the law. Theories reflect physiological, sociological, and psychological biases (Gold & Petronio, 1980). Newman & Newman (1986) describe five identifiable groups of delinquents. They are: 1) the psychopathic delinquent, described as having personality characteristics that include "impulsiveness, defiance, absence of guilt feelings, inability to learn from experience, and the inability to maintain close social relationships"; 2) the neurotic delinquent, where "delinquent behavior is thought to arise from psychological conflict and anxiety"; 3) the psychotic delinquent, reflecting an inability to test reality, control personal impulses, and utilize good judgment; 4) the organic delinquent, resulting from mental retardation and/or brain damage; and 5) the gang delinquent whose membership in a group meets the delinquent's need for "status, resources, and relationship." Although theories about delinquency exist, none is definitive. Young offenders often initially resist adult intrusion and control in their lives. When charged with an offence, the youth has been placed by a person in authority (policeman, judge), under the control of another authority figure such as a child care professional. The involuntary nature of this relationship requires patience, skill, and knowledge to overcome the resistance and hostility that the youth may experience. Recognition of this sense of powerlessness is therefore essential in dealing with the behaviors that the youth worker encounters, behaviors that range from subtle cries for help to overt hostility. One aspect of the work with young offenders requires that workers be familiar with relevant legislation and procedures within the youth justice system.

THE YOUNG OFFENDERS ACT

The Y.O.A. is federal legislation enacted in 1984 by the Canadian parliament. To understand the relationship between federal and provincial legislation, it is essential to outline the relationship between the powers of the federal parliament and the provincial governments.

The *Constitution Act*, 1982 (formerly the *British North America Act*, 1867) sets out the division of powers between the federal and provincial governments. This is done in a way that subjects every person to the laws of two authorities, the parliament of Canada and the legislature of the province. As Hogg (1985) states, "the central authority and the regional authorities are 'co-ordinate,' that is to say, neither is subordinate to the other" (p. 30). Under the *Constitution Act,* one authority does not have the power to enact legislation in "classes of subjects" assigned to the other. Section 91 of the act enables the national parliament to enact laws for the "Peace, Order and good Government of Canada." Under the "classes of subjects" are, for example, "Unemployment Insurance" and "the Criminal Law." Section 92 lists the "classes of subjects" which the *Constitution Act* assigns exclusively to the provinces. These include "the Administration of Justice in the Province including the Constitution, Maintenance and Organization of Provincial Courts, both the Civil and of Criminal Jurisdiction."

The federal government enacts the criminal law (the criminal code) and is responsible for making laws establishing the procedure to be followed in criminal matters (such as the Y.O.A.). The provinces, on the other hand, are responsible for passing laws with respect to "the administration of Justice in the Provinces," and for the purpose of establishing, maintaining, and managing the provincial courts. The provinces establish court procedures in civil matters; the federal government defines procedure in relation to criminal matters. In addition to the administration of justice through the court system, provincial governments are responsible for general policing and services to young offenders. Procedural legislation determines the function of the other three components of the system: the police, the courts, and the services to youths who have come into conflict with the law.

Offence legislation sets out what behavior is unlawful and enables the system to intervene in the life of a youth. Thus, it is the youth who is the first, and key, component of the youth justice system.

The relationships between procedural and offence legislation under the federal and provincial governments and their effect on the four components of the youth justice system are presented in Figure 2.

The Operation of the Y.O.A.

Like most other pieces of legislation, the Y.O.A. defines, empowers, and limits actions and behaviors. However, no longer do we speak of "juveniles," "juvenile delinquents," "juvenile court," or "industrial schools." The *Juvenile Delinquents Act* (1908) embodying the fundamental principles of the "child saving movement," provided for a separate court and special court procedures for young people charged with committing "delinquencies," as well as for the development of a probation service.[2] For seventy-six years, this act has had a pervasive effect on shaping youth corrections in this country. The Y.O.A. is the result of twenty years of public debate, undergoing many revisions in response to changes within society.

Under the Y.O.A., a young person is anyone between 12 and 18 years of age. Previously, considerable age variation existed among provinces: in some provinces, persons aged 16 or 17 years were governed by adult criminal law. As children under age 12 cannot be prosecuted for committing an offence, they cannot be held criminally responsible.

For a young person to appear in "youth court" under the Y.O.A., he must be charged with a violation of a federal statute, such as the Criminal Code, Narcotic Control Act, or Food and Drug Act. Other crimes not included in federal statutes include truancy, driving, and liquor offences. Each province has its own legislation and penalties for these offences; all

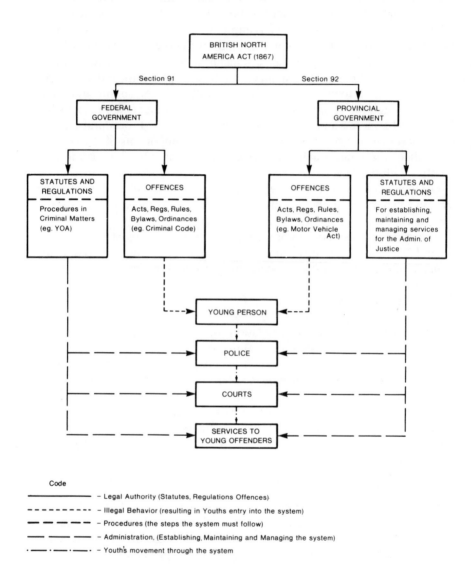

FIGURE 2. The Relationship Between Various Aspects of the Legislation and the Young Offender

Courtesy of the Legal Services Society of British Columbia.

are tried in youth courts. The following is a summary of the main aspects of the Y.O.A.

Philosophy and Intent

The Declaration of Principle clearly sets out the philosophy and intent of the act (Sec. 3) and provides basic principles for interpretation and application. One such principle is that the young person is seen as having the same rights and protections under the law as adults. However, no longer does the court act in the role of a kindly parent in a relatively informal setting. Youth courts, like adult courts, are open to the public, which allows for public scrutiny and awareness of matters relating to young offenders. There are some instances where young persons are given special protection. For instance, names of young persons charged with or convicted of offences cannot be published (Sec. 38(1)).

According to the Declaration of Principle, young persons have the right to be informed (Sec. 3(1)(g)), to be heard in court, and to participate in the processes leading to decisions that affect them. Responsibilities in this area fall to police, judges, staff of detention and custody facilities, probation officers, child welfare workers, and all other persons and agencies who are involved in the youth justice system. Sections 11 and 12 of the Y.O.A. ensure that a young person must be informed upon arrest, at all court appearances, and on court documents of his right to be represented by counsel. Section 56 requires that police officers take special steps to inform a young person of his rights prior to taking a statement.

The Y.O.A. also guarantees counsel for the young person. This provision might be used, for example, in situations where the young person and his parents are not in agreement. The Y.O.A. provides for copies of court reports, such as dispositional reports and medical/psychological reports, to be given to the young person. However, the judge may decide to exclude the youth from receiving all or part of the report if considered injurious. In addition to the range of court dispositions available, the Y.O.A. reflects concern for minimal intervention through other provisions, such as alternative measures.[3] Thus, there has been a movement from a preoccupation with the young offender's needs to a focus on the nature of the young person's offending behavior.

Responsibility and Accountability

The notion of "mitigated accountability," or lessened accountability, is reflected in the maximum length of disposition available under the

Y.O.A.: two years for a probation order or two or three years for a custody order, depending on the seriousness of the offence (Sec. 20). Also, provisions for community service and personal service provide an opportunity for the young person to work off his debt to the community in general or to the victim. This is a departure from the *Juvenile Delinquents Act,* where the juvenile was depicted as a "misguided, misdirected youth."

Special Needs

Although the act focusses on the nature and seriousness of deeds, the Declaration of Principle states that both the needs of the young person and the interests of his or her family should also be taken into consideration at the time of disposition. For example, removing the child from the home can have a dramatic effect on both the child and the family. This must be weighed against society's need for protection. Recognition of the special needs of the young person reflects a major distinction between the youth justice and adult corrections systems. These needs arise out of the young person's state of dependence and his maturity. The act not only recognizes that young offenders require "supervision, discipline and control," but also underlines the need for "guidance and assistance" (Sec. 3(1)(c)).

There is a considerable amount of flexibility in the Y.O.A. to assist young persons with special needs through the wide range of dispositional alternatives, including treatment orders.

The provision for various predispositional and medical/psychological reports affords the opportunity for opinion by social work, child care, psychological, and psychiatric professionals. This provides the youth court judge with information about the personal profile of the young person. In this way, the disposition of the court, following a finding of guilt, is able to balance the seriousness of the offense with the needs of the young person.

Parental Rights and Responsibilities

Parents or guardians are considered responsible for the care and supervision of their children; for this reason, young persons should be removed from parental supervision "only when measures that provide for continuing parental supervision are inappropriate" (Sec. 3(1)(b)). Parents receive notice of all court proceedings and copies of reports prepared for the youth court. Parents who attend proceedings under the Y.O.A. are not parties to the proceedings, but they are assured an opportunity to be heard. Furthermore, the courts can compel a parent to attend proceedings. In some cases, parents may reject the child because of embarrassment experienced as a result of the child's behavior. This sense of failure may also show through in their relationships with professional staff. It is also important to note that an order to detain a young person for treatment cannot be made without the consent of the parent where the parent is taking an active interest. This encourages the involvement of parents in decision making.

Child care professionals working in treatment programs may have to account to the parents for what they do with the child. This may be seen by the professional as interference in the treatment process rather than constructive involvement by the parent. At minimum, parents may wish to become informed of the intended outcome of a particular program before they involve their child.

Rights of Society

The Y.O.A. also articulates that society has a right to be protected from illegal behavior. For the first time, legislation has concerned itself with the victims of youth crime. Although not essential, there is provision in the act for the results of an interview with the victim to be attached in predispositional reports that go before the court. Where an order is made that the young person must make compensation in kind to the victim (known as "personal service order"), the victim must be aware of and agree to the terms. Not only does this "repay" the victim for the damage done, but it also makes the youth more aware of the impact of his behavior on another person.

Dispositions

Section 20 of the Y.O.A. sets out all of the dispositional options available to the youth court judge, including maximum limits pertaining to each disposition. The range of dispositions can be grouped in two categories: community dispositions (including detention for treatment), and custody dispositions.

Within the range of community dispositions, there is provision for orders involving financial payment and compensation or return of property. For instance, the Y.O.A. allows for a fine of up to $1,000 to be paid "at such times and on such terms as the court may fix" (Sec. 20(1)(b)). There is also provision for orders involving service to the community (community service) and service to the victim (personal service). Probation is another community disposition under the Y.O.A. and is limited to a maximum period of two years. The role of the "youth worker," as defined by the Y.O.A., is to supervize the young person in complying with the conditions of a probation order and to assist the young person until the disposition has been completed. The youth court may also order that a young person be detained for in-patient treatment. This disposition must be preceded by a medical/psychological report recommending that the young person undergo treatment for any of the following conditions: a physical illness or disorder, a mental illness or disorder, a psychological disorder, an emotional disturbance, a learning disability, or mental retardation.

The range of custody dispositions reflects two types of custody, open and secure. Like community dispositions, all custody dispositions are prescribed for a definite period of time. Generally, custody dispositions are not to exceed two years in length. However, custody dispositions may be for periods of up to three years for offences punishable by life imprisonment under the Criminal Code, or when the young person has committed more than one crime. Whether we speak of open or secure custody, the Y.O.A. requires that the young person be held separate and apart from any adult charged or convicted of an offence. Section 24(1) defines open custody as a community residential center, group home, child care institution, or wilderness camp. Secure custody, on the other hand, is defined as a "place of secure containment or restraint." Each province has made its own policy decisions regarding the designation of open and secure custody.

Professionals involved with young offenders in custody settings should also be familiar with the provisions regarding "temporary release" from custody (Sec. 35). Releases may be granted for medical, compassionate, or humanitarian grounds, rehabilitation, reintegration into the community, education, and employment (for periods not exceeding fifteen days). Under this section the young person may be released with or without escort.

Transfers to Ordinary Court

There is provision for transfer to ordinary adult court if the person was 14 years of age or over when the alleged offence was committed. The transfer hearing is not a trial. Rather, it is a hearing to determine whether the interests of society might better be served if this matter went to trial in the adult court. If the matter is transferred to adult court, the sanctions of the adult law apply.

Reviews

The act details the grounds for reviews, defines who is eligible to apply and when, and delineates the possible outcomes. It is particularly important that child care professionals working with young persons in custody settings or on probation orders be aware of the purpose, mechanics, and implications of reviews. These professionals are often assisted by representatives from the local probation office or from the local Crown's office, who detail the provisions, policies, and procedures relative to reviews.

Figure 3 provides an operational description of the Y.O.A. by identifying the process through which the young offender passes. It includes the various stages, decision points, and alternatives from the occurrence of an alleged offence through to the court's final disposition. This also describes the "activities" that take place in the youth justice system and the relationships of the various components. As this is an overview, slight variations may be seen between provinces, depending on the youth justice model adopted.

In summary, marked alteration in the treatment of young persons before and under the law have occurred. Proclamation of the Y.O.A. has resulted in a number of changes to the youth justice system; these are reflected in terminology, attitude, theme, and philosophy. In addition to the young offender, new procedures, including ongoing changes to the Y.O.A., affect all persons involved in the youth justice system.[4]

THE STRUCTURE OF THE YOUTH JUSTICE SYSTEM

The *Young Offenders Act* describes the roles, responsibilities, and relationships of various aspects of the youth justice system. As referred to previously, it has four primary components. Programs may be provided directly by provincial governments or through private or non-profit agencies funded by contracts, grants, or fee for service arrangements. Custody programs are generally provided as a direct service of government and tend to be the best known aspect of youth programming. However, there are a range of programs providing care, treatment, custody, and control for young persons charged with or found guilty of an offence. The most common include secure and open custody, institutional and community treatment, probation, counseling, education, and work experience.

Many provincial government services to young offenders have evolved through circumstance, tradition, or political expedience, as op-

The Legal Process for Young Offenders

This is a general framework only

Criminal (Ordinary) Court

Appeal — Permission Not Required

Trial

Transfer Hearing

Further Appearances (If Necessary)

Dispositions Available to Youth Court
Absolute discharge
Orders
- Fine up to $1,000
- Compensation
- Restitution
- Third party compensation
- Personal service in lieu of above
- Community service
- Prohibition; seizure, forfeiture
- Treatment (with consent)
Probation (with conditions)
- Attendance programs
Custody
- Open
- Secure

Accused Pleads Guilty — Disposition or Disposition Date Set

First Appearance
- Arraignment
- Application to transfer to ordinary court
- Request for court-appointed counsel
- Judicial interim release hearing
- Warrant or resummons if accused fails to appear

Youth Court
The youth court is a division of Provincial Court which has exclusive jurisdiction in young offender matters. A young offender is a young person between the ages of 12 and 17 who has committed a criminal offence.

Community

Letter to Parents

Alternative Measures

Information Sworn/Summons Issued

Information Sworn/Summons Issued

Information Sworn — Accused Remanded in Custody or Released on U.T.A. or Recognizance

Justice of the Peace

Crown Counsel Decision

Crown Counsel Decision

Crown Counsel Decision

Crown Counsel

Absolute Right to Counsel
Before entering a plea or at any court hearing (including application to transfer to ordinary court, trial, appeal, and review of disposition), the accused has an absolute right to be represented by a lawyer. That is, if a lawyer has not been retained, the judge will appoint counsel on request to be paid for by the state.

Police Report to Crown Counsel

Police Report to Crown Counsel

Police Report to Crown Counsel

No Further Action

Accused Released on P.T.A., Recognizance, or with Intent to Summons

Police Discretion

Investigation — Accused Not Arrested

Accused Arrested with or without Warrant

Police
If the accused can be charged with an indictable offence, the police may fingerprint and photograph, by force if necessary.

Right to Counsel
From the time of arrest or a request by the police for a statement, the accused has the right to consult a lawyer and/or parents or a suitable adult of the young person's choice.
This right to counsel is not an absolute right, i.e., the accused has a right to obtain a lawyer but the state has no obligation to provide one.

Offence Alleged

FIGURE 3.

Courtesy of the Justice Institute of British Columbia

posed to a planned and deliberate structuring of an efficient and effective service delivery system. Each province is autonomous in the way it deals with young offenders. Three types of service delivery models have evolved across Canada.

The Integrated Model

In this structure, services to young offenders are included as part of a children and family services ministry or division; resources for children and their families are administered under one broad organizational structure. Ontario, the Northwest Territories, and the Yukon have adopted this model in which child welfare, youth correctional programs, and health services to young offenders all fall within the same administrative structure, although Ontario is currently providing services to 16- and 17-year-old offenders under the Ministry of Correctional Services (adult correction).

The Social Welfare Model

Services to young offenders in this model are included under the department or ministry providing social or welfare services. An example may be seen in Quebec, where the youth justice system is included under the Ministry of Social Services. Other provinces to adopt this approach are Manitoba, Newfoundland, Nova Scotia, and Saskatchewan.

The Corrections Model

All correctional services for both young offenders and adults are provided under a corrections ministry, department, or branch of government. For example, in British Columbia all services to young offenders are provided under the Corrections Branch, a department of the Ministry of the Attorney General. Youth corrections, therefore, is within the same structure that administers adult corrections. Alberta, New Brunswick, and Prince Edward Island have also adopted a similar model.

Advantages and Disadvantages of these Models

The integrated model provides the opportunity for better co-ordination of youth services. This system has one organizational structure providing all services to a particular youth, rather than multiple systems. The advantages of these programs include:

More effective problem solving. A single organizational structure has within it the authority to resolve problems quickly. When a problem crosses ministry or departmental boundaries, the process for resolving the issue can be slow and cumbersome.

Less disruptive transition between programs. The various programs within the integrated system tend to flow more smoothly from one to another; transitions can be done in a planned way with minimum disruption. The youth is less likely to become lost in the gaps between the programs in which he is participating.

Improved information sharing. Information is shared through a formal structure rather than informally between systems.

Better funding. The allocation of financial resources determines the quality and quantity of programs and services provided. This decision is to some extent based on the strength of the ministries' representation at the political level. It could be argued that it is politically more acceptable to lobby for children's programs in general than for programs for young offenders who are part of a larger corrections ministry.

The integrated model has at least one major disadvantage. If a particular service is not part of its mandate, there may be no other system available to provide it. For example, if alternative educational programs for behaviorally disturbed youths are not available within a family and child services ministry, and this ministry is responsible for young offenders, then young offenders may not receive this service. The criteria for gaining entry to many programs may disqualify youths who exhibit disruptive behavior. Alternatively, professionals working with youths may prefer those who are more amenable to treatment. This process may result in a greater number of young offenders being placed in institutions rather than in community programs.

The social welfare model provides services to young offenders under the umbrella of a social welfare ministry or department. Health services, for example, are not usually included under this ministry. Although not as wide-ranging in scope as the integrated system, it does provide services to a broader range of clients as compared to the corrections model. The social welfare model may provide foster programs, child welfare, and services to children, families, and young offenders. Because a social services system generally provides a wide range of services, it may be able to respond more effectively to the needs of the child than the narrower focus of the corrections model. However, there is a danger that, like the integrated model, programs provided through a social welfare system may overlook the needs of young offenders.

The corrections model, sometimes referred to as the justice or responsibility model, provides services to young offenders in terms of custody and control. This model often involves placing young offenders under the administrative umbrella of adult corrections. There is reduced emphasis on the prevention of offending behavior and increased emphasis on the protection of society. However, programs developed within the corrections system specifically for young offenders are more likely to focus on aggressive behavior. In this system, the special needs of youth for health care (physical and psychological) and social services, such as release planning, are provided through ministries, departments, or agencies outside the corrections system. This approach relies to some extent on goodwill between the various components of the system, rather than on a formal organizational structure. An advantage of the corrections model is that its role is clear. There is less likelihood that corrections will become the broad net catching youths who are experiencing behavior problems but are not a danger to the community. In this system there may be a tendency to minimize the importance of the youth's needs. Consequently, services could become more control-oriented.

Policies emanating from the senior levels of complex organizations are likely to be general and all-encompassing. For example, consider the statement contained in the Youth Correctional Manual of the British Columbia Corrections Branch (1984). "The director shall establish procedures for grievances and they shall be included in the information provided to each youth upon admission" (Sec. c1, 2.01, p.2). The person responsible for the program then must ensure that a policy is in place that specifies when and how the information is communicated to the youth and the steps that must be followed by staff in processing a youth's grievance. The operational policy of the program is much more specific than the general policy of the organization.

TRENDS WITHIN SOCIETY AND THE WORK OF THE CHILD CARE WORKER

The Y.O.A. has shifted the emphasis away from preoccupation with rehabilitation toward concern for the protection of the public. Inherent is the danger that provinces may interpret this shift as justification for moving away from a developmental approach (that is, treatment and rehabilitation) toward a custodial stand (control, containment, and lockup). In practical terms, this approach is cost-effective (at least in the shortterm), is easily understood, and avoids viewing corrections as rehabilitation. This position is consistent with Martinson (1974) who stated, "with few and isolated exceptions, the rehabilitative efforts that have been reported so far have had no appreciable effect on recidivision" (p. 22). In a later publication, Martinson (1976) commented that "correctional treatment is about nine-tenths pageantry, rumination, and rubbish" (p. 180). Although this "nothing works" debate has centered largely on adult corrections, such thinking has also permeated youth corrections. However, many administrators and the majority of professionals working with young offenders believe that young people have particular needs which require special care. Administrators and professionals must continue to assert that the system has as one of its objectives the growth and development of the youth.

The role of the child care professional will naturally be affected by the philosophy of the organization in which the professional is employed. If the agency or ministry providing the services stresses the needs of the youth, then much of the training that child care professionals receive will be compatible with the goals of the system. However, if the organization sees its role primarily as protection for society through the control of the youth's behavior for the duration of the judicial order, then child care professionals will be required to function in an environment which may conflict with their training and orientation.

Child care professionals working with young offenders must come to terms with a number of expectations from society, government, senior administration, colleagues, and academics. They can be summarized as follows:

Rehabilitation

This has as its objective the behavior change of the youth so that future offences will not be committed. If the youth does not commit further offences then it can be assumed that "rehabilitation" has occurred. Child care professionals may enter this system with the assumption that if the young offender is brough before the court and sentenced to probation or institutional confinement, it is the responsibility of both the system and the professional to elicit this change.

Retribution

This objective assumes that, as the young offender has broken the law, he must be punished. In contrast, programs that have as their objective the "treatment" of the offender may be seen as too soft or even pleasant. However the acceptance of punishment as an objective leaves open the possibility for allegations of staff abuse. The Y.O.A. states that "while young persons should not in all instances be held accountable in the same manner or suffer the same consequences for their behaviour as adults, young persons who commit offences should nonetheless bear responsibility for their contraventions'' (Sec. 3(1)(a)). The act further states that ''young persons who commit offences require supervision, discipline and control'' (Sec. 3(1)(c)). Accountability and punishment are not synonomous, nor does the Act suggest that the objective of a disposition, whether custodial or non-custodial, is punishment. Similarly, discipline and control do not give staff in a custodial setting license to exercise power in a way that is inhumane or otherwise punitive. Although the term discipline may be closely aligned with punishment, it more generally refers to the rules governing conduct. Its use in the Act does not appear to refer to the imposition of punishment for breaking the law.

Control

This differs from rehabilitation in that the control exercised is to prevent further delinquencies from occuring during the period of the disposition. Emphasis is placed on protecting society by removing the youth from the community. The proponents of the control approach look to the section of the act that states, ''society must . . . be afforded the necessary protection from illegal behaviour'' (Sec. 3(1)(b)). This section of the act taken out of context and not applied in relation to the needs of youth may result in the propagation of an expectation prominent in adult correctional circles. This refers to the ''warehousing'' of the offender for the duration of the sentence with minimal involvement by others, other than the provision of food, shelter, and basic activities such as work and education.

Normalization

The fourth expectation is that the young offender will be provided with a humane environment with the same general conditions and services that would be available in the community. The only limitation should be the degree of restriction on the young person's freedom required to protect society from illegal behavior. This meets both the requirement of Y.O.A. and one of the underlying tenets of the child care profession; it emphasizes the importance of meeting the special needs of youth in an effort to maximize the individual's potential.

Regardless of the exact youth justice model adopted by the province, or the expectations placed on the child care professional, youths have rights guaranteed by the *Canadian Charter of Rights and Freedoms*

(1982) and the *Canadian Bill of Rights* (1960). Child care professionals working with young offenders need to have some understanding of issues involving these rights. Coughlin (1973) identifies three areas. The first right involves "a moral power in virtue of which human beings may make just claims to certain things" (p. 8). An example is the right of a six-year-old to claim the candy which he is holding and not be forced to give it up. Secondly, natural rights or human rights belong to a person, "by reason of his very existence as a human person, and therefore is not conferred upon him by parents or church or state or any other individual or community of men" (p. 8). These unconditional rights include the right to, "life, food, drink, shelter and certain level of physical, emotional, intellectual, and spiritual growth" (p. 9). The third area involves civil rights, which are based "on natural rights and are the state's explicit enunciation of rights that it guarantees to every citizen" (p. 9). The *Canadian Charter of Rights and Freedoms* and the *Canadian Bill of Rights* outline civil rights. Other declarations of rights that have been adopted by the United Nations include the *Declaration of Rights of the Child* (1959), *Standard Minimum Rules for the Treatment of Prisoners* (1955), and the *Universal Declaration of Human Rights* (1948). Although these documents do not have the force of law, they stress the importance of ensuring that the rights of the individual are maintained.

Child care professionals working within the youth justice system will be confronted with the issue of children's rights balanced against the conditions within restrictive environments. The youth is an involuntary participant in the system and can only be released into the community if certain conditions are met. Limitations on freedom are imposed in order to maintain the care, custody, and security of the resident and the protection of staff. Control is required to maintain the rights of the other residents and the staff and provide a reasonable living environment. Not only does the Y.O.A. state that young offenders have the "right to be heard and included in the decisions affecting them" (Sec. 3(1)(3)), but also the right "to the least possible interference with freedom bearing in mind the needs of young persons and the interest of their families" (Sec. 3(1)(f)). Within policy regulations and rules, there still remains some discretion in decision making by staff working with young offenders.

The principles of administrative fairness must apply to all decisions made by a child care worker supervising young persons, whether on probation, in community programs, or in secure institutions. Criteria can be applied to all decisions to determine level of fairness. Fairness is determined by whether the decision is contrary to law, unjust, oppressive, discriminatory, arbitrary, unreasonable, or is not explained appropriately.

In summary, the youth justice system exists because of society's perceived need to be protected from the illegal behavior of young people. Thus, laws representing these interests are enacted to enable society to deal with illegal behavior. The law requires a system for young offenders that is separate from the adult criminal justice system, and the Y.O.A. provides the basis for dealing with offences committed by youth in Canada.

THE RELATIONSHIP BETWEEN THE CHILD CARE PROFESSIONAL AND YOUNG OFFENDER

The third component of working with young offenders involves the professional skills and abilities of the child care practitioner and the type of relationship with the young offender. Positions within the youth justice system may range from counseling in a diversion program to working in a secure custody centre. In most cases, the practitioner has two equally important but divergent roles. He must ensure that the youth is abiding by the court order, yet he must also provide the youth with support, direction, and guidance. Although these goals are often in conflict, and the time available to spend with the youth may be minimal, the relationship between youth and worker can be rewarding and productive. Success depends upon the worker's skill at non-judgmental listening, involving the youth in making decisions and ensuring that expectations are clearly defined. The initial contact with the worker will be affected by the emotional state and attitude of the youth. The message to the youth must be that ''I accept you as a person even if your behavior is unacceptable.''

With a progression through the system from lesser degrees of control (such as alternative measures) towards greater control (such as custody), the role of the child care professional becomes more intrusive in the life of the youth. In most larger urban communities, a wide range of services are established and available to young offenders. Community service, restitution, diversionary counseling, and other programs are provided as alternative measures. Dispositional options ordered by the court include community programs, probation supervision, treatment, and open and secure custody. However, in many of the more remote or rural areas, there may be few programs for youths. Subsequently, individualized programs need to be developed to accommodate dispositions and the need for care and control.

Often there is a definite increase in the level of control imposed on the young offender when the intervention is court-ordered. The consequences for violating a court-ordered disposition are serious, and the court can impose heavy restrictions on the freedom of the youth. Youths in secure custody have often "run the gamut" of available programs, having had numerous court appearances and perhaps having committed serious crimes such as robbery or murder. This environment generally provides minimal freedom, all staff represent total control, and all doors to the outside are locked. The routine is regimented and opportunities for youths to make decisions are severely curtailed. Rigid behavior control, peer pressure, the multiplicity of interactions between staff and residents, the lack of privacy, and the loss of freedom often combine to make the institution a dehumanizing and destructive place. However, secure custody is sometimes the only way of protecting society from aggressive or violent behavior. It is the single most restrictive disposition available to the youth court under the Y.O.A. and is intended for a minority of offenders for whom there is no other option.

In a recent discussion with residents in a secure custody facility, one of the authors asked a number of youths to describe the most effective staff member. The "best" staff member was described as follows:

> Every youth stated that the staff member really cared about him. There was also a perception that the staff member "liked kids" in general.
>
> Each youth made some reference to fair discipline and treatment; that is, when asking the child to do something the staff member explained why it should be done.
>
> Most youths commented on the staff member's availability and willingness to listen when they had a problem. This is reflected by one youth who added, "he seemed to know when something was bothering me and we would talk about it."
>
> The staff member did extra things outside normal working hours. For example, one youth had been taken by an off-duty staff member into the community for a family visit. He commented that the staff member realized how important it was to visit with family and trusted that he would not run away.

The same youths were also asked to describe the worst staff member. Comments included: "doesn't like kids," "only comes to work for the pay," "plays head games," "sits in the office," "pokes fun at me," and "calls me down in front of everybody." This information suggests that any worker in this setting is being observed and under close scrutiny. These comments by youths of the "best" and "worst" staff members are supported by Gold & Petronio (1980), who identify two themes of effective interventions: the support of warm, accepting relationships with adults, and the enhancement of adolescents' self-images as autonomous and effective individuals in the present and future (p. 523).

The relationship between workers and youths within these settings may be limited by time, routines, the dynamics of the existing peer group, and the degree to which meaningful relationships have been established in the past. Each worker, for example, has acquired a range of knowledge gained through education, training, and past experience. Knowledge from the youth justice field includes restrictions imposed by law, decisions handed down by the courts, policies, procedures and verbal instructions from supervisors, youth assessments and reports, and ideas from the youth's family, the victim and other professionals. However, a critical component in the transition of this knowledge to action involves the values of the worker. Like the physical properties of a prism that refract and disperse the sun's rays into a spectrum of color, the actions of the individual worker in relation to the client are focussed, filtered, and diffused during this transition.

Similarly, the young offender will see and interpret the decisions, actions, and intentions of the child care professional through the prism of his own value system. This information will, in part, be translated into behavior. This behavior in turn provides clues for the worker to incorporate into his repertoire of experience, thus completing the cycle. Finally, it should be understood that the application of various procedures in this setting may take on some degree of flexibility. The same policy applied by different staff members may initiate differing reactions in youths, from compliance, resistance and hesitation to anger.

The following describes one application of professional skills, knowledge, and attitudes within a closed custody setting.

> It's 6:45 AM. You arrive at the institution and an on-duty staff member unlocks the door and lets you in. Upon arrival you are assigned to a unit. On the unit you are briefed by the off-going staff as to problems or noteworthy events occurring during night shift. You receive your keys and check each room, counting the number of youths in care and their condition. At 7:30 AM you wake the residents and ask them to shower. After showers, breakfast is served and after breakfast the group must be prepared for school. Prior to school, residents are expected to tidy their rooms and make their beds. The schedule follows through lunch, the afternoon activities and at 3:00 PM the next shift comes on duty.

This work involves the constant supervision of the activities and behavior of the youths. Consequently, the potential for conflict is very high. Some youths are cheerful in the morning, but for some it's the most difficult part of the day. For those not in school there are work programs or other activities. Workers are involved in the continual process of balancing the demands of the organization (that is, get him to school on time) against the needs of the youth (for example, "I didn't get much sleep last night because I'm worried about something that's happening at home and I want to deal with it right now"). The worker can take a moment to talk with the youth about his problem or can react under the pressure of the moment and use authority to impose control. The latter approach will probably result in a struggle for power. Mismanaged conflict often results in escalating tension, beginning with defiance, then shouting, and finally either a voluntary retreat by the youth to his room, or a physical demonstration. If the youth becomes physically aggressive, staff may need to be summoned. If the youth is not intimidated into submission by the show of force, he may be restrained and physically placed in a secure room. This is a "no-win" outcome, as the resident ends up missing school and the staff member hasn't accomplished the objective of getting him there.

Sometimes there are no alternatives to physical control. Child care professionals working in settings where physical control may be required should keep in mind five basic tests to be applied when use of force is required.[5]

> 1) The objectives must be lawful. There must be an act or regulation that permits the use of force to obtain compliance or control. The legal authority for use of force should be reflected in agency policy.
> 2) The resistance to the attainment of the lawful objective must be evident. The degree of force required must be linked to the resistance. Resistance may be either verbal or physical.
> 3) Reasonable alternatives to the use of force must be either unavailable or have been tried and proven unsuccessful. Force should be used as a last resort and then only to the extent necessary to effect control. The resident should be given "space" and time to "cool off" in an effort to avoid the use of physical force. If force is required, the resident should be advised in advance that force will be used.
> 4) The force used must be minimal (that is, no more force than is required to overcome the resistance or to effect control). Force may be incrementally escalated as the resistance by the resident increases. The force used involves "restraint"; not strikes, blows, arm-bending, headlocks, other methods of inflicting pain. Inflicting pain is not an acceptable means of control or restraint for youth. It in-

creases anger and hostility and makes physically hurting others an acceptable practice.

5) The force used must be directly related or limited to the attainment of the lawful objective. For example, if staff are moving a resident to a secure room because he is destroying the furniture, once in the secure room he must be free to move about. Physically restraining him for an additional period of time to ''get the point across'' is not acceptable (pp. 63–65).

It is often when staff perceive minor issues as serious that hostile and aggressive incidents result. Such incidents are unlikely to occur when the staff member is nonjudgmental, capable of handling minor frustrations, and able to open channels of communication, allowing problems to be resolved in a mature and constructive manner. Patience, sensitivity, a sense of humor, and the ability not to feel threatened when challenged can make working with young offenders an enjoyable, productive, and rewarding experience.

It is very important that the child care professionals working with young offenders acknowledge the *dignity* and *self-worth* of every youth. In addition, it is the professional's responsibility to do his part to ensure that the institutional landscape is dominated by the intention to provide the most humane and caring environment possible within what can otherwise become a coercive, restrictive, and dehumanizing existence for both residents and staff.

SUMMARY

This chapter has provided an overview of three basic components essential to the practice of child care in the youth justice field:

1) Knowledge of the *Young Offenders Act* and how it affects the young offender, the system, and the child care profession.
2) Knowledge of how the various components of the system, such as the youth, family, police, courts, and services, interact.
3) Discussion of the skills and approaches required by child care professionals within settings in which young offenders are placed.

It is important that the child care professional working closely with young offenders separates who he is from what he does. By recognizing and respecting the power and authority vested in this position, the professional is less likely to become embroiled in power struggles with youths and, consequently, is less likely to become involved in destructive or abusive relationships. The rejection, rule-breaking, and inappropriate behavior of a youth can have significant impact on the emotions of the professional worker.

The *Young Offenders Act,* like any new legislation, will undergo an interpretation period over a number of years. The adoption of the *Canadian Charter of Rights and Freedoms* has also had an impact on the development and interpretation of the *Young Offenders Act.* The youth justice system in Canada is experiencing a significant period of transition. As changes have taken place in the system, so has the child care profession been gaining recognition and status. Skilled practitioners are being recruited in ever-increasing numbers. This provides child care professionals with the opportunity both to influence and impact youth justice in Canada.

NOTES

1. These statistics, however, do not reflect the current uniform age for young offenders. Effective 1 April 1985 (tentative) the age range under the Y.O.A. is 12 to 17 years inclusive. Up to 1 April 1985, the lower age limit of young offenders was 7. In Alberta and Ontario young persons committing offences after their 16th birthday were tried in adult court and in Manitoba and Quebec offenders were considered "adult" when they turned 18.
2. Canada's first national legislation dealing with young offenders was passed in 1894. This act made it mandatory that persons under 16 years of age be tried separately from other accused persons and without publicity. The act did not provide for any special court procedures for young offenders. Although tried separately, young offenders were subject to court process and procedures applied to adults. This act also provided for separate pre-trial and post-trial custody (McGrath, 1965, p. 10).
3. Alternative measures are measures other than judicial proceedings used to deal with a young person alleged to have committed an offence under the Young Offenders Act. In a sense, Y.O.A. legislates a concept of "diversion." However, not all diversion programs are to be considered alternative measures programs. Many diversion programs do not comply with the rigid legislative provisions which apply to alternative measures programs. For a program to be considered an alternative measure program, it must be formally designated as such by provincial authorities. The Y.O.A. allows each province to determine whether it wishes to implement alternative measures programs and provides flexibility for the development of different types of programs in response to needs, interests, and resources. The reader is advised to contact local provincial authorities to determine the status and scope of alternative measure programs in his province.
4. During February 1986 it was announced that further amendments to the Y.O.A. would be considered. The amendments are in the final stages of parliamentary approval with proclamation scheduled for the early Fall. Many of the amendments are technical in nature, but several are more substantive. The following summarizes a number of these areas:

    1) the substitution of offence provisions will permit arrest for a breach of probation without a warrant.

2) temporary restraint provisions will permit young persons to be held in police cells where custody facilities are not available.
3) with judicial approval the name of a youth can be published if the youth is at large and the court considers the youth a danger to the community.
4) record maintenance and destruction amendments now emphasize prohibition on use rather than destruction. Young offender records can be revived and used in adult court under certain conditions with judicial approval.
5) changes to the criminal code will enable an adult or young person to be charged for aiding and abetting a child under the age of 12 to commit an offence.
6) consecutive sentences beyond the three-year maximum limit will be permitted. For example, if a youth is placed in secure custody for three years for murder, escapes, then commits an armed robbery, he/she may be given another secure custody disposition of up to three years, consecutive to the first. The young offender would have to complete the time remaining in the first term prior to serving the additional three years.

5. These five points were originally taken from documents from the Office of the Ombudsman, Hawaii (1983).

REFERENCES

British Columbia (1984). Ministry of the Attorney General, Corrections Branch. Youth Correctional Manual, Sect. Cl, 2.01, p. 2.

Coughlin, B. (1973). The rights of children. In A. Wilderson (Ed.) *The rights of children: Emergent concepts in law and society* (pp. 7–23). Philadelphia: Temple University Press.

Canada. (1908). Laws and Statutes. Juvenile Delinquents Act. 7–8 Edward VII, C-40.

Canada. (1960). Bill of Rights. 8–9. Eliz II, c. 44. (R.S.C., 1970, Appendix 3).

Canada. (1970). Law and Statutes. Criminal Code. RSC. C-34.

Canada. (1982). Charter of Rights and Freedoms. 30–31. Eliz II–11–Sch.B; 1 (U.K.).

Canada. (1982). Laws and Statutes. Young Offenders Act. S.C. 1980–81–82, Eliz II, c. 110, proclaimed 2 April 1984.

Gold, M. & Petronio, R. J. (1980). Delinquent behavior in adolescents. In J. Adelson (Ed.) *Handbook of adolescent psychology* (pp. 495–535). New York: Wiley.

Hogg, P. (1985). *Constitutional law of Canada.* Toronto: Carswell.

McGrath, W. T. (Ed.) *Crime and its treatment in Canada.* Toronto: Macmillan.

Martinson, R. (1974). What works? Questions and answers about prison reform. *Public Interest, 35,* 22–54.

Martinson, R. (1976). California research at the crossroads. *Crime and Delinquency, 22,* 180–191.

Newman, B. M. & Newman, P. R. (1986). *Adolescent development.* Ohio: Merril.

Office of the Ombudsman, British Columbia. (1985). *The Willingdon Case.* Public Report No. 13.

Office of the Ombudsman, Hawaii. (1983). *Investigation of allegations of the use of unreasonable force against inmates during the shakedown of the Oahu Community Correctional Centre from December 14th through December 18th, 1981.*

Statistics Canada. (1983). Canadian Centre for Justice Statistics, Ministry of Supply and Services, Pub. No. 85-X-202, Juvenile Delinquents.

United Kingdom Laws and Statutes. (1867). British North America Act. 30 & 31 Victoria, c. 3.

United Nations. (1948). Universal declaration of human rights. United Nations Document A/811.

United Nations. (1955). Standard minimum rules for treatment of prisoners. First United Nations Congress on the Prevention of Crime and the Treatment of Offenders. Geneva A. conf. 6 Li7.

United Nations. (1959). Declarations of the rights of the child. General Assembly Resolution, 1386 (viv), November 20th. Official Records of the General Assembly, Fourteenth Session Supplement, No. 16, 1960, p. 19.

ADDITIONAL READINGS

Bala, N. & Heino, L. (1982). *Young offenders act annotated.* Solicitor General Canada.

Bala, N., Heino, L. & Thomson, G. M. (1982). *Canadian children's law: cases, notes and materials.* Toronto: Butterworth.

Brownlie, I. (Ed.) (1981). *Basic documents on human rights* (2d ed.). Oxford: Clarendon Press.

Corrada, R. R., LeBlanc, M. & Trepanier, J. (Eds.) (1983). *Current issues in juvenile justice,* Toronto: Butterworth.

Hackler, J. (1978). *The prevention of youthful crime: The great stumble forward.* Toronto: Methuen.

Jenkins, R. L., Heidemann, P. H. & Caputo, J. H. (1958). *No single cause: Juvenile delinquency and the search for effective treatment.* Maryland and Virginia: Maryland Correctional Association.

Leon, J. S. (1977). The development of Canadian juvenile justice: A background for reform. *U Grad Hall Law Journal, 15,* 71.

Leyton, E. (1979). *The myths of delinquency: An anatomy of juvenile delinquency*. New York: Oxford University Press.

Lundman, R. (1984). *Prevention and control of juvenile delinquency*. New York: Oxford University Press.

Millar, L. (1986). *The Young Offenders Act*. Toronto: Guidance and Counselling, Guidance Centre, University of Toronto Press.

Parker, G. (1976). The juvenile court movement. *University of Toronto Law Journal, 26,* 40.

Platt, A. M. (1969). *The child savers: The invention of delinquency*. Chicago: University of Chicago Press.

Reid, S. & Reitsma-Street, M. (1984). Assumptions and implications of new Canadian legislation for young offenders. *Canadian Criminology Forum, 7,* 1–19.

West, W. G. (1984). *Young offenders and the state: A Canadian perspective on delinquency*. Toronto: Butterworth.

Wilson, L. C. (1982). *Juvenile courts in Canada*. Toronto: Carswell.

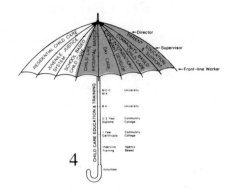

4

Canadian School-Based Child Care

CAREY DENHOLM AND DAVID WATKINS

INTRODUCTION

In the past twenty-five years, child care in the Canadian educational system has neither followed a carefully scripted master plan, nor has it emerged as a result of intentional national legislation. What is termed "Canadian school-based child care" refers to a myriad of programs containing individual histories, emphases, therapeutic and educational aims, supported by differing structural and administrative frameworks, all occurring within a variety of environments.

Although the area of school-based child care has received scant attention in the professional child care journals[1] and texts,[2] child care work in Canadian schools is now extensive and well-established.[3] The impetus for the development of individual school-based child care programs may have been in response to a heartfelt community need, an act of desperation on the part of the school principal, or simply an administrative directive. Thus, many of these programs have their own unique history. This may suggest that attempts to establish a national perspective would be fragmented and disparate. However, a number of inter-related yet separate factors occurring within the last two decades have provided the substance and credibility for the movement to establish child care services within the Canadian education system.

KEY INFLUENCES WITHIN CANADIAN EDUCATION

The CELDIC Report

Clearly the most influential document produced in recent years was the report by the Commission on Emotional and Learning Disorders in Children (CELDIC) (1970). Entitled *One Million Children*, this report focussed attention on the urgency to develop new approaches to meet the "special needs" of children and youth. Of specific relevance to the emergence of school-based child care programs was the stated need to develop methods "to provide continuity of care and immediate help . . . by people close to the child in his home, school and community" (Lazure, 1970, p. 8). The report continues:

> We were frequently distressed by the isolation of the school from other sources of help in the community. This provides an example of the division that we saw between many of the services and the helping professions who were all working separately to aid children. We are convinced that these divisions are intolerable. They lead to a partial, fragmented effort when a total coordinated drive is required (p. 4).

Prior to this report, other reports supported this approach. For example the Hall-Dennis Report (1968), commissioned by the Ontario Ministry of Education, stressed that "there no longer be a distinction between one type of student and another; that education for an individual should progress along a continuum with the choices of experiences and rate of progress depending respectively on student's needs, interests and his/her own rate of maturing" (p. 150). Subsequently, two fundamental principles for governing school education in the province of Ontario were made. These were: 1) the right of every individual to have equal access to the learning experience best suited to his needs, and 2) the responsibility of every school authority to provide a child-centered learning continuum that invites learning by individual discovery and inquiry (p. 150).

One example of the impact of the CELDIC report is recorded by Haberlin (1976) who outlines the initial beginnings of the Kitsilano Elementary Child Care Program in Vancouver. In 1974, the Vancouver Resources Board made a decision to follow one of the recommendations of the CELDIC Report by placing three child care workers into three elementary schools. This program was in response to the needs of a very visible group of pre-delinquent boys who were causing havoc in their school. By 1977, grants were approved to place six workers in six elementary schools. The concept, states Neil (1981), of placing social services-oriented counselors in schools was also strongly supported by a Report by the Educational Research Institute of British Columbia (Laycock & Finlay, 1974). The primary role of the elementary school child care worker was to focus on specific social functioning and school-related behaviors which were affecting academic learning.

The CELDIC report provided the philosophical "groundwork" for a review of educational services for Canadian children, youth, and their families and for the legitimization of child care services in schools. Two implications emerged from this review. The first was whether it was the responsibility of the school to assume responsibility for the emotional and/or associated learning problems of all children; the second questioned the type and quality of service needed for exceptional students (Klassen, 1981).

Normalization and Integration

"Normalization" is a broad principle of human management initially outlined in the Scandinavian literature in the late 1960s. It is defined as: "utilization of means which are as culturally normative as possible, in order to establish and/or maintain personal behaviors and characteristics which are as culturally normative as possible" (Wolfensberger, 1972, p. 28). One of the major adaptions of this principle in North America involved the examination of the philosophical tenets and types of programs in which mentally handicapped children and adults were being placed. One related effect of this movement was the shift away from institutional care of handicapped children in large residential centers to supportive care within their home environment. Subsequently, a vast body of approaches relating to the management of handicapped children at home (Porter & Coleman, 1978; Wolfensberger, 1983), provision of parent support (Standifer, 1964; Wolfensberger & Menolascino, 1970), and societal implications (Wolfensberger, 1980; Wolfensberger & Thomas, 1980) were developed.

When U.S. President Gerald Ford signed the *Education for All Handicapped Children Act*, PL94-142 ("Education of Handicapped Children," 1977) an educational trend within the United States had received federal sanction (Strain and Kerr, 1981). In essence, the principle was to "educate handicapped children in the least restrictive environment, as close as possible to their non-handicapped peers" (Kameen, 1979). The "least restrictive environment" is explained as follows:

1) That to the maximum extent appropriate, handicapped children, including children in public or private institutions or other care facili-

ties, are educated with children who are not handicapped, and
2) That special classes, separate schooling or other removal of handicapped children from the regular educational environment occurs
only when the nature or severity of the handicap is such that education in regular classes with the use of supplementary aids and services cannot be achieved satisfactorily (23 August 1977, p. 42497).

Subsequently, many school board administrators in the United States
and Canada "leaped on the bandwagon without providing adequate
teacher support or inservice training and without thoroughly examining
the concept" (Allan, 1980, p. 15). Acceptance of both the philosophy
and implications of normalization had a direct impact on local schools,
often forcing untrained staff to learn to cope with severely handicapped
children and adolescents within the normal school setting. Thus the opportunity for community agencies and boards to establish and manage
child care services in these educational programs commenced. This
opened a new avenue for the introduction of the child care role to administrators, teachers, and parents.

Climate of Social and Educational Change

During the late 1960s, Canadian provinces experienced an increase in
the number of training programs offered and taken by school counselors,
learning assistants, special education teachers, and child care workers.
Community and parent groups continued the trend established in the
United States for involvement and active participation in public education. In response, "experimental" educational programs grew more acceptable, if not fashionable and perhaps trendy. This developed into a
plethora of "alternate" education programs attempting to expand learning options within the public school system.

What emerged then were: 1) "integrated" programs, designed to integrate subject areas within the regular school; 2) "enriched" programs,
emphasizing community spirit and enriched classroom learning; 3)
"alternate" schools, with a humanistic orientation and heavy involvement in student decision-making; and 4) "rehabilitation" programs,
aimed at potential or actual "dropouts." Those programs classified as
"alternate" and "rehabilitative" were more likely to have child care
professionals (usually funded by other non-education ministries) on the
staff. One reason for their involvement was "to enable children or youth
who are experiencing great difficulty at school for social and/or emotional reasons or who have dropped out of school, to acquire basic skills
which will make it possible for them to re-enter the school system or pro-
ceed to further training or employment" (GAIN, 1978, 2.183).

School programs catering to the individual learning needs of students emerged; within many of these programs, positions for child care workers were created. The establishment and solidification of these programs came about as part of the trend towards a more humanistic, child-centered approach and the establishment of divergent educational programs. The rehabilitation practitioner, who is employed to assist the integration of developmentally handicapped individuals within society, also appeared at this time. As will be evident later in this chapter, many of the central functions of the child care worker and the rehabilitation practitioner are similar. In fact, many of the recently developed models of vocational training, social education, home living, and leisure time for handicapped young adults (Brown & Hughson, 1980; DuRand & Newfeldt, 1975; Marlett & Hughson, 1979) can be applied to a wide variety of child care work.

In summary, a number of events occurred during the 1960s and 1970s: the trend to decentralize large institutions and the evolution of more community-based programs; the impact of integration and parental demand for quality care of handicapped children; increased training and educational opportunities for child care professionals; the attention of the media on the need to develop more meaningful educational progams for children; the impact within the education system of the works of Neill (1960) and Holt (1964); and the relative prosperity of provincial governments. Although many of these factors can be examined separately, it should be seen that the interplay has been dramatic and pervasive, contributing in their own special way to the establishment of varying types of child care programs within this system.

MODELS OF CANADIAN SCHOOL-BASED PROGRAMS

The following is an outline of eight major types or models of Canadian child care programs. Variations within provinces are evident in terms of location, student population size, staff complement, and funding structure and mandate; hence their title may not indicate the category into which they may fall or the underlying structure of each program. For example, the authors have met child care workers from programs having the following names: The Warehouse School, Eastside, Multiple Choice, New Dimensions, Total Education, Options for Pregnant Teenagers, Up-Town, Girls Alternative Program, Outreach, Bridge, 8J9J, and Sunrise East.

The following models illustrate the central differences among programs employing child care professionals. It should be noted that this list is not exhaustive and local variations will be evident.

Model No. 1

In this model, one child care worker is assigned to either a regular elementary, junior secondary, or secondary school with the primary responsibility of working with non-handicapped children and their parents (Neil, 1981; Klassen, 1981). The worker may be supervised directly by the school principal or a person external to the school. They may be expected to perform a variety of functions, work during non-school hours, have their own office, and be responsible to administer their own budget for materials and equipment. This is similar to the position of the home-school liaison worker in Ontario.

Model No. 2

The only difference between this and Model No. 1 is that the child care worker is assigned one or several handicapped children throughout the entire day. These workers are often attached to special education classes or classes for the mentally handicapped. Specific functions may include transportation, teaching and supporting the student throughout the day, conducting parent counseling, and designing the student's individual learning plan. In Alberta, the work of the rehabilitation practitioner is similar to this model.

Model No. 3

This model involves one or more child care workers assigned to several schools. Again, these may be regular elementary, junior secondary, or secondary schools, with the principal and/or the sponsoring agency/board supervising and implementing the program (McMorran, 1981; Hubbard & Phillips, 1981). The worker may be called a youth counselor, adolescent care worker, or child care worker and may also be required to monitor attendance and help irregular attenders increase their involvement and participation.

Model No. 4

Child care workers also become involved within the school system on an itinerant basis. In this situation, the worker is hired by a community agency/board to provide child service to families within a designated area. Contact must be made with the school principal, relevant teachers, and school counselors concerning referred clients, and the school may provide counseling facilities for the worker (Klassen, 1981). The child

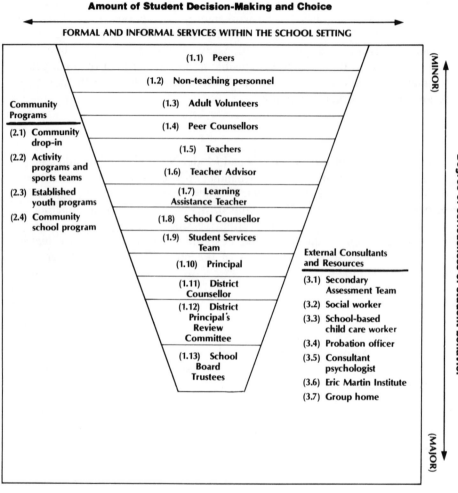

FIGURE 1. The Structure of Student Support Services at Shoreline Community School

care worker as one of many external consultants and resource personnel within the network of student services at a community school is presented in Figure 1 (Nordstrom & Denholm, 1986). In this particular situation, the worker maintains an indirect relationship with the school and is contracted on a request/referral basis.

Model No. 5

The "alternate" program setting has a number of variations, but in most cases it occurs in one specific location. In this model the building and program are attached to an existing junior or senior secondary school. The staff are directly responsible to the school principal, and students for the program (primarily adolescents) come from within this school population. The child care staff may or may not be direct employees of the school district.

Model No. 6

A variation on the previous model uses the same staffing arrangement, but the building is physically separate from the "parent" school; in some cases it is up to five miles away. The students are usually referred from specific neighboring schools.

Model No. 7

In this type, building and program are autonomous; the education staff are employees of the school district, and the child care staff are responsible to a community agency or board of directors. The teachers and academic program are the responsibility of a supervising principal appointed by the school district. Child care supervision is established jointly by a personnel committee comprised of board members and/or representatives from the relevant ministry responsible for the funding (Figure 2). Students may apply to attend from any school and admission screening takes place internally.

Model No. 8

This variation is to be found within the day clinic/center where children and/or adolescents are placed for shortterm intervention and later returned to their regular school program. This is generally a nonresidential program; child care intervention may involve family counseling and support, child assessment, and teacher education. The demon-

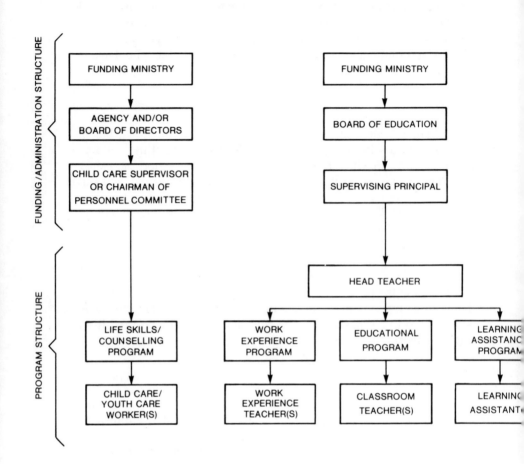

FIGURE 2. Organizational and Funding Structure of Alternate Program

stration of effective intervention techniques from a clearly articulated theoretical base may also be required of staff.

In summary, a number of existing models exist, differing in program organization, description, mandate, and staffing structure. It should also be noted that programs may appear to be one particular model, but they may not be as easily identifiable as has been suggested here. Differences may be found in terms of size of student body, historical development, style, and educational goals.

FUNCTIONS OF SCHOOL-BASED CHILD CARE WORKERS

What exactly do child care workers do in schools? One sample response which may serve as a starting point for discussion is as follows: "The primary role of the child care worker within the educational setting is to promote behavioral change and personal growth in children and adolescents who are having difficulties coping within this setting as a result of social, emotional and physical problems, and to assist in their academic success." Single sentence definitions, however, only assist in providing direction, not substance. For example, it would be difficult to establish a full-time, accountable school-based child care position on the basis of this definition. In order to provide a more definitive response and to discover exactly what school-based child care workers are doing, a compilation was made. This was extracted from published works (Anglin, 1983; Denholm, 1981a; Denholm, 1983; Houndle & Ricks, 1981; Klassen, 1981; McMorran, 1981; Neil, 1981), from established guidelines in provincial education ministry and school district policy handbooks,[4] from various program documents,[5] and from personal discussions with school-based child care workers over the past eleven years.

Variations in the functions of workers were seen. These were related to the size of the program, type of structure/setting and funding arrangements, length of time established, type of student service, and educational level of the child care worker. One clear trend emerged: the higher the educational level of the worker, the more clearly documented and specific were the established functions. It should be noted that these functions are not grouped into categories as in Anglin (1983), nor are they listed in order of significance. In addition, no one child care worker position ever encompassed this complete list of functions. Only those that were consistently mentioned have been included; they will almost certainly occur within the majority of educational programs employing Canadian school-based child care workers. They are classified into five main areas.

School-related Functions

1) working in the classroom with the primary objectives of behavioral change, improvement of self-concept, and the development of social skills in individual students or the entire class. Also included may be the demonstration of individual and group management techniques to teachers and parents, the modeling of specific approaches with problem students, and the presentation of programs which focus on affective and social skills education.

2) assisting individual teachers in the preparation of recommendations on individuals or groups of students (or their families) for case conferences. Depending on any subsequent recommendations, this assistance may continue during the implementation and/or the evaluation phases, referred to later in this chapter.

3) collecting information for school staff on classroom environments and the student population. Activities include the preparation of such information as the socioeconomic and geographic makeup of the community, the availability and limitations of community resources, relevant coming events, and position papers on research supporting a particular therapeutic approach. In response to the expressed needs of teachers concerning information on the social and/or emotional development of children or adolescents, the workers may also be requested to make the necessary arrangements for guest presentations, films, and the circulation of relevant literature.

4) co-ordinating case consultation and team meetings. In co-operation with the school principal, who may assume responsibility for conducting the meeting, the school-based child care worker often organizes times, informs parents and other appropriate members about the conference, and ensures that all relevant information and reports are ready for that meeting.

5) participating in school-related meetings. These include regular staff meetings, consultations with administration, school-based child care team meetings, representations to government officials, professional workshops, school-initiated parent consultations, and membership in ad-hoc commitees, such as curriculum planning and school discipline.

Individual Student Functions

1) identifying and providing a suitably in-depth assessment of individual children and adolescents. This involves planned observations within the classroom, school and/or home environment using formal assessment tools, conducting individual sessions with identified students, preparing confidential reports (including practical in-class suggestions), and communicating recommendations to teachers, the school principal, and students (if appropriate).

2) designing, implementing, and evaluating interventions to assist students (and families if necessary) in dealing with specific school related issues. The implementation stage may require brief counseling or a series of planned interventions. The integration of handicapped students, organization of new student admissions, or assistance for students experiencing a death in the family may all require both counseling and intervention strategies.

3) referring students and their families to relevant social service agencies and medical/dental personnel. This requires that the worker act as student advocate to ensure prompt attention and adequate delivery of services.

4) placing students in community-based programs and organizations. The intent is to enhance student self-esteem in relation to newly acquired physical, social, and living skills. Follow-up support is also conducted with those who require more intensive care to facilitate the successful bridge between the existing program and these resources.

5) participating in the existing work experience program. This may be in co-operation with the work experience teacher by assisting students to meet set objectives, assessing the individual needs of students, and developing individual programs for students within specific work settings.

6) attending to the overall integration of one or several handicapped students to whom they are assigned for the entire school day. This includes the supervision and/or provision of physical care such as feeding, toileting, and maintaining general physical comfort. Invariably, the worker becomes involved in the education of teachers and fellow students concerning the strengths, limitations, and developmental needs of the student and may also have to become proficient in the language used by the student, such as Bliss symbolics, sign language, or Braille.

Group Intervention Functions

1) assessing and preparing students for shortterm group counseling with the focus on the development of social skills. Involved in the establishment of specific groups (such as for anger management, relaxation training, or problem solving) is the responsibility to conduct these groups and to evaluate individual progress.

2) assessing, preparing, intervening, and evaluating "identified" students for longterm group counseling. Topics may include life skills training, self-esteem development, peer counseling, and support for students with a handicap or a chronic illness.

3) initiating and involving groups in recreational and other activities. These may include athletics, games, crafts, camping, and outdoor education, with the emphasis on self-reliance and socializaion.

4) developing programs in response to student request or assessed need with both "normal" and "special needs" students in order to promote the integration of special needs and normal children. An example would be the involvement of handicapped children in regular sports and general age-appropriate activities with their non-handicapped peers.

Family-related Functions

1) conducting parent education programs. Examples include Parent Effectiveness Training (Gordon, 1975), Systematic Training for Effective Parenting (Dinkmeyer & McKay, 1976), and Systematic Training for Effective Parenting of Teenagers (Dinkmeyer & McKay, 1983).

2) providing long- and shortterm support to families. Examples may include providing information concerning financial problems or helping change a difficult living situation. This function is not as intense as family therapy but serves to facilitate family interpersonal communication and problem solving skills.

3) referring parents who are in need of longterm counseling and support to a social service agency.

4) co-ordinating parent and family activity nights. The focus would be assisting potentially isolated families (that is, immigrants, recent arrivals, parents of handicapped students) to make contact with other families in order to promote family growth and development.

Community Functions

1) consulting with other professionals in the community. This may involve being an active board member of a community program, being involved with community centers, community care teams, and other social service agencies, and co-operating and consulting with officials from services such as health and police departments. Also included is liaison with residential care workers in an effort to maintain a consistent child management model across environments.

2) promoting inter-agency co-operation within the community. This would primarily be in response to specific situations which may affect the management and organization of the school.

IMPLICATIONS FOR CURRENT PRACTICE

One immediate implication addresses all college and university child care training programs. It is vital that school-based child care workers have adequate preparatory knowledge and skill in the areas of individual and group assessment, intervention and evaluation, counseling, recreational leadership, program planning and professional consultation. In addition, it would be advisable for the student intending to seek employment in this environment to have had a minimum of two supervised practica with school-based child care workers in different school settings.

During that time the student should have had the opportunity to work with a number of teachers in different programs, deal with students exhibiting a range of problems, be involved in report writing and case consultations, and accompany the worker on home visits.

With special emphasis and skills in the areas of child and family development, child care workers offer a range of non-educational functions within the school setting. Their role is to meet the student's behavioral needs, thereby enhancing the student's ability to benefit from the educational program. One of the many strengths of this role is that professional child care workers have the conceptual and theoretical background, coupled with a pragmatic understanding of the various systems which may affect the student or family. These competencies allow workers to move across the boundaries of government ministries in order to coordinate the total care system for the student. Information on several Canadian programs involved in the preparation of school-based personnel is described elsewhere (Brown & Hughson, 1980; Denholm, in press).

Regardless of a list of clearly defined functions, an effective child care presence within any school and school district comes about only through careful planning, preparation, and on-going support. Hence, the successful maintenance of this service requires that both school personnel and child care workers maintain an open and equal relationship. In order to facilitate the acceptance and potential of child care work in the schools, child care workers need to: 1) know and understand the academic experience of teachers; 2) be aware of the special demands and stresses placed on teachers by the education system; and 3) understand how intervention and management techniques must be modified in order to suit the classroom and school environment.

Teachers and other school personnel need to: 1) know and understand the academic and practical experience of school-based child care workers; 2) be aware of the special demands and stresses placed on child care workers by parents, students, the school system, and external supervisors and boards; and 3) be willing to listen and openly discuss child care perspectives and approaches in relation to parents, students, and the school system.

PUTTING THEORY INTO PRACTICE

Knowing what Canadian school-based child care workers do is only the first step. Several vital and related aspects remain to be addressed involving the actual implentation of these theories. Acceptance of the child care presence within any school does not come about simply through a written job description, although a clear outline of what the worker is able to do and expected to perform is a prerequisite for success. It is important that the actual process of introducing a child care worker into a school is attempted only with prior planning, organization, and diplomacy. For, as will be indicated, loss of support and alienation by staff are potential hazards. Perhaps the effectiveness of the service will depend on the degree to which the presence of the child care worker is accepted personally and professionally by the staff, as well as the degree to which the role is accepted by the parents and the school administration.

The following five-phase approach may serve as a focal point for those child care professionals who are contemplating working within this system. Although a number of issues relate to all workers entering schools, this approach is primarily designed for full-time, school-based child care workers. It is also noted that this process is not considered prescriptive; adaptations will need to be made in relation to individual program needs.

Phase 1: Orientation, or "Earning the Right to Help"

Many of the functions described in this chapter have, as their common element, involvement with people (student, teachers, parents, community resource personnel). Therefore, the first step in beginning a child care program in a school involves getting to know the people and establishing a productive working relationship. This relationship must be earned (Parsons & Meyers, 1984). Earning the right to help means the child care worker must accept the stated goals of the school and be an active participant in helping students and teachers achieve these goals.

The child care worker's orientation to students and to the school, then, must be clearly demonstrated as one of service. Although the school and the worker are allies and share many common objectives, approaches to the provision of "service" to students may differ. In order to understand and work effectively with this potential conflict, the worker may function as if the school and student body are potential clients. Implied here is the need to begin serving the school and individuals in practical ways. This should be done in areas in which there is a visible need and the activity can be considered non-threatening to the roles and tasks of others. The following are examples of service/helping activities appropriate to this orientation phase.

> Your school is hosting a basketball tournament this weekend. You offer to help paint posters welcoming visiting teams.
> You observe in a meeting of the student government, the treasurer is having trouble keeping the statement of accounts in order. You offer to assist.

Litter has collected at the back of the school and you organize a group of students to clear it up.

During this phase, the focus is on the functions of the child care worker as a professional who works with people in visible ways and who is serious about making a commitment to service within the school, to its staff and students. It should be noted that this phase has no specific time period. That is, many of these activities should occur on a regular basis after the right to help has been earned. It is the child care worker who needs to seize the opportunity to remain visible within this setting and must continue to make a positive statement concerning the degree to which he or she is committed to the school.

Phase 2: Data Gathering, or "Determining What is Needed"

The functions of the child care worker encompass a range of activities beyond the abilities of any one person. It is unrealistic to expect one individual to attend to them all with any degree of effectiveness. To avoid a haphazard selection, the functions relevant to each school should be identified in the form of a cluster of manageable tasks. Those relevant function statements should be related to the needs of the students within the setting and should be in harmony with the established guidelines and philosophy of their particular school.

In an attempt to place the most relevant functions into a comprehensive job description, the worker should gather data to determine which functions reflect the greatest need. Data can be compiled in a variety of ways, including the administration of carefully designed questionnaires, interviews with former workers and allied professionals (such as the nurse or psychologist), informal discussions with teachers, counselors, and administrators, and feedback from parents. Regardless of the degree of formality and the time taken for data collection, all results should be documented accurately and presented in a professional manner to the principal. This documentation should then form the basis for the next step: priorization.

Workers should also prepare an outline of the possible activities in which they consider themselves competent. Included in this document might be relevant past experiences, special skills, preferred method of counseling and intervention, and a copy of any written material (personal or from your professional association) which might further explain your potential role. Publications assisting in understanding the change process within school (Apter, 1982) and human service settings (Egan, 1985), theoretical bases for behavioral change (Kanfer & Goldstein, 1984) and practical applications within the classroom (Cartledge & Milburn, 1985;

Jarrett & Klassen, 1986), would serve as appropriate sources and could be purchased to form a part of the child care worker's professional library.

Phase 3: Planning and Priorization, or "Who Needs Help First?"

Using the data relating to role definition and service delivery tasks within this system, child care functions need to be put into an hierarchical order. This could involve lists of daily, weekly, or monthly tasks. When potentially conflicting demands and expectations arise, the lists will assist the worker in appropriate time allocation. It is stressed that the process of data gathering, followed by planning and priorization, must be done in consultation with the school administrative personnel and other staff such as school counselors. The possibilities for success in this position will be enhanced when effective communication with these individuals has been established and they demonstrate understanding, agreement, and commitment to each of the child care worker's priorized functions.

Phase 4: Implementation, or "Doing It"

With the role, functions, and priorities clearly established and supported, the child care worker is now in a position to become "fully operational." That is, the theoretical descriptions of these functions can now be translated into practice. At this point, a number of suggestions can be made which might further facilitate the implementation phase and enhance the credibility of the worker within this system. For example, it is suggested that the worker:

> become familiar with the provincial legislation, policies and regulations relating to the particular school district, school routine, and procedures and note the laws and regulations concerning such as the transportation of students;
> clearly describe the referral process for students, staff and parents for child care services;
> be sensitive to those matters which may create tension between themselves and students or staff members (such as flexible work schedule, dress code, having an office and telephone);
> keep the staff informed about their work load and timetable. It is suggested that beginning workers offer an introductory workshop for teachers on the theory and practice of child care, develop a brochure clearly describing the child care role, attend staff meetings to give brief reports and answer questions, and learn about the operation of the school;

always give teachers advance notice about any activities which may affect their teaching duties or schedule;

familiarize themselves with other school-based programs and their mode of operation; and

keep a copy of a daily diary which is placed with the school secretary indicating the location and phone number of various appointments.

Phase 5: Evaluation, or "Where Was I Least and Most Effective?"

An important task is the establishment of criteria for success both in relation to the role description and to individual and group interventions. Self-report as well as external evaluation procedures should be completed on a regular basis. Included within the evaluation file should be teacher evaluations of presentations, copies of written parent feedback, and supervisory notes.

A self-evaluation component is necessary for two reasons. First, feedback is the link between past and future performance, enabling the worker to adjust, correct, and improve the quality of service. Second, evaluation measures provide an excellent source of data with which to establish a level of accountability. Workers should expect that documented evidence of satisfactory performance will be required at some point.

The child care worker, in consultation with school administration, will need to consider carefully the characteristics of the setting in which this service will be provided and make appropriate decisions concerning these phases. Such decisions would concern the needs within each phase and the amount of time allotted to each. For example, the first phase might be successfully achieved within several weeks, depending on the particular setting. It may also be an ongoing process in some situations, as the worker is repeatedly required to reorient him or herself and re-earn the right to help. Another consideration is that the child care worker may be involved with more than one school, requiring the application of different approaches to child care services within each school.

CRITICAL ISSUES IN CANADIAN SCHOOL-BASED CHILD CARE

School-based child care work brings with it a variety of interesting issues. Some are the articulation of the role of child care in relation to the purpose or "mission" of the school, while others relate to the emergence of child care within this system. This section briefly describes several current issues frequently discussed in educational settings.

Issue 1: Financial, or "Who Pays the Piper?"

Who should bear the financial responsibility for the provision of child care services? One perspective maintains that child care is supplementary to the instructional component. Continuing with this position, the primary purpose for child care services is to be supportive of the delivery of educational services. Therefore, as a supportive service (as distinct from a service providing "a direct educational benefit" to students), the cost of this service is not a proper charge to the educational budget. The cost of such supportive services, it is argued, cannot be borne by the educational tax dollar.

It is here that the issue of financial constraints and education "cutbacks" become a factor. The funding formula applied to schools is often tied to school size. With declining populations, services seen as additional to classroom teaching (such as librarian, learning assistance, child care) are often reduced. Thus, child care workers need to maintain an active, visible, and accountable role within the school and community in order to combat this trend. Perhaps the recent unionization of non-teaching assistants at a number of boards of education in Ontario is one way of developing some level of career attractiveness and permanent status.

Alternately, when child care is seen as integral to the school system, the functions of the worker become a necessary extension of activities and experiences designed to benefit the "whole" child. The activities of child care professionals are seen not as supportive to teachers but as a specialized component of teaching. Therefore, the provision of these services in a school setting is a legitimate and proper expenditure of educational dollars.

Each of these perspectives brings with it differing implications for school-based child care workers. In the former, the role of the worker may be one of separation from school staff, whereas in the latter, the role brings with it a potentially closer relationship with educational and administrative staff.

Issue 2: Supervision, or "Who Calls the Tune?"

When funding for a child care position originates from another government department outside the education system, the host funding agency will typically establish guidelines relating to terms and conditions of employment. These guidelines will also be found when the funding source provides money through an intermediary agency such as a local board or non-profit society. Included within this document is the child care job description, the decision-making process determining the policies and regulations governing the activities of the worker, and, possibly, limitations on certain activities, such as outdoor education experiences.

The management model within which the child care worker must work may be more complex compared to that applied to teachers. For example, it is not unusual that permission must be obtained from two or three "levels" in order to undertake a project or activity. These levels might include the school principal, the society or board administering the funds, and representatives from the relevant government department. In these circumstances, considerable effort must be taken to obtain clarification and agreements concerning management and decision-making issues. Some examples of these issues can be suggested as a series of questions:

> Who is responsible for supervising the day to day activities of the child care worker?
> Other than the child care worker, who is responsible and accountable for the activities of the child care worker and the success of this program?
> How are decisions concerning the child care worker's role, duties, and activities made?
> How does the child care position fit into the formal organization of the school?

The experience of working in a school and having supervision and management external to this system may be cumbersome and may serve to inhibit the implementation of various programs. On the other hand, with these types of external review procedures, the worker does have additional support and guidance.

Issue 3: Employment, or "Who Wants to Dance?"

The introduction of child care services in the school setting will raise a variety of personal and professional issues. These are matters which child care workers contemplating work in this system should consider. For those with community college training and certification as a child care worker, the issue of professionalization and the gaining of status in a "B.A./B.Ed.-crazed world" may prove taxing. This, it would seem, is one of those issues which refuses to go away. With the development of more Canadian university child care programs, perhaps this issue will reduce in intensity. A related component is the issue of increased lobbying of support within universities for more generous transfer credit for college training, thus increasing opportunities for "horizontal" academic advancement within the profession.

Regardless of the educational preparation, it would seem a constant that Canadian child care workers are paid less than teachers and yet work equal hours and have an equal number of expectations placed on them. The following questions are representative of areas that school-based child care professionals may need to address.

> What are the financial rewards? Are they going to be adequate and acceptable?
> What opportunities exist for promotion and advancement?
> Will the work be interesting, challenging, and satisfying?
> What will be the sources of frustration?
> What status does this position have? Is status of concern to me?
> What is the future security in the position?
> What benefits, such as pension and medical plans, are typically available?
> Will I be able to handle the personal stress and professional demands of this position?

One's responses to these and other issues may indicate the appropriateness and actual desire to be involved as a school-based child care worker.

SUMMARY

This chapter has attempted to demonstrate that child care work in Canadian schools consists of a diverse series of unique and largely unconnected programs. In comparison, child care professionals in schools in the United States have traditionally worked within residential facilities for emotionally disturbed children (Alwon, 1979; Goocher, 1975; Meisels, 1975; Trieschman, 1976). The role usually involves dealing with crisis-oriented situations, within activity programs, and during after-school hours.

The reader will be aware that within Canadian schools, the child care task may range from crisis work to preventive care, requiring individual and group approaches working with a wide range in a variety of settings. Although an overview of the current situation can be established at one moment, change and expansion continues to alter the character of work within this setting. This fact alone may offer the allure, intrigue, and professional challenge required for successful school-based child care.

NOTES

1. From a review of the three journals most heavily influencing the child care profession in North America (*Child Care Quarterly, Child Welfare,* and *Journal of Child Care*), no article focussed exclusively on the work of the school-based child care professional.
2. Most major texts used in child care training programs and considered pivotal to the field (Klein, 1975; Krueger, 1980; Mayer, 1958; Treischman, Whittaker and Bendtro, 1969; Whittaker, 1979), fail to isolate and discuss this area of child care work.
3. For example, in British Columbia, 142 programs were listed in 1979, while 180 were recorded in 1982 in the Directory of British Columbia Alternative Rehabilitative Programs, Victoria, BC. This would suggest that in this province there are between 300–500 child care professionals associated on a full- or part-time basis in educational settings.
4. School District Policy from the Ministry of Education (British Columbia), Calgary Board of Education Special Education Handbook (1981), Medicine Hat Public School Policy Handbook (1983), Ontario Ministry of Community and Social Services and Ontario Ministry of Education Administrative Guidelines (1981).
5. Papers and informal notes from the archives of the Ministry of Human Resources, Region 2 (Vancouver); Nanaimo Family Life Association; Victoria Girls Alternative Program, Edwin Parr Community School, Athabasca.

REFERENCES

Allan, J. (1980). Integration and mainstreaming in the elementary schools: Facts, problems and solutions. *British Columbia Counsellor, 2* (2), 15–27.

Alwon, B. (1979). An after school activity program. *Child Care Quarterly, 8* (4), 266–278.

Anglin, J. (1983). Setting the sights: An assessment of child care job functions and training needs in British Columbia. In C. Denholm, R. Ferguson and A. Pence (Eds.) *The scope of professional child care in British Columbia.* (pp. 7–24). Victoria: University of Victoria.

Apter, S. (1982). *Troubled children: Troubled system.* New York: Pergamon.

Brown, R. I. & Hughson, E. A. (1980). *Training the developmentally handicapped adult.* Illinois: Thomas.

Cartledge, G. & Milburn, J. F. (Eds.) (1980). *Teaching social skills to children.* New York: Pergamon.

Denholm, C. (1981a). *Canadian trends in school-based child care.* Victoria: Fotoprint.

Denholm, C. (1981b). School based child care in British Columbia. In C. Denholm (Ed.) *Canadian trends in school-based child care* (pp. 1–17). Victoria: Fotoprint.

Denholm, C. (1983). Beyond the three r's: Child care in educational settings. In C. Denholm, R. Ferguson & A. Pence (Eds.) *The scope of professional child care in British Columbia* (pp. 59–72). Victoria: University of Victoria.

Denholm, C. (in press). Child care workers in Canadian schools: What do they do? *Journal of Child Care*.

Denholm, C., Ferguson, R. & Pence, A. (Eds.) (1983). *The scope of professional child care in British Columbia*. Victoria: University of Victoria.

Dinkmeyer, D. & McKay, G. (1976). *Systematic training for effective parenting*. Minnesota: American Guidance Service.

Dinkmeyer, D. & McKay, G. (1983). *Systematic training for effective parenting of teenagers*. Minnesota: American Guidance Service.

DuRand, J. & Newfeldt, A. H. (1975). *Comprehensive vocational service systems*. Toronto: National Institute on Mental Retardation.

Egan, G. (1985). *Change agent skills in helping and human service settings*. California: Brooks/Cole.

GAIN Act of 1978, Section 2, subsections 1 & 2: Section II, British Columbia: Family and Childrens' Resources, Ministry of Human Resources.

Goocher, B. E. (1975). Behavioral applications of an educateur model in child care. *Child Care Quarterly, 4* (2), 84–92.

Gordon, T. (1975). *Parent effectiveness training*. New York: Signet.

Haberlin, L. (1976). *Child care workers in elementary schools: A developmental model*. Unpublished manuscript.

Hall, E. M. & Dennis, A. A. (Eds.) (1968). *The report of the provincial committee on aims and objectives of education in the schools in Ontario: Living and learning*. Ontario: Ministry of Education.

Holt, J. (1974). *How children fail*. New York: Dell.

Houndle, C. & Ricks, F. (1981). Child care workers in school settings. In C. Denholm (Ed.) *Canadian trends in school based child care* (pp. 33–38). Victoria: Fotoprint.

Hubbard, B. & Phillips, S. (1981). Child care workers and school counsellors within the traditional school: A process model. In C. Denholm (Ed.) *Canadian trends in school based child care* (pp. 51–60). Victoria: Fotoprint.

Jarrett, A. S. & Klassen, T. (1986). *Planning for positive behavior in the classroom*. Toronto: Dellcrest Resource Centre.

Kameen, M. (1979). Guest editorial. *Elementary School Guidance and Counselling, 13,* 150–151.

Kanfer, F. H. & Goldstein, A. P. (1984). *Helping people change*. New York: Pergamon.

Klassen, T. (1981). School based child service in Ontario: A provincial overview. In C. Denholm (Ed.) *Canadian trends in school based child care* (pp. 18–32). Victoria: Fotoprint.

Klein, A. F. (1975). *The professional child care worker: A guide to skills, knowledge techniques and attitudes.* New York: Association Press.

Krueger, M. (1980. *Intervention techniques for child care workers.* Wisconsin: J. Tall.

Laycock, S. R. & Findlay, J. A. (1971). *Educational needs of emotionally disturbed children in the schools of British Columbia.* Educational Research Insitute of British Columbia, Report No. 5.

Lazure, D. & Roberts, C. A. (Co-Chairmen). (1970). *One million children.* Ottawa: Commission of Emotional and Learning Disabilities in Children.

McMorran, S. (1981). Student perceptions of school counsellors and child care workers in school settings. In C. Denholm (Ed.) *Canadian trends in school-based child care* (pp. 39–50). Victoria: Fotoprint.

Marlett, N. J. & Hughson, E. A. (1979). *Rehabilitation programs manual.* Calgary: The Vocational and Rehabilitation Research Institute.

Mayer, M. F. (1958). *A guide for child care workers.* New York: Child Welfare League of America.

Meisels, L. (1975). The disturbing child and social competence in the classroom: Implications for child care workers. *Child Care Quarterly, 4* (4), 231–240.

Neil, R. (1981). Child care counsellors in public elementary schools: A model for the team approach. In C. Denholm (Ed.) *Canadian trends in school-based child care* (pp. 61–84). Victoria: Fotoprint.

Neill, A. S. (1980). *Summerhill.* New York: Hart.

Nordstrom, G. & Denholm, C. J. (1986). Student contact, counseling and support: The Shoreline Community School approach. *The British Columbia School Counselor, 7* (2), 31–37.

Parsons, R. O. & Meyers, J. (1984). Consultation stages and dynamics. In *Developing consultation skills* (pp. 99–121). New York: Jossey-Bass.

Porter, F. & Coleman, R. (1978). *The pilot parent program: A design for developing a program for parents of handicapped children.* Omaha, Nebraska: Greater Omaha Association for Retarded Citizens.

Standifer, F. R. (1964). Pilot parent program: Parents helping parents. *Mental Retardation, 2,* (5), 304–307.

Strain, P. S. & Kerr, M. M. (1981). *Mainstreaming of children in schools: Research and programmatic issues.* New York: Academic Press.

Trieschman, A. E. (1976). The Walker school: An education-based model. *Child Care Quarterly, 5* (2), 123–135.

Trieschman, A. E., Whittaker, J. K. & Bendtro, L. K. (1969). *The other twenty-three hours: Child care work in a therapeutic milieu.* Chicago: Aldine.

Whittaker, J. K. (1979). *Caring for toubled children: Residential treatment in a community context.* San Francisco: Jossey-Bass.

Wolfensberger, W. (1972). *Normalization.* New York: National Institute on Mental Retardation.

Wolfensberger, W. (1980). The definition of normalization: Update, problems, disagreements, and misunderstandings. In R. J. Flynn & K. E. Nitsch (Eds.) *Normalization, social integration, and community services* (pp. 71–115). Baltimore: University Park Press.

Wolfensberger, W. (1983). *Normalization-based guidance, education and supports for families of handicapped people.* Toronto: National Institute on Mental Retardation.

Wolfensberger, W. & Menolcascino, F. J. (1970). A theoretical framework for the management of parents of the mentally retarded. In F. Menolascino (Ed.) *Psychiatric approaches to mental retardation* (pp. 663–689). New York: Basic Books.

Wolfensberger, W. & Thomas, S. (1980). *Program analysis of service systems' implementation of normalization goals.* New York: Training Institute for Human Service Planning, Leadership and Change Agency.

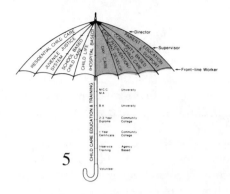

5

Child Life Programs: Meeting Developmental Needs of Children and Families in Medical Settings

ROY FERGUSON AND CAROLYN LARSEN

INTRODUCTION

Child life programs have been emerging thoughout Canada during the last five decades; the majority have developed over the past twenty years. These programs are designed to meet the developmental and emotional needs of children and families in medical settings and have been based primarily in acute care pediatric hospitals. However, we are beginning to see child life programs developing in a greater number of pediatric units in general hospitals, in long-term care hospitals for children, and in out-patient health care services for children and families. Throughout these health care facilities, child life programs have been developed to meet three primary goals: 1) to minimize the stress and anxiety experienced by children and adolescents; 2) to provide life experiences essential to healthy development; and 3) to provide opportunities to retain self-esteem and appropriate independence (Association for the Care of Children's Health, 1977).

This chapter will begin with an examination of the changing philosophy of health care, followed by a review of the short- and long-term effects of hospitalization and illness on children. The role and function of child life programs and the populations served will then be outlined. The chapter will conclude with a look at the historical development of child life programs in Canada and education and training programs for child life personnel.

THE CHANGING PHILOSOPHY OF HEALTH CARE

During the past quarter century numerous medical, scientific, and technological advances have had a significant impact on the care of hospitalized children. This progress has tended to be primarily in the area of physical care, with less attention being paid to the developmental and psychological needs of children and families within the health care system. Health care facilities are no longer only concerned with the treatment of disease; in recent years considerable attention has been directed toward disease prevention and health promotion. This shift in emphasis is reflected in the frequently quoted objective within the Constitution of the World Health Organization: "Health is a state of complete physical, mental, and social well-being and not merely the absence of disease and infirmity" (Dunn, 1959, p. 213).

Szasz (1974) points out that "it is not enough that we in the health professions do a technically competent job of healing the patient's body; we must do an equally competent job at safeguarding his dignity and self-esteem" (p. 544). As these views became more prevalent, we began to see within the health care system a shift from a traditional medical model to a more holistic one in which consideration is given to the interaction between the individual and his or her psychosocial environment, while recognizing mind and body function as an integrated unit. Health care is increasingly regarded as an enterprise where "humanism and science must be inextricably intertwined" (Turner & Mapa, 1979, p. xi). Within this context child life programs began to flourish.

In the *Directory of Child Life Programs in North America* (1984), published by the Association for the Care of Children's Health, there is a list of over 342 programs. A survey conducted by Rutkowski (1978) indicated that the peak period for the establishment of new programs was in the late 1960s and early 1970s. However, the fact that 25 per cent of the programs listed in the 1984 directory have been established within the past five years, despite a tight economic climate, suggests that the evolution of child life programs is still in an early stage.

Two other major trends in children's health care, concurruent with the child life movement, have been toward a greater emphasis on family-centered care and an increase in outpatient alternatives to hospitalization. These, in turn, have been associated with a broader scope of child life practice. We will examine some of the major findings reported in the literature which have influenced these general trends as well as the nature of child life practice.

THE EFFECTS OF HOSPITALIZATION AND ILLNESS ON CHILDREN

The Association for the Care of Children's Health, in a statement of policy for the care of children and families in health care settings (1977), outlines the situation as follows:

> Threats posed to the emotional security and development of many children and their families by serious illness, disability, disfigurement, treatment, interrupted human relationships and nonsupportive environments have been clearly demonstrated by worldwide research studies. The outcomes can range from temporary but frequently overwhelming anxiety and emotional suffering to long-standing or permanent developmental handicaps. (p. 1)

Prevalence of Psychological Distress From Hospitalization

By the age of seven, a large number of the children in the country will have been hospitalized and/or will have experienced outpatient care of one form or another. Hospitalization, in particular, is a stressful event for preschool and school-aged children, since it is a situation with which they usually have had little or no previous experience. A significant proportion of all children who are hospitalized encounter some form of psychological distress (Petrillo & Sanger, 1980).

In examining the effects of hospitalization, Sides (1977) identified 63 per cent of his subjects (aged 1 month to 15 years) as having negative psychological sequelae in relation to their hospitalization. In another study, Jessner, Bloom & Waldfogel (1977) found that approximately 20 per cent of children who were hospitalized for surgical procedures (tonsillectomy and adenoidectomy) demonstrated severe postoperative reactions such as eating, sleep, and speech disturbances, tics and mannerisms, fears, and regressive behavior.

Types of Reactions to Hospitalization

The negative psychological effects of hospitalization on children is manifest in a variety of reactions which Thompson and Stanford (1981) organize into three broad categories. The first of these response categories is the overt or *active* response: this would include behaviors such as crying, clinging to parents, resisting treatment, and being destructive to self or to the environment.

The second broad category of reaction includes the *passive* responses, where the child withdraws from human interaction or discontinues previously typical activities. Examples would be excessive sleeping or a marked decrease in physical activity, communication, or appetite.

Lastly, evidence of psychological upset may appear as *regressive* behavior, such as changes in habits and daily patterns of functioning. Tension, anxiety, restlessness, fears, compulsive behaviors and shifts in eating or sleeping patterns are typical reactions observed in this broad category.

It has been noted that any of these responses can occur during hospitalization (Prugh et al., 1953; Oremland & Oremland, 1973; Klinzing & Klinzing, 1977) or after the child has returned home (Eckenhoff, 1953; Blom, 1958; Vernon, Schulman & Foley, 1966). Responses can vary in intensity and duration from mild, transitory episodes (Vernon, Foley, Sipowicz & Schulman, 1965) to behavioral disturbances lasting for years (Douglas, 1975; Quinton & Rutter, 1976).

FACTORS RELATED TO PSYCHOLOGICAL UPSET IN HOSPITALIZED
CHILDREN

Four basic elements have been suggested (Vernon et al., 1965) as determinants of the amount of psychological upset which hospitalization will produce in the child.

Unfamiliarity

When hospitalized, the child is confronted with an unfamiliar physical setting, a large number of unknown people, and a variety of new procedures. The child is usually unsure of his or her role in this new setting and how he is supposed to behave. This physical, social, procedural, and behavioral unfamiliarity upsets children and affects parents by increasing their level of anxiety so that they are less able to support their child effectively.

Separation

The second determinant of psychological distress from hospitalization is the separation of the child from his parents. For young children, hospitalization may be the first time they separate from their parents; the resulting feelings are of abandonment and helplessness. The work of Bowlby (1960) describes a series of three stages which characterize a young child's response to separation: *protest, despair,* and *detachment,* the latter viewed as having permanent effects on the child's ability to form later close relationships.

Age

The third variable which determines the degree of psychological upset in children who are hospitalized is age. Generally, it appears that the relationship between age and psychological upset is curvilinear: children between the age of approximately seven months to three or four years are particularly vulnerable (Prugh et al., 1953; Vernon et al., 1965). Children who are younger than seven months appear to be less disturbed by the disappearance of their primary caregivers (Schaffer & Callender, 1950); reported signs of psychological upset during and after hospitalization are relatively uncommon. The next most vulnerable group are children aged four to six years; adverse reactions to hospitalization usually diminish after the child reaches school age (Vernon et al., 1965). However, this is not to say that there are no instances where school-age children and adolescents experience adverse reactions to hospitalization.

Personality and Life Experience

The last predictor of psychological upset is the child's personality and life experiences. Stacey, Dearden, Pill and Robinson (1970) observed that children who make poor relationships with others and are socially inhibited, uncommunicative, and aggressive, are the ones most likely to be disturbed by a hospitalization. Further, they reported that only children, youngest children, children from extended families, and children whose mothers are either overly anxious or very bland about the hospital admission to be at greater risk. The number of previous hospitalizations experienced by the child is also considered to be a predictive factor with respect to the likelihood of hospitalization creating psychological distress (Douglas, 1975; Quinton & Rutter, 1976; Sides, 1977).

Pre-hospital Status

A large proportion of infants, children, and youth admitted to hospital or attending emergency departments and clinics for what would appear to be primarily a physical illness or accident are at the same time experiencing major social and familial upheaval. An example might be the seriously burned young child whose parents are experiencing marital difficulties and have recently separated. An epidemiological study by Heisel et al. (1973) demonstrated that children admitted to hospital with various medical, surgical, and psychiatric problems had experienced two to three times more social and emotional change during the year prior to admission than in a control sample of children.

Thus, in addition to the fact that hospital, medical, and illness experiences render children more psychologically vulnerable, it seems that a large percentage arrive for care in a predisposed state.

CHILD LIFE INTERVENTIONS AND SERVICES

Basic Interventions

The basic child life service available to all or most of the children and families in a staffed clinical unit generally consists of the following components: 1) ample oportunities for normal and satisfying play and other age-appropriate activities; 2) therapeutic play or dialogue; 3) various functions to foster family comfort, independence, involvement, and education; 4) a significant relationship with the child life specialist; 5) acts to render the overall physical and social environment as receptive and responsive as possible to the needs of children and parents; and 6) ongoing informal assessment of emotional and developmental status in the child. These components of basic child life services are an integral part of each of the following areas to be considered.

A Safe, Accepting, "Normal" Environment

The central focus of child life programming is the provision of a safe and accepting atmosphere and environment in which children are encouraged to play and engage in various activities which reduce tension, foster individual expression, and contribute to learning and developmental progress. The core ingredient of such an environment is the day-to-day interaction with a familiar and trusted adult whose behavior fosters a sense of security.

Play programs, in particular, continue to be a basic component of child life practice in the majority of settings because of the rich opportunity they provide for addressing a wide spectrum of needs within a relaxed atmosphere. The power of appropriate play experiences to resolve emotional conflict while promoting mastery and self-esteem in the hospitalized child has long been documented (Barton, 1962; Brooks, 1970; Dimock, 1959; Erickson, 1959; Jolly, 1968; Lindquist, 1977; Plank, 1962; Tisza & Angoff, 1957).

The play or activity room usually serves as the central working environment of the child life specialist and as the hub of ward or group activities for the children. In this area, over which the child life service has primary jurisdiction, physical safety is fostered through the selection of appropriate furnishings, equipment, materials, and activities adapted to the needs and particular vulnerabilities of the children on the ward.

It is the emphasis on creating and maintaining environments which are psychologically safe which most typifies the child life mandate. Within the confines of the play or activity area, this entails providing a milieu in which normal and pleasurable activities will help offset the unsettling and often frightening effects of other hospital experiences. The psychological relief experienced by children who feel they are in a safe place where they can be themselves without having constantly to be on guard is also assured by the establishment of a policy which preserves the playroom as a haven in which medical procedures and rounds are not permitted to take place. However, time spent by physicians, nurses, and other treatment staff interacting in a personal way with the child in this setting can help to convey their interest in the child as an individual and to deepen the child's trust in those who must dispense care which can be anxiety provoking. The participation of parents and siblings in the playroom can also enhance emotional security in the hospitalized child, as well as providing opportunities for the child life specialist to support the family members in helping the child to cope.

A supportive social and physical environment, with provision for involvement in normal life activities, may be all that certain children and their families require. However, many depend on the child life specialist for more intensive support and guidance. The degree of involvement can range from on-the-spot problem solving to frequent and continuing contacts designed with both short- and longterm goals.

Coping with Medical Procedures and Major Life Changes

Children and youth who are adequately prepared for new, potentially stressful experiences are considered psychologically safer. Child life specialists have begun to contribute to the literature on this topic (Alcock, 1984; Droske & Francis, 1981). Certain diagnostic and therapeutic types of play experiences, such as "hospital" or "medical" play (Doak & Wallace, 1975), specialized puppetry (Letts, Stevens, Coleman & Kettner, 1983), and other approaches are used in an effort to determine a child's expectations, perceptions, misperceptions, and attitudes regarding medical procedures, illness, or hospitalization.

Specific stress-reducing techniques, such as physical relaxation, guided imagery, or cognitive restructuring might be used to help selected children and youth cope more effectively and independently with pain or medical experiences (Alcock, 1984).

Family-Centered Care

As might be expected of specialists whose primary training is in child development, child life professionals have long been associated with family-oriented care. One of the earliest "mother live-in programs" was co-ordinated under the auspices of the Child Life Department at the Johns Hopkins Hospital in Baltimore, Maryland, during the mid-1960s. Those in the field today continue to work for the establishment of policies, facilities, and approaches which favor family involvement in a child's hospital experience.

Direct supportive contacts with parents are a natural part of the daily routine of a hospitalized child. Parents, like their children, are often initially ill at ease in hospital environments. If their child is very sick, they, too, are under considerable stress and require support and guidance. Professionals help the parents to encourage their child's participation in usual kinds of activities, and they help explore broader child rearing issues.

Case Illustrations

Two case examples (modified from an exerpt first appearing in the 1977 Fall edition of the Montreal Children's Hospital newletter, *Children's News*) illustrate various aspects of the child life role. The first involves a child whose life circumstances had been altered so drastically that individual attention was required for an extended period of time.

> Paul, aged seven, had been very badly burned. Most of his skin which had not been damaged was used for grafting onto the burned areas of his body. His arms and hands had become contracted from the tense position in which he kept them. Movement was confined to his face, from which angry and frightened eyes looked out, and to his head, which he could turn. All nourishment came through tubes and for several months he was confined to his isolation room.
>
> Although there was little response to the child life worker's daily visits during the early weeks, Paul made it clear that he wanted her there. Her early work involved establishing an emotional bond which could help him to cope with the many difficult experiences yet to be faced, and would be a motivating force for involvement in activities essential to healthy development.
>
> An early source of comfort was just having the child life worker's hand on his or having his temple gently stroked as she tried to understand his feelings and verbalize them for him. She worked to make his bedside environment visually stimulating and personal, while

fostering his identity as a vital member of his family. She gradually stimulated his involvement in a variety of play experiences. His active participation, in spite of major restrictions, helped to restore a feeling of hope and wholeness and to provide a sense of accomplishment, independence, and improved self-esteem.

Although Paul rejected all initial attempts to accept food by mouth, he was thrilled about doing some cooking in his isolation room. Enthusiastically, he ordered that the weiners which the child life worker had helped him to fry be cut up and given to many of the nurses, physicians, and others on his ward.

Paul eventually accepted little nibbles of whatever food they had prepared in his room. Cooking was to become one of his greatest sources of pleasure. Towards the end of his stay he even baked bread, wearing a chef's hat his aunt made.

Paul's first days out of his isolation room and in the ward playroom were both exciting and anxious. Paul could not relax, fearing the pain resulting from another child bumping into his wheelchair. With some rearrangement of furniture, a protected corner was made in the little playroom.

The next hurdle was coping with the stares and questions of the other children, who were mostly in the hospital for brief stays. The child life worker helped Paul learn how to handle this situation while at the same time allaying the anxieties of other children and parents. Resocialization with other children was yet another rehabilitative task, and the playroom served as an important testing ground for Paul's anticipated re-entry into his family and community life.

In another example, an early intervention role is illustrated through the case of a severely delayed and withdrawn 20-month-old blind boy of a single mother who was overwhelmed and without resources to cope. The child life specialist, after much reading and consultation, developed a daily handicap-specific stimulation program for the child, along with regular encouragement for the mother's efforts and periodic video filming to document progress. These films, shared with the mother, became an invaluable tool for both the staff member and mother in the assessment and modification of their approaches to the child. The boy made remarkable progress in his development, while the mother gained increased confidence and commitment in caring for her son, to the point where she stimulated the formation of a support group for parents of young, blind children. Teamwork with the social worker resulted in a creative solution permitting a return to home four days a week and placement in a supportive foster family on the other days while the mother worked. The boy was enrolled in a preschool for blind children, first attending while still in the hospital and continuing once he returned home.

This all took place as part of the regular service on a non-surgical inpatient unit for about twenty infants and toddlers. At any time, approximately one-third of these young children and their families can be identified as experiencing serious social problems, ranging from illness associated with poor lifestyles to child abuse. Similar findings were reported by Stocking et al. (1972) in a study carried out in another pediatric setting.

A significant contribution can also be made by the child life specialist to the care of infants or toddlers admitted because of child abuse or failure to thrive (Elver, 1982); these are often considered priority groups for child life services.

ADVOCACY AND HOSPITAL PLANNING

Children and families commonly share their fears and concerns with child life specialists; as a result, the professional often advocates on behalf of patients and families; especially for those who are less able to represent their own needs because of age, cultural differences, unfamiliarity with the hospital system, limited mental resources, or diminished personal strengths.

In addition to direct interventions with children, youth, and family members, child life personnel are usually involved in a variety of indirect care activities which help make the hospital a more humane and supportive environment. As front-line caregivers with constant exposure to the experiences of children and families, child life staff generally become active participants in the interdisciplinary process of establishing policies and facilities. The film "Adolescents Speak Out," produced by the Child Life department at the Isaak Walton Killam Hospital in Halifax in 1983, is one example of this advocacy. These two aspects of the child life role, categorized as case advocacy and class advocacy, are thoroughly addressed by Thompson and Stanford (1981).

TEACHING AND CONSULTATION

Much teaching takes place on an informal level through modeling mechanisms or discussing the child's needs and approaches to meeting them with parents or team members.

Child life staff frequently participate in the orientation and inservice education of fellow professionals in addition to providing supervised field work experiences for students in their own and other disciplines. Formal teaching appointments may be held by child life personnel in medical schools, as at McMaster University and the University of Winnipeg, or in a variety of other university departments.

Child life personnel have been involved with interdisciplinary community planning groups in developing new resources for handicapped children as well as with provincial and national bodies developing guidelines to meet the special needs of children (Canada, 1985; Quebec, 1983).

CURRENT PRACTICE

The functions and interventions described in this chapter reflect fairly standard practice across most Canadian child life programs. The most common program design is the long-term assignment of one child life specialist to a particular inpatient ward or outpatient service. The regular availability of the staff member permits the establishment of trusting relationships, the ability to respond to on-the-spot needs, and the provision of normal and familiar activities. The work with the children and families may take place in the designated play or activity center, at the bedside, in the treatment room, or outside the clinical area. Occasionally, home or school visits might be made, such as to meet classmates and teachers of a child returning to school following the treatment of cancer.

Some hospitals also have regular centralized group programs, such as weekend recreational programs for adolescents from various treatment units. Child life programs exist for the majority of patients from infancy to late adolescence.

At present, most programs provide services predominantly, if not entirely, to inpatients. The number of beds on a ward could range from 15 to 40; more often than not there is only one child life staff member on a ward regardless of its size. Recommended ratios of child life staff to patients are between 1:5 and 1:15 (Veenneklaas, 1971; ACCH, 1977 & 1981). In those Canadian programs listed in the only available directory (ACCH, 1984), the number of pediatric beds per child life professional range from 4 to 63. The actual number of staff to inpatients ratio cannot be determined, since some of these staff work only with outpatients.

Within the context of these general organizational characteristics, the following represents some of the current child life program areas.

Inpatients

In addition to the emphasis on helping children and families cope with the medically related aspects of the hospital experience, the child life program is also the principle resource for meeting the child's and youth's need to explore, learn, create, express, achieve, make friends, and so forth. It is common for the majority of a ward's active, mobile children, especially those from early preschool to late school age, to spend a large part of the day participating in activities organized and supervised by child life personnel. Although the primary reason most children are admitted to hospital is to receive medical diagnosis and treatment, a very small percentage of their time is actually taken up by medical activities.

Two separate, unpublished studies carried out at the Montreal Children's Hospital by G. Kolyvas in 1978 and D. Scanlan in 1980 documented how, and with whom, patients spent their daytime weekday hours. Findings indicated that an average of 6.2 and 7.8 per cent of the day on each ward (the first medical, the second orthopedic surgical) was spent in medical care, which was defined as: all contacts with physicians including time off the unit for surgery, all medical aspects of nursing care, all diagnostic procedures, physical therapies, and so on. The average time per patient spent in child life care was 30.4 per cent on the medical and 13.2 per cent on the orthopedic surgical wards. Patients in the former group were mostly ambulatory preschool and school-age children, while the orthopedic patients were primarily immobilized and included a large number of adolescents.

Many patients require "one-on-one" time, such as those who are isolated for infection control, attached to life-support equipment in the intensive care unit, or whose psychological status requires individual interventions. Thirty per cent of the child life programs in acute care pediatric hospitals report providing a service to premature newborns as well (ACCH, 1984).

Another area of the hospital involving child life activities is the operating room reception area. Six per cent of Canadian hospitals report having child life programs in these areas (ACCH, 1984).

Outpatients

Child life services in outpatient areas are becoming increasingly common and may be confined to specific populations, such as those attending emergency departments (Alcock, 1984), or clinics treating children with particular chronic diseases, such as cancer (Larsen, 1983). Adams (1978) describes the core team members in the cancer clinic as the physician, the social worker, and the child life worker. Likewise, outpatient child life services might be offered to children attending any of the many other clinics which exist throughout Canada. Approximately 15 per cent of Canadian child life programs offer services for both outpatient clinics and emergency departments, while about six per cent provide services within admitting departments (ACCH, 1984).

Preadmission Preparation

Other populations for whom a child life program might be established are patients prior to an anticipated admission, siblings of patients, and well children in the community who are learning about hospital experiences. Preadmission preparation programs may be provided by the child life staff, frequently in conjunction with nursing staff (Alcock, 1977; Ferguson, 1979; Ferguson & Robertson, 1979). Individual referrals might be made by psychologists, other health professionals, or directly by parents requesting preadmission preparation for their children.

Services for siblings are generally of three types. Most common is the incorporation of siblings into the group program in the ward or clinic. More unique is the provision of a "drop-in" type of day care facility, such as exists at Ste. Justine Hospital in Montreal, or a special support group for siblings of patients with long or serious illnesses.

Well children in the community might have the opportunity to participate in an educational hospital orientation program developed by child life staff either within the hospital or in the community school or nursery.

School

The Canadian child life programs listed in the aforementioned ACCH directory (1984) assume responsibility for the co-ordination of 36 per cent of school teaching programs located in children's hospitals and 10.5 per cent of school programs located on pediatric units in general hospitals. The importance of hospital school programs are discussed by Alcock (1981).

Generally, teachers are assigned to the hospital school by a local school board. At the Isaak Walton Killam Hospital for Children in Halifax, however, child life teachers are hired directly by the hospital with funding provided by the ministry of education.

Libraries

There are three types of libraries which might be part of the child life department's responsibilities: 1) the regular, leisure reading type of library; 2) a family resource library; and 3) a toy lending library.

The family resource library, such as at the Children's Hospital of Eastern Ontario, is one which includes special books, films, and videotapes for both children and parents which focus on a wide variety of issues related to health, illness, and disability. Various health professionals can refer families to specific resource materials which might be of interest to them.

Toy lending libraries, such as the ones at the Alberta Children's Hospital in Calgary and Ste. Justine Hospital in Montreal, provide a source of toys and games for both recreational and therapeutic purposes. Child life specialists and other health professionals, such as occupational therapists, will assist parents in selecting appropriate toys for their children as well as providing instruction in the developmental application of the materials.

In-house Television Programming

Child life specialists are increasingly involved in live, closed-circuit television programming featuring interaction with patients as well as in the production of taped programs of both an entertaining and educational nature. This form of televison is viewed as an important alternative to regular commercial programming and is an effective way of contributing to the well-being of large numbers of children. Part-time staff are employed specifically for this purpose at the Health Sciences Centre for Children in Winnipeg, where a research project documented viewing patterns of patients prior to and following the establishment of the center's own closed-circuit system (Guttentag et al., 1983).

Playgrounds

Outdoor play areas are also commonly established, maintained and staffed by the child life service as described by Alcock (1978). Students are frequently hired in the summer to staff these areas, some of which have been designed specifically for the hospitalized child.

Activity Specialists

Some child life departments, such as the one at the Alberta Children's Hospital, include persons with recreation or therapeutic recreation backgrounds. These departments might also include specialists in the expressive therapies who utilize music, art, and dance within child life programming as a way to encourage individual expression.

CHILD LIFE PROFESSIONAL ISSUES

Standards

In North America, several leading organizations, such as the American Academy of Pediatrics (1978), the Canadian Pediatric Society (1979), the Canadian Institute of Child Health (1979), and the Association for the Care of Children's Health (1977), have recommended the inclusion of child life programs in hospital settings for children. The last organization has been publishing guidelines for these programs since 1971. Recent Canada Health and Welfare ministry publications have also recommended that child life programs form a part of the overall services for children and youth in hospitals (1982, 1985). The first textbook on child life practice, published in 1981 (Thompson and Stanford), is another valuable source of guidelines for students and practitioners as well as administrators establishing new programs.

Most child life services function in similar ways whether in the pediatric unit of a general hospital (Crossley, 1975), an acute care children's hospital, or an extended care hospital for children (Ferguson & McNamara, 1983). However, it is important to acknowledge the existence of individual variations in program design, interventions employed, and special programs and resources offered. Key factors contributing to the nature of particular programs include: the general philosophy of care prevailing in the institution as a whole, the training and caliber of the child life staff, the ratio of staff to patients, and the administrative placement and resources of the program (Larsen, 1980).

No enforceable standards exist in any province or territory through legislation or in the requirements of hospital accrediting bodies. Adherence to existing recommendations or guidelines is purely voluntary. The Child Life Council of the Association for the Care of Children's Health is making steady progress, however, in defining and establishing standards through its work on a peer program review system, quality assurance guidelines, and a mechanism for the certification of practitioners in the field. Certification procedures, effective in October 1986, will ensure that those certified possess the specified minimum theoretical and practical preparation for professional child life practice.

The Association for the Care of Children's Health

The first professional meeting for child life personnel was held in 1965. Two years later a multidisciplinary organization, originally called the Association for the Care of Children in Hospitals, was founded. The name was later changed to the Association for the Care of Children's Health, reflecting a broader concept of health care. This multidisciplinary, international organization is dedicated to promoting the health and well-being of children and families in health care settings by education, multidisciplinary interaction, and research. The head office for the association is located in Washington, DC, with regional affiliates established across the U.S. and Canada. There is a total membership of over 2,500. ACCH produces a quarterly journal called *Children's Health Care* as well as a number of position papers and policy statements on a variety of topics such as the roles and functions of child life programs, the care of adolescents, the involvement of parents and families in health care settings, and hospital environmental considerations. The association also maintains a central resource library, sponsors task forces, and organizes a large, annual conference.

In 1982, the association established the Child Life Council to serve as a structure for dealing with child life professional issues. This created a mechanism within the larger, multidisciplinary organization dedicated specifically to the needs of those employed directly in child life programs. The Child Life Council is actively working towards developing program and practitioner standards as well as guidelines for the education and training of child life professionals.

In addition to being actively involved in the Child Life Council, the directors of child life programs across Canada also meet on an annual basis to exchange information, review issues of common interest, and undertake specific projects which further the development of child life activities and programs within the country.

Education and Training of Child Life Personnel

In a position paper formulated by ACCH (1981) it was recommended that a *Child Life Specialist* should have academic preparation at a bachelor's degree level with supervised experience in the health care field as well as competence in a variety of areas, such as growth and development, family dynamics, interpersonal communication, group process, and behavior management. A *Child Life Assistant* would work only under the direct supervision of a child life specialist and would have a diploma in an appropriately related field. A *Child Life Administrator* would have a master's degree and, in addition to the competencies required at the baccalaureate level, would be competent in a variety of administrative and managerial areas.

Two studies (McCue, Wagner, Hansen, & Rigler, 1978; Rutkowski, 1978) indicate that child life programs in North America have involved staff with various backgrounds such as child development, education, recreation, psychology, nursing, and other fields. The Child Life Council has developed a list of competencies necessary in order to function as a child life specialist. A review of them indicates that approximately 80 per cent are generic in nature and would be appropriate to practitioners in any child care setting. The remaining 20 per cent are specific to working with children and families in health care settings. Child development would be an example of one of the generic competency areas.

A study reported by Crowley-Gannon & Robinson at the ACCH conference in Seattle in 1982 combined competency lists developed by task forces of ACCH and the National Therapeutic Recreation Society and asked respondents from therapeutic recreation programs and child life programs to rate the importance of each of the 40 competencies. It was interesting to note that the majority of the competencies were considered important by both groups.

An increasing emphasis is being placed upon standardizing the training of child life personnel (Stanford, 1980). Degree-granting child life preparation programs have been established at colleges and universities such as Wheelock College (Boston), Mills College (Davis, California), Utica College (Utica, New York), Northeastern Illinois University (Chicago), Bowling Green State University (Ohio), Case Western Reserve University (Cleveland, Ohio) and Edgewood College (Madison, Wisconsin). In Canada, the only training programs which exists at the present time are at the School of Child Care at the University of Victoria and within the post-graduate Clinical Behavioural Sciences Program at McMaster University in Hamilton, Ontario. In addition, the University of Montreal offers guided field work for selected students in education (preschool and primary educational science).

CONCLUSION

The face of health care in Canada has been changing rapidly during the past few decades. As a result, the developmental and psychological needs of children and youth are now more carefully considered in the design and delivery of health care services. Child life programs have been a major force in this movement towards a better integration of physical and psychosocial care.

The well-established professional child life program is an important hospital resource in the prevention (Wilson, 1979), early detection, and early treatment of problems affecting social, psychological, and cognitive development in children and youth. It is conceivable that in the future child life professionals, with their increasing expertise at helping children and families overcome barriers to normal development, will begin to move beyond the hospital setting, establishing closer links with early intervention programs in the community.

The Child Life Council is actively working to establish standards of practice for hospital programs as well as guidelines for the training of professionals. Canadians have played an active role within this body from the beginning; they demonstrate strong leadership in the quest for standards both through the council and in annual meetings of Canadian child life department heads.

The field is at an exciting stage of its development, building service structures and preparing its practitioners to help ensure that the developmental and emotional needs of children and their families in health care settings are being met.

REFERENCES

Adams, D. (1979). *Childhood malignancy: The psychosocial care of the child and his family*. Springfield: Charles C. Thomas.

Alcock, D. (1977). Hey, what about the kids?: A child life program in action. *The Canadian Nurse, 73,* (11), 38–43.

Alcock, D. (1978). Developing an outdoor playground. *Dimensions in health services: Journal of the Canadian Hospital Association*.

Alcock, D. (1981). School programs for hospitalized children. *The Journal of the Canadian Association for Young Children,* 44–49.

Alcock, D. et al. (1984). Child life intervention in the emergency department. *Children's Health Care, 12,* 130–136.

American Academy of Pediatrics. (1978). *Hospital care of children and youth*. Evanston, Illinois: AAP.

Association for the Care of Children's Health. (1977). *Statements of policy for the care of children and families in health care settings*. Washington, DC. ACCH.

Association for the Care of Children's Health. (1984). *Guidelines for the development of child life programs*. Washington, DC. ACCH.

Association for the Care of Children's Health. (1984). *Directory of child life programs in North America*. Washington, DC. ACCH.

Barton, P. (1962). Play as a tool of nursing. *Nursing Outlook, 10,* 162.

Blom, G. E. (1958). The reactions of hospitalized children to illness. *Pediatrics, 22,* 590–600.

Bowlby, J. (1960). Separation anxiety. *International Journal of Psychoanalysis, 41,* 89–113.

Brooks, M. (1970). Why play in hospital? *Nursing Clinics of North America, 5,* 431–441.

Canada, Health and Welfare. (1982). *Child and adolescent services in general hospitals.* Ottawa: Health Services Directorate.

Canada, Health and Welfare. (1985). *Child and youth long term services.* Ottawa: Health Services Directorate.

Canadian Institute of Child Health. (1979). *Care of children in health care settings: A resource and self-evaluation guide.* Ottawa: CICH.

Canadian Paediatric Society. (1979). Resolution on the child in hospital. *Dimensions in Health Services: Journal of the Canadian Hospital Association, 8,* 52–67.

Children's News (The). (1977). The invaluable role of child life workers. Montreal Children's Hospital, pamphlet.

Crossley, V. (1975). Child life programs: An essential ingredient to good patient care. *Hospital Administration in Canada, 17* (2), 20–24.

Crowley-Gannon, M. & Robinson, M. E. (1982). *Competencies for pediatric play program workers as perceived by specialists in child life and therapeutic recreation.* Paper presented an Association for the Care of Children's Health Conference, Seattle, Washington.

Dimock, H. G. (1959). *The child in hospital: A study of his emotional and social well-being.* Toronto: MacMillan.

Doak, S. & Wallace, N. (1975). The doctors wear pajamas. *Journal of the Association for the Care of Children in Hospitals, 3* (8), 13–20.

Douglas, J. W. B. (1975). Early hospital admissions and later disturbances of behavior and learning. *Developmental Medicine and Child Neurology, 17,* 456–480.

Droske, S. & Francis, S. (1981). *Pediatric diagnosis procedures with guidelines for preparing children for clinical tests.* New York: Wiley and Sons.

Dunn, H. L. (1959). High level wellness for man and society. *American Journal of Public Health, 49,* 786-792.

Eckenhoff, J. E. (1953). Relationship of anesthesia to postoperative personality changes in children. *American Journal of the Diseases of Children, 86,* 587–591.

Erickson, F. (1958). Play interviews for four-year old hospitalized children. *Monographs of the Society for Research in Child Development.*

Evler, G. L. (1982). Nonmedical management of the failure-to-thrive child in pediatric inpatient setting. In P. Accardo (Ed.) *Failure to thrive in infancy and early childhood.* (pp. 243–263). Baltimore: University Park Press.

Ferguson, B. F. (1979). Preparing young children for hospitalization: A comparison of two methods. *Pediatrics, 64,* 656–664.

Ferguson, B. F. & Robertson, J. (1979). Making hospital preparation child-centered (with a little help from Emily). *Journal of the Association for the Care of Children in Hospitals, 8* (2), 27–31.

Ferguson, R. V. & McNamara, P. (1983). Child life programs in hospitals: Meeting the non-medical needs of children and families. In C. Denholm, A. Pence and R. Ferguson (Eds.), *The scope of professional child care in British Columbia.* Victoria: University of Victoria.

Guttentag, D. N. W., Albritation, W. L. and Kettner, R. B. (1983). Daytime television programming. *Pediatrics, 71* (4), 620–625.

Heisel, J. S. et al. (1973). The significance of life events as contributing

factors in the diseases of children. *Journal of Pediatrics, 83,* 119–123.

Jessner, L., Bloom, G. D. & Waldfogel, S. (1977). Emotional implications of tonsillectomy and adenoidectomy on children. In R. S. Eissler et al. (Eds.), *Physical illness and handicap in children.* New Haven: Yale University Press.

Jolly, H. (1968). Play and the sick child. *Lancet, 2,* 1286.

Klinzing, D. R. & Klinzing, D. G. (1977). *The hospitalized child.* Englewood Cliffs: Prentice Hall.

Larsen, C. A. (1980). The child life professions: Today and tomorrow. *Child life activities: An overview.* Association for the Care of Children's Health, Washington, DC. ACCH.

Larsen, C. A. (1983). The child life worker's contribution within an oncology setting. In J. E. Schowalter et al. (Eds.), *The child and death.* (pp. 293–302). New York: Columbia University Press.

Letts, M., Stevens, L., Coleman, J. & Kettner, R. (1983). Puppetry and doll play as an adjunct to pediatric orthopedics. *Journal of Pediatric Orthopedics, 3,* 605–609.

Lindquist, I. (1977). *Therapy through play.* London: Arlington Books.

McCue, K., Wagner, M., Hansen, H. & Rigler, D. (1978). Survey of a developing health care profession: Hospital "play" programs. *Journal of the Association for the Care of Children in Hospitals, 7* (1), 15–22.

Oremland, E. K. & Oremland, J. D. (Eds.), (1973). *The effects of hospitalization on children,* Springfield: Charles Thomas.
Petrillo, M. & Sanger, S. (1980). *Emotional care of hospitalized children.* Philadelphia: Lippincott.
Plank, E. (1970). *Working with children in hospitals.* (2d. ed.). Cleveland: Case Western Reserve University Press.
Prugh, D. G., Straub, E. M., Sands, H. H., Kirshbaum, R. M. & Lenihan, E. A. (1953). A study of the emotional reactions of children and their families to hospitalization and illness. *American Journal of Orthopsychiatry, 23,* 70–106.
Quebec. (1983). *Impact des garderies sur les jeunes enfants: Où va le Québec?* Gouvernement du Québec.
Quinton, D. & Rutter, M. (1976). Early hospital admissions and later disturbances of behavior: An attempted replication of Douglas' findings. *Developmental Medicine and Child Neurology, 18,* 447–459.
Rutkowski, J. (1978). A survey of child life programs. *Journal of the Association for the Care of Children in Hospitals, 6* (4), 11–16.
Schaffer, H. R. & Callender, W. J. (1959). Psychological effects of hospitalization in infancy. *Pediatrics, 24,* 528–539.
Sides, J. P. (1977). *Emotional responses of children to physical illness and hospitalization.* Unpublished Ph.D. diss., Department of Psychology, Auburn University.
Stacey, M., Dearden, R., Rill, R. & Robinson, D. (1970). *Hospitals, children and their families.* London: Routledge.
Stanford, G. (1980). Now is the time: The professionalization of child life workers. *Journal of the Association for the Care of Children in Hospitals, 8* (3), 55–59.
Stocking, M. (1972). Psychopathology in the pediatric hospital: implications for community health. *American Journal of Public Health, 62,* 551–556.
Szasz, T. S. (1974). Illness and indignity. *The Journal of the American Medical Association, 5,* 543–545.
Thompson, R. H. & Stanford, G. (1981). *Child life in hospitals: Theory and practice.* Springfield, Illinois: Charles C. Thomas.
Tisza, V. B. & Angoff, K. (1957). A play program and its function in pediatric hospital. *Pediatrics, 19,* 293.
Turner, G. T. & Mapa, J. (1979). *Humanizing hospital care.* Toronto: McGraw-Hill Ryerson.
Vanek, E. P. & Yanda, C. P. (1981). Academic programming for child life education: a case study. *Children's Health Care, 10* (2), 53–57.

Vernon, D. T. A., Foley, J. M., Sipowicz, R. R. & Schulman, J. L. (1965). *The psychological responses of children to hospitalization and illness.* Springfield, Illinois: Charles C. Thomas.

Vernon, D. T. A., Schulman, J. L. & Foley, J. M. (1966). Changes in children's behavior after hospitalization. *American Journal of Diseases of Children, 111,* 581–593.

Wilson, J. M. (1979). Child life. In P. J. Vallettutti & F. Christopolos (Eds.), *Preventing physical and mental disabilities: Multidisciplinary approaches,* (pp. 65–89). Baltimore: University Park Press.

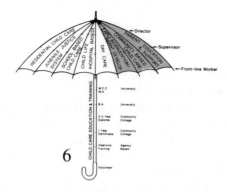

6

Day Care in Canada: A Child Care Perspective

ALAN R. PENCE AND PATRICIA CANNING

Day care, the full or part-time care of children of working parents by persons other than their own parents, is one of the oldest child care programs in Canada. This chapter will review the history and the present status of *group-based (center) day care in Canada,* its role in relationship to families and the labor force, its changing importance in contemporary society, its service and regulatory structures, and its training requirements as viewed from a child care perspective.[1]

HISTORY

The history of organized, group day care in Canada goes back over 160 years to the 1820s. Infant Schools were the first group day care centers supported from sources other than parental payment alone and intended, in part, to serve the child caring needs of working parents. The Infant Schools established in both Canada and in the United States were based on earlier British models; the "golden age" of the Infant School movement in North America was in the late 1820s and the early 1830s. The factors contributing to the development of these early day care programs and those effecting their demise have in large part continued to exist throughout the long history of day care in Canada. These influencing factors have contributed to day care's unique, multifaceted identity today. Various aspects of that unique identity will be considered briefly in the following section.

By 1830 Infant Schools had developed three specific models, each appealing to or developed for a different stratum of society or for a different child propulation. The three models were: Robert Owen's model; the London Infant School Society model; and the North American conception/reaction (Pence, 1986).

Owen's model, the earliest of the three, was the most closely tied to familial needs arising from increased industrial labor force participation. During the early part of the industrial revolution women were viewed as integral members of the new labor force. Robert Owen, an industrialist in the early 1800s, had purchased a textile mill in New Lanark, Scotland. In his desire to make New Lanark a model industrial town, he established an "institution for the formation of Character." This institution, or school, contained in it an Infant School for the children of the families working in the New Lanark mill. Children from the "age at which they could walk" were able to attend the school while their parents worked (Owen, 1841). The plan was conceived both as a service to the working families and a positive learning environment for the young children. Owen was quite specific in his directions to the male and female teacher hired to work in the infant school. In strong contrast with the public school practices of that time, the children were not to be beaten or forced to engage in rote activities. Song, dance, and outside exercise were all parts of Owen's established curriculum.

Owen's experiment attracted attention both within and outside Britain. It had particular appeal for a group of London philanthropists who visited New Lanark on several occasions and who ultimately hired Owen's own infant school instructor, Mr. Buchanan, to be the first instructor in a London-based infant school. Other programs in London soon followed. However, the motivation for the creation of the London-based programs was considerably different from that of Owen's experiments. Well-to-do Londoners were extremely concerned about the large numbers of young children who populated the streets and who learned various means — most often illegal — to survive on the streets. These children were major contributors to London's high crime rates. To many of the good citizens of London, the Infant Schools represented both a means of getting these children off the streets and, not incidentally, a way of instructing these children about issues near to the heart of the city fathers, such as property rights and the ways of good citizenry. Lord Brougham, one of the philanthropists responsible for bringing Buchanan to London, noted that "planting a sufficient number of Infant Schools for training and instructing those classes of the people will at once solve the problem of prevention" (Roberts, 1972, p. 155). These programs of social control and instruction can be considered the "London model."

The principal advocate of the London model was Samuel Wilderspin, an individual engaged by the London Infant School Society to travel throughout the British Isles propagating the model and its accompanying rationale. The pedagogical approach utilized by Wilderspin was adapted from the Lancasterian or monitorial model of instruction, whereby older child monitors were appointed to watch over groups of younger children while a central instructor lectured about the focal topic. Wilderspin noted in one of his publications that by such means, "it is possible to have two-hundred or even three-hundred children assembled together, the oldest not more than six years of age, and yet not have one of them cry for a whole day" (Albany Infant School Society, 1829, p. 7, as taken from Wilderspin).

Knowledge of the Infant Schools came to North America in the mid-1820s and was represented by both the Owenite and the London models. Because the London model was better documented in a larger number of magazines and newspapers, it became a more common base for North American programs. In North America, however, another factor influenced the creation of these programs, as was summarized in the editorial of an 1820s Boston newspaper article: "at the age of entering primary schools these *poor* children will assuredly be the *richest* scholars. And why should a plan which promises so many advantages, independent of merely relieving the mother from her charge, be confined to children of the indigent?" (May & Vinovskis, 1976, p. 79). Given this additional impetus, Infant Schools rapidly spread the length of the Atlantic seaboard, "from Halifax to Charleston."

Many of the program variants and impetuses for the creation of early childhood/day care programs that are familiar today were evident in North America as early as the 1830s. Then, as now, programs were developed as a resource for working parents or as a way to ensure that children received the benefits of "early instruction." In addition, similar to the current attempts to correct the effects of a "deprived" or "disadvantaged" environment on young children, programs were often designed to "reform" children from poor home situations.

The flowering of day care under a variety of sponsors and using a variety of approaches was short-lived in North America. By 1840 virtually all infant school programs had ceased to function, the result of fundamental changes in family and economic life in the mid-1800s.

The early nineteenth century in both Great Britain and in North America witnessed a significant shift in both the location and the economic base of family life, away from rural settings with largely self-sufficient households toward urban locations of wage-based employment. The onset of industrialization brought with it major expansion of urban centers and fundamental, significant shifts in family structure and responsibilities. Initially, as seen in New Lanark, it appeared that women as well as men would no longer be at home with their children but would be employed in the factories. It was necessary to provide alternate care for the children of these workers. During this period, day care received the support of the public and politicians. However, after an initial movement towards both male and female occupation outside of the home in urban centers, requirements for female labor lessened and a new model of the family emerged. This change in family models lessened the need for day care services and indelibly stamped one particular family model on the North American psyche.

The new family model, termed the Victorian family by some (Strickland, 1984), defined specific spheres of influence for men and women. Men (fathers) became the breadwinners while women (mothers) became the keepers of the house. The world of men was that of business and competition, "the turmoil and bustle of an active, selfish world"; women were the domesticators, they themselves as delicate and refined as the "haven from strife" for which they alone had responsibility (Kraditor, 1968, p. 47). Part of the responsibility of mothers within the family circle was as caregivers of their children; insofar as mothers were expected to be their children's primary caregivers there was no need for such programs outside the home. Thus, the creation and popularization of the Victorian family spelled the destruction of the Infant School movement.

The Victorian family model, with its tightly defined roles and responsibilities for both parents and children, remained the dominant family ideal throughout the remainder of the nineteenth century and well past the midway point of the twentieth century. In Canada, the rurally based, domestically centered family was numerically larger than families reflecting the Victorian model, but the latter had enormous power as a model to be emulated. Most of us, our parents, and our grandparents were reared within its symbolic sway, and it is difficult for many to imagine social stability without its enforcing structure.

A change in acceptable male and female roles, albeit a temporary one, occurred during the Second World War. In addition to taking men far away from their homes, the war brought with it a need for women in Canadian industrialized urban centers to work in factories and other "out-of-home" places that had traditionally been the domain of men. If women had to work, their children would need caregivers. Day care again became a national rather than a personal familial need. The federal government offered cost sharing of day care services with the provincial governments. The two most industrialized provinces—Ontario and Quebec—signed agreements. That this support of day care was for the "war effort" and not to support working parents is evidenced by the fact that in order to receive support, at least 75 per cent of the children in the programs had to have mothers working in "essential industries" (that is, essential to the war effort). By 1946, the federal government had withdrawn all such funding; this reflected the general belief that now that the war was over families would return to "normal": with father at work and mother at home caring for the children.

THE CONTEMPORARY NORTH AMERICAN FAMILY

Although the Victorian family model existed in fact and in ideal for a century and a half in North America, its zenith was probably reached in the post Second World War period of 1945 to 1955. In the flush of excitement accompanying a return to home, normalcy, and stability, families sought and found security in the roles of male-breadwinner and female-nurturing childrearer. The baby boom of the late 1940s and early 1950s was in part an affirmation of this return to established ideals and roles for the Victorian model.

This peak lasted for approximately one childrearing generation; by the mid 1960s the children of that return to "normalcy" were themselves of child bearing age, and deep shifts in values and ideals, which would have profound effects on families and children, were becoming evident. There was an increase in marriage and divorce rates, a decline in typical family size and fertility rates, a significant increase in the number of female-headed, single-parent families, and a major increase in the number of married women in the out-of-home, paid labor force. Statistics covering these demographic changes will be briefly considered.

Marriage in Canada is presently a popular institution. In the late 1970s approximately 65 per cent of the adult population were married, as compared with 50 per cent in the late 1920s, and 52 per cent at the turn of the century (Statistics Canada, *Canada's Families,* 1979, p. 3).

Divorce also has become more popular in recent years. During the 1920s, the divorce rate per 100,000 was less than 8 per annum. A fairly stable divorce plateau was reached in the 1950s and early 1960s, when rates stood at between 35 and 40 per 100,000. Subsequent to the divorce act of 1968, which considerably broadened Canadian legal grounds for divorce, the rate soared: 148 in 1972; 235 in 1976; and almost 280 per 100,000 in 1981 (Statistics Canada, *Divorce: Law and the Family in Canada,* 1983, pp. 59–61).

While an increasing number of Canadians are getting married and divorced, the average household size is decreasing; it has declined from 3.7 people in 1971 to 3.5 people in 1976 and 3.3 in 1981. The number of families having four or more children has decreased from 16.4 per cent in 1961 to 8.7 per cent in 1981 (Statistics Canada, *Canada's Families, 1981*, p. 4).

The increase in divorce in recent years has resulted in an increase in single-parent families, the vast majority of which are headed by females. While the number of male-headed families has remained fairly constant over the last twenty years, female-headed families have increased by almost 30 per cent. Recent data (Perreault & George, 1982) suggest that Canada is on a steady course toward more single heads of families and that by 1991 almost 15 per cent of families will be headed by one parent; of these 80 per cent will be women.

Beginning in the late 1950s and accelerating through the 1960s and 1970s, the entry of an increasing number of women—more specifically, of mothers—into the labor force has been one of the most significant transformations in North American society in this century. Increasingly, women are offered the opportunity and are choosing to participate in out-of-home work in much the same way as men. Women now account for over 41 per cent of the total Canadian labor force. Within the ranks of women engaged in the paid labor force, the fastest growing segment has been married women with children, and the younger the age of the child the more rapid has been that group's increase in the labor force over the last ten years. These trends reflect both the economic necessity of two salaries to raise a family, as well as changes in the roles of women which have occurred over the past twenty years. For whatever reason women with children choose to work, their increasing numbers indicate an increasing need for day care services.

With the dramatic increase in both the overall number and proportion of families with working mothers, there has been a re-evaluation of the role that day care plays in Canadian society. Since the 1840s, day care has been considered by most Canadians as a welfare-related service for that minority of families who did not fit the Victorian ideal. However, the Victorian model has now become the *minority* phenomenon; working mothers are part of the *majority* of families. The need for day care is no longer restricted to the few but is a necessary service for the many. As a result of this major and significant change in the Canadian family life, day care has assumed a level of social and political importance heretofore unknown in Canada.

Beginning with the 1970 report by the Royal Commission on the Status of Women, followed closely with the First National Canadian Conference on Day Care in 1972, the issue of day care has become an increasingly important policy issue. This is especially true in the 1980s, as ever-increasing numbers of mothers join the out-of-home labor force and require preschool and day care services. Commencing with the Second

National Day Care Conference in Winnipeg in 1982, issues related to women in the labor force and the consequent need for child care assistance have been covered heavily in the popular media and are the subject of several 1980's Child Care Task Forces. The Liberal government established a Task Force on Child Care within the Status of Women Office in May 1984. At the same time, an interprovincial Task Force on Child Care was also created, linking the provincial ministries responsible for the Status of Women. In November 1985, a special Parliamentary Committee on Child Care was formally announced by the Conservative government of Brian Mulroney. Reports and studies from these various task forces make a significant contribution to our greater understanding of the complex relationships among families, labor force participation, and child care needs.

Not since the period of the Infant School movement a century and a half ago has there been such a high level of interest in and support for child care. And now, as then, the interest extends beyond the provision of specific services for children of working parents to a more general discussion of the effects of various pedagogical approaches and to the effects of such care and early education on special needs, non-special needs, and advantaged children. In addition, the current debates and discussions go beyond the question of increased services to examine the broader (and ultimately more significant) social policy question of how parents (in the complex demographic diversity of Canada), can best be supported in their child rearing activities. Changes in governmental and employer benefit structures, such as extensions of maternity and paternity leave, leave for child sickness days, assured labor force re-entry after extended time taken off for parenting duties, and changes in the tax structure supportive of parent options must all be considered in the debates regarding the future of child care in Canada.

Although the broader parental benefits and services picture is part of child care discussions of the 1980s, the focus for this chapter will remain on the more limited aspect of day care *services* and, more specifically yet, on day care centers in Canada. The following section will provide an overview of the Canadian day care services structure, noting in particular the federal-provincial partnership which characterizes it.

CANADIAN DAY CARE SERVICES: A FEDERAL-PROVINCIAL
PARTNERSHIP

As noted earlier in this chapter, the creation and development of day care services is intimately linked to family form and function and to labor force characteristics and expectations. The shifts over the last two to three decades in these two major socioeconomic variables have altered the basis on which arguments for increased day care services are being made. However, those arguments have yet to alter fundamentally the funding and regulatory systems on which such services have traditionally been based.

It is difficult to generalize about the Canadian day care system because of its decentralized nature and the diversity of its composition and regulation across the provinces. The act by which Canada was declared a country, the *British North America Act* (B.N.A. Act), designated what services were to be the responsibility of the Canadian federal government (such as defense and transportation) and those which were to be primarily the responsibility of the provinces (such as welfare and education). Since services to children and families were viewed as "welfare" issues, these were considered a provincial matter.

A century later, this welfare orientation was reflected in the Canada Assistance Plan (C.A.P.) passed by the Canadian parliament in 1966. This plan provided for assistance to needy Canadians "who require financial assistance or who require social services to prevent, overcome, or alleviate the causes and effects of poverty or child neglect" (Department of National Health and Welfare, 1974, p. 2). Under this act, the federal government agreed to provide matching funds to the provinces for various services, including day care services to "needy" Canadian families. Since day care is no longer considered by many as a "welfare" service but rather one needed by the majority of Canadian families, regardless of income, C.A.P. has come under increasing attack as an inappropriate funding vehicle. In addition, C.A.P. enables the richer provinces to obtain more federal "matching" dollars than poorer provinces. Day care services then become yet another reflection of regional disparities.

Since the provinces and territories are responsible for regulations governing day care services, not only are regulations distinct and different from province to province, but so too are the goals espoused by these various provincial governments. The two tables on pages 120 to 123 demonstrate aspects of that range and diversity.

Given this diversity in programs, regulations, and monies available in the provinces for day care, a major debate in Canada has centered on the question of the quality that such care represents. Traditionally, discussions of quality in child care have centered on the regulations and the power of government to close facilities not meeting those guidelines. Typically, regulations establish a "minimal" level of acceptable care, below which programs will not be allowed to remain open. Adequate funding to ensure enforcement of even those basic standards is, however, often lacking. The public may then be provided with a false sense of security regarding what the possession of a license actually indicates and how well enforced those regulations may be.

Even when adequate funding is available for monitoring compliance with regulations, major questions are often raised regarding the mechanical nature of regulations: square footage space requirements, number of toilet facilities, staff-child ratios, lighting, heating, and so on. The desirable aspect of such regulations is that they are measurable. However, what can be missed in such "measurables" are the nature and quality of staff-child and child-child interaction, which generally are far more dependent upon the psychological aspect of caregiving than upon space requirements alone.

Even if it were possible to add this interactional element to the regulatory guidelines, the direct measure of such an element would be extremely difficult, if not impossible, to monitor. No doubt it would take away significantly from the already inadequate funds available for day care services. One way to create higher quality care for young children is to provide better trained professional caregivers.

TRAINING FOR DAY CARE EMPLOYMENT

The knowledge we have accumulated in the past half-century highlights the need to consider caring for young children in groups as professional work. Such work requires specialized knowledge and training. However, the job of the day care worker has not been and is still not perceived in all quarters as being a "professional" career. This is clearly reflected in the fact that in many places in Canada only limited, if any, formal education or professional training is required for day care employment.

While there is no one kind of environment which is right for the needs of all children, we can say with some confidence that there are certain characteristics, both physical and human, that need to be present in all good environments for children. The quality and organization of physical space, the availability of materials, and the numbers and abilities of the adults involved are all related to quality care (Day & Sheehan, 1974). It is the caregiver, however, who is the linchpin in the environment.

It is widely reported and accepted that the quality of the staff determine to a high degree the quality of the program (Decker & Decker, 1978). According to the National Day Care Study (Ruopp, Travers, Glantz & Collen, 1979) conducted in the United States, one important factor which determined the quality of a program was the presence of

Ratios Staff/Child	(1) B.C.	(2) ALTA.	(3) SASK.	MAN.	(4) ONT.	(5) QUE.	N.B.	(6) N.S.	P.E.I.	(7) NFLD.	YUKON	N.W.T.
1:3		0–18m			(4)		2m–24m		0–2y			
1:4	18m–3y			0–2y	(4)				mixed under 3y			
1:5		19m–35m	18m–30m		(4)		2m–3y		2y			0–18m
1:6										2y&3y	0–2y	18m–36m
1:7					(4)	0–2y		-5y				
1:8	3y & up	3y–4y		2y–5y	(4)					3y–sch.	2y–6y	
1:9					(4)							36m–6y
1:10		5y	30m–6y			2–10y	4y & 5y		3y & 4y			
1:11									mixed over 3y			
1:12									5y & 6y			
1:15			5y–12y	6y–12y		5 & up	6y–12y	5y & up	7y & up	sch. & up		6y–12y

Notes:

(1) Regulations do not permit group day care for children under 18 months. Maximum center size for children 3 years to school age is 75, and 36 for children under 3 years. The maximum group size for children under 3 years is 12; and for 3 years to school age, 25.

(2) Maximum center size: 80. Maximum group size for children 0–18 months = 6; 19–35 months = 10; 3–4 years = 16; and for 5 years = 20.

(3) Maximum center size = 60.

(4) The following ratios apply:

	No. of Staff	Ratio
Up to 10 children, under 18 mos.	3	1:3.3
Up to 14 children, 18–24 mos.	3	1:4.7
Up to 15 children, 2–4 yrs.	3	1:5.0
16 to 34 children, 2–4 yrs.	4	1:8.5
35 to 45 children, 2–4 yrs.	5	1:9.0
Up to 25 children, 5 yrs. old	3	1:8.3
26 to 35 children, 5 yrs. old	3	1:7.0
26 to 45 children, 5 yrs. old	4	1:9.0

Maximum number of children per room—babies, 10; 18–24 mos., 14; 2 yrs. to school age, 25; school age, 30.

(5) L'Office des services de garde à l'enfance has proposed the following staff/child ratios: 0–13 months, 1:5; 18 months to 5 years, 1:8; and 5 years and older, 1:15. Maximum center size, 60.

(6) Maximum group size 25 children.

(7) Regulations do not allow group day care for children under 2 years. Maximum center size is 50. There cannot be more than one center per building/dwelling.

Source: National Day Care Information Centre, Health and Welfare Canada (1982)

TABLE 1. Minimum Staff/Child Ratios by Age of Child

Synopsis	B.C.	ALTA.	SASK.	MAN.	ONT.	QUE.	N.B.	N.S.	P.E.I.	NFLD.	N.W.T.	YUKON
Supervisory Positions												
A.*Educational Level*												
Basic Minimum Training	*											
Letter of Qualification	*											
Training Program			*									
Grade 11 Standing				*								
Satisfactory Training				*								
Specialized Knowledge						*		*				
Completed E.C.E. Program						*						
Diploma							*					
Certificate	*						*					
Univ. Diploma							*					
E.C.E. Training Highly Recommended									*			
Knowledge in Child Development									*			
Baccalaureate Degree										*		
B.*Experience*												
12 Months Experience	*											
Several Years Experience	*											
Adequate Experience						*		*				
2 Years						*						
3 Years							*					
C.*Administrative Training*												
Administrative Abilities	*			*								
D.*Personal Qualities*												
Personal Suitability	*			*				*				
E.*Health*												
Suitable Health								*				
F.*Age*	19y	18y		18y								18y

TABLE 2. Summary: Day Care Staff Qualifications (Interprovincial Comparisons)

Table 2: Continued

Synopsis	B.C.	ALTA.	SASK.	MAN.	ONT.	QUE.	N.B.	N.S.	P.E.I.	NFLD.	N.W.T.	YUKON
Staff Positions												
A.*Educational Level*												
Training Commenced	*											
Training Program			*									
Grade 11 Standing				*								
Training in Child Development				*								
Univ. Degree.				*								
College Diploma				*		*						
College Extension Certificate				*								
Specialized Knowledge					*							
Completed E.C.E. Program					*							
Univ. Diploma						*						
Training Recommended									*			
Encouraged to Participate in Training										*		
B.*Experience*												
Experience				*								
Adequate Experience					*							
3 Years Experience						*						
C.*Personal Qualities*												
Personal Suitability	*				*							
D.*Age*			16 y									

Source: Kava, T., British Columbia Ministry of Education (1982).

staff with specialized knowledge of child development, early childhood education, or day care. The understanding and specialized knowledge gained through professional training were essential.

As we have seen in earlier sections, an examination of the existing requirements for the education and training of day care workers in Canada shows no standard qualification accepted throughout the country. Several provinces do require a certain level of training for particular positions, while others require that a certain percentage of day care workers in each center be qualified. For example, in a number of provinces (such as Ontario and Manitoba) supervisors of centers are required to be graduates of recognized training programs and must possess prior day care work experience. Others (such as Nova Scotia and P.E.I.) require, or are going to require, that a certain percentage of day care workers in each center be qualified, while still others (such as N.B., Nfld. and Yukon) require only good health and suitable personal qualities. This disparity in regulations is reflected in the diverse day care training programs available.

The education of day care personnel is carried out through a variety of educational institutions operating at a number of levels. There are continuing education programs for those already in the workplace; vocational school programs, usually of less than a year's duration; one-, two-, and three-year community college certification and diploma programs; and four-year baccalaureate and post-graduate programs available to those pursuing a career with young children in groups. Most often the disciplinary context of these training programs is early childhood education. However, within the early childhood education field a distinction between teacher training for elementary school settings and preparation for preschool/day care settings is and should be made. Although there is a certain amount of overlap in background knowledge requirements for elementary education and preschool/day care practice, the fundamental thrust and objectives of the two settings are quite different. As will be discussed in some detail later in this section, a holistic view of the child as part of a complex set of interactive family and social systems is one critical aspect of training for day care work—a characteristic that day care shares with other fields of child care employment.

The "typical" day care worker may have been through any one or none of these programs. The need for a government commitment to establish the professional qualifications for day care workers and the need for standardization of these qualifications across jurisdictions is great.

It would be appropriate for there to be a number of different levels of qualification acceptable for different positions within the child care/day care profession. Program directors, supervisors, and organizers should be educated at least to a baccalaureate level, while other qualifications may be appropriate for teachers, child care workers, or assistants. The profession at present has little in the way of a career structure to motivate those working within it to improve and upgrade qualifications.

There is a recognized need to increase the knowledge and skills of day care personnel at all levels. The following description highlights the essential components of the education and training needs in order to plan and implement programs for young children. All child care programs preparing people to work with groups of young children in day care should cover at least four essential curriculum areas: 1) liberal education; 2) human development within the context of family and society; 3) knowledge specific to the day care profession; and 4) a substantive field placement experience.

Liberal Education

Professional programs must be based on a belief in the value of a liberal education. This is not exclusive to child care but is true for all professions. A general education helps to promote the improvement and the advancement of any profession and indirectly affects the service provided by professionals. Liberal arts courses enhance students' breadth of knowledge, help to develop the ability to think critically and analytically, and enhance problem-solving and communication skills. Regardless of place or level of education, all students of child care should endeavor to enhance their general education.

Human Development within the Context of Family and Society

Specific professional education in child care has been expanding significantly in recent years. Traditionally, programs attempted to educate people to meet the needs of children within the day care environment without reference to outside factors. The increasing knowledge of human development, and enormous changes in the family and our society, necessitate an ever expanding professional knowledge base in order to meet the needs of children. Care must be taken to educate generally enough to meet the demands of modern society, yet the training of day care personnel must address three specific areas. First, day care workers must be knowledgeable about human development in order to provide a safe, stimulating, and appropriate environment for young children. Second, education and training must encompass an understanding of the family, its changing roles and needs, and the role of the day care worker in supporting the family. Third, the day care worker must be prepared as a ''professional'' with a broad understanding of both social issues and changes that have direct relevance to the lives of children and the ways in which public policies affecting children evolve and are implemented.

a. human development.   The essential component of the professional study of day care is a sound knowledge of human growth and development, both normal and atypical. Human development courses must address the physical, cognitive, linguistic, social, and emotional aspects of development. Different theories on learning and development need to be examined.

Education and care at all levels have been influenced by different perspectives and a changing knowledge base. The study of human development must include an examination of its social, cultural, and political contexts. Students should remember that knowledge is constantly evolving and not accept it as "truth." A critical examination of all knowledge is required of any discipline, and knowledge of the issues and questions as yet unanswered is as essential as knowing what has been explained.

Students must be familiar with the norms of development from birth through the early childhood years. The continuous, gradual, and orderly sequence of development as well as the variation in growth and development among individuals needs to be stressed, lest we "shift from the child and his needs to the adult and his expectation" (Hirsch, 1983). Typical and expected behavior of two-, three-, and four- or five-year olds is critical knowledge for those working with groups of children. In a recent study, Canning & Lyon (1984) reported a disproportionately high incidence of suspected behaviorally/emotionally troubled children being identified by day care teachers as compared to teachers of older children. In this case, such findings underscored the importance of ensuring that day care personnel know what constitutes appropriate behavior for young children lest children be given inappropriate activities or are perceived as having problems because workers lack knowledge of normal development and behavior.

Knowledge of normal development is also essential to an understanding of atypical development. Day care centers are places for all children. Increasing numbers of children with suspected or identified handicapping conditions (that is, physical and/or sensory disabilities; developmental disabilities; mental retardation; speech and language problems; emotional disturbance; or special needs arising from abusing or neglecting families) are being enrolled in them. To ensure appropriate services and programs, day care care personnel must be able to work with other professionals to identify problems, interpret assessments, and initiate programs for each child and family in need of this special effort.

We cannot state with any certainty what the effects of group care will be for any individual child or group of children. Nevertheless, anyone providing such care must examine the research investigating the effects of different kinds of "out-of-home" care on child development and the potential implications of these findings.

b. family.   However long a child spends in day care centers, the family remains the primary socializer (Bronfenbrenner, 1974, 1979). According to the Federal Interagency Day Care Requirements (1980), day care must not only focus on and meet the needs of children enrolled but must also have a social services component that supports family functioning. Support and supervision of day care in Canada is generally the responsibility of provincial departments or ministries of social services. Administratively, it is perceived as a service to families as well as children.

Families exist in many forms. The recent changes in family structure and composition, especially the increase in single-parent families, highlights the need for an increasing sensitivity to children's home backgrounds. The changing nature of families must be recognized and understood by professionals working with children. But regardless of the form families may take, the function that they play in the child's life and socialization are nevertheless similar.

Nuclear families often do not function well in isolation, yet many families in today's mobile society lack any kind of extended family or neighborhood support system; day care may be their only or most important support. It is becoming increasingly difficult for parents to find the support they need. In order to understand the modern family and establish positive and supportive relationships with families, day care workers must be aware of other services available for families in their community. Courses in the sociology of the family, families in different cultures and societies, the socialization of the child, or parent-child relations should be included in the core curriculum.

c. society.   It is also important that students understand and examine factors in the child's wider social environment. The multicultural nature of Canadian society necessitates an awareness of the ethnic and cultural backgrounds from which children come. Women's roles and the sex roles that are considered appropriate are changing. Technology is changing society and the needs of individuals. Values have changed and continue to do so. Students must develop some understanding of the way in which attitudes towards children and families are translated into the kinds of services provided. They must also know how policies for children and families have evolved and are implemented within the federal and provincial political structure in order to be able to work effectively to improve services. Courses or components in government administration, social policy, contemporary society, and social issues, including an examination of ethical issues involved in providing group care and the laws and regulations affecting this provision, should be included.

Knowledge Specific to the Child Care Profession

The goal of the applied curriculum is to provide the students with the skills required to develop and implement high quality programs for young children, which are premised on the basis of knowledge of human growth and development, the family, and society. A mentally and physically healthy and stimulating environment for young children does not happen by chance but requires short- and longterm goal setting and planning and sound organization and evaluation. Day care workers must be able to meet each child's social, emotional, and physical needs and be able to manage groups of children effectively.

The day care setting itself can be viewed as an ecological system in which all the elements influence the child's development. Many areas must be included in the professional preparation of day care personnel. Courses or components in the following areas should be included in the core curriculum: 1) organizing a healthy and safe environment for young children; 2) meeting children's nutritional needs; 3) group management; 4) planning and implementing activities for young children; 5) curriculum development; 6) observation and assessment techniques; 7) techniques for evaluating children and programs; and 8) program administration.

Students need to develop skills which enable them to involve parents in the childrens' program. Day care personnel must be responsible partners with parents and must consider parents' circumstances and desires. This is essential if the program is to benefit the child. At the very least, good communication with parents must be established so that they feel that day care is an adjunct to, and not a substitute for, their care. Ideally, involvement will go much further.

Day care personnel should be knowledgeable enough to offer support to parents. Parent education is the term most often used in this respect, but this education or help must be in response to the parents' own perceived needs and not a professional "how to parent" exercise. Sensitivity to parents' positions and circumstances and an accurate awareness of the day care provider role is essential.

Students need to develop good oral and written communication skills in practical situations. As well as working and communicating effectively with children and parents, day care personnel must be able to work effectively as a member of the staff and also with other professionals in the community.

The urgent need for improvement in the status and salaries of those caring for young children and in the funding of programs for children and families necessitates that day care personnel are encouraged to first see themselves as "professionals" and work towards being recognized as such. An integral part of professionals' responsibility is lobbying effectively and acting as advocates for the services and programs in which they work. Since day care is itself part of the emerging profession of child care, professional and advocacy skills should be a priority.

Field Placement

Although few scientific evaluations of training are available, it is generally recognized that an essential component of day care training is actual work in centers providing child care. Field work may be given concurrently with classroom training, or it may be provided in blocks of time during which there are no classes. Careful planning, co-ordination and supervision are needed to maximize the learning potential of field work.

Care must be taken in choosing the centers in which students are placed. Much of what the student will learn in the center will be done through modeling the caregiver. The student needs to be in an atmosphere which encourages learning through personal experience and also provides appropriate guidance. Expectations for the students must be consistent with their education and prior experience.

In order to assist the co-operating centers, the educational institution must provide clear goals and expectations for students and supervisors in written as well as oral form. The educational institution supervisor should be one who is familiar with both the academic program and the actual work site. Major responsibility for student supervision should be assumed by those providing the direct service, with clear guidelines for evaluation provided by the institution and the day care in which the student is placed, preferably facilitated by onsite visits from the institution's supervisor.

The institutions seeking co-operating day care centers must also recognize and acknowledge the extra work required of day care personnel when students join them. Some institutions offer small monetary rewards to centers, while others provide course credits at their institutions. Regardless of the form it takes, appreciation of the value placed on the professional contribution of day care personnel to educating future professions must be fully recognized.

SUMMARY

Day care is not a recent phenomenon in Canadian society. Its beginnings go back well over a century. Child care programs based primarily on the British Infant School system were in existence as early as the 1820s. In fact, during the 1820s and 1830s there was interest and development in the child care field, in some respects not unlike what we are experiencing today. Similarly at that time, there were also significant changes occurring in family structure and responsibility which required both mothers and fathers to work outside the home and left children to be cared for in schools or day care centers. By the 1840s, however, the Victorian family model with its specific and different roles for mothers and fathers was seen as the ideal family form. Women were staying at home and caring for children. This situation continued for over a century, with only a minor interruption during the war years when women were required to replace men in working outside the home. Society responded by establishing day care centers for children. At war's end, however, women quickly returned to the home to care for their children; day care centers closed abruptly. By the 1960s, society was once again going through changes that greatly affected family and work and which have resulted in an increasing interest in and need for day care provision.

The postwar generation were reaching maturity and were beginning families by the mid- to late-1960s. In contrast to the period of relative calm during the early postwar years, the 1960s brought significant changes in society which greatly affected the family structure. There was an increase in marriage, remarriage, and divorce rates. Families were smaller, and there was an increase in the number of single-parent families, headed mostly by females who were required to seek employment outside the home in order to support their families. Married women with young children, particularly those with preschool children, were also joining the work force in unprecedented numbers: a result of both the women's movement and an economic situation which increasingly necessitated two salaries to support a family. These trends are continuing and are expected to do so into the twenty-first century.

Care for children outside the home is a necessity for the majority of families with young children in Canada today. Many families require support in raising their children. Such support was once provided by the extended family and the community, but in our highly urban, mobile society, that function must be assumed by other agencies. However, most of the children are cared for not in day care centers but in informal babysitting arrangements. No financial support is available to families using this kind of care, which may be unreliable or of uneven quality.

While it may be easier to control the quality of group care of young children, there is as yet little information on this topic. Day care regulations do not adequately address the issue of quality. Regulations vary from province to province, but in all provinces they deal predominantly with such factors as space, lighting, heating, and staff-child ratios without attention to additional variables which may be more indicative of the actual quality of the care being provided.

One way to increase the quality of care provided to day care centers is by the education and training of the day care staff. All provinces now provide training in this area. Programs vary, but it is possible to offer general guidelines for educating and training. Basic to any program preparing students to work with young children is an ecological approach. A child is a member of a society as well as a family and must be understood and cared for in relation to the society as a whole. To be adequately prepared to care for children in groups, four main areas must be included in the curriculum. They are: 1) liberal education; 2) human development within the context of family and society; 3) knowledge specific to the child care profession and; 4) a substantive field placement.

NOTES

1. It should be noted that while this chapter focuses primarily on center-based day care services, the majority of day care in Canada is provided by home-based caregivers, most of whom are unlicensed.

REFERENCES

Albany Infant School Society. (1829). *Proceedings*. Albany: Albany Christian Register.

Bower, E. M. (1971). "K.I.S.S. and kids: A model for prevention (key integrative social systems)." *American Journal of Orthopsychiatry, 42* (4), 556–565.

Brontenbrenner, U. (1974). "Developmental research, public policy, and the ecology of childhood." *Child Development, 45*: 1–5.

Brontenbrenner, U. (1979). *The ecology of childhood*. Cambridge, MA: Harvard University Press.

Canada. (1970). *Report of the royal commission on the status of women in Canada*. Ottawa: Information Canada.

Canada. Department of Health and Welfare, National Day Care Information Centre. (1973–1983). *Status of day care in Canada*. Ottawa: Health and Welfare Canada.

Canning, P. & Lyon, M. (1984). *Community service needs of pre-school children and their families*. Unpublished manuscript, Mount Saint Vincent University, Halifax, Nova Scotia.

Day, D. & Sheehan, R. (1974). Elements of a better school. *Young Children,* 30 (1), 15–23.

Decker, C. A. & Decker, J. R. (1978). *Planning and administering early childhood programmes*. Columbus, Ohio: Charles B. Mont.

Dowley, E. (1971). Perspectives on early childhood education. In B. A. Anderson & H. J. Shane (Eds.) *As the twig is bent* (pp. 12–21). Boston: Houghton-Mifflin.

Federal Interagency Day Care Requirement — F.I.D.C.R. (1980). Washington, DC: U.S. Department of Health, Education & Welfare.

Fitzpatrick, E. A. (1911). *Educational views and influence of DeWitt Clinton*. New York: Teachers College Press.

Hirsch, E. (1983). *Problems of early childhood: An annotated bibliography and guide*. New York: Garland.

Kamerman, S. B. & Kahn, A. J. (1977). The day care debate: a wider view. *The Public Interest,* 54 (1).

Kava, T. (1982). *Report on program standards for children in day care and day care staff qualifications*. Victoria: Ministry of Education.

Kraditor, A. S. (Ed.) (1968). *Up From The Pedestal*. New York: Quadrangle Book Co.

Manitoba. (1983). Manitoba regulation 148. *The community and day care standards act*. (Sec. 6).

May, D. L. & Vinovskis, M. A. (1977). A ray of millennial light: Early education and social reform in the infant school movement in Massachusetts 1826–1840. In T. Haraven (Ed.) *Family and kin in urban communities*. New York: New Viewpoints.

New Brunswick. (1984). *Standards for day care facilities*. Fredericton: Department of Social Services.

Nova Scotia. (1978). Day care act and regulations. *Statutes of Nova Scotia*. Halifax: Queen's Printer.

Ontario. (1984). *Standards for day care nurseries*. Toronto: Ministry of Social and Community Services.

Owen, R. (1841). *Address on opening the institution for the formation of character at New Lanark, delivered on the first day of January, 1816: Being the first public announcement of the discovery of the infant school system.* London: Home Colonization Society.

Pence, A. (1986). Infant schools in North America, 1825–1840. In S. Kilmer (Ed.) *Advances in early education and day care,* vol. 4 (pp. 1–25). Greenwich, Conn. J.A.I. Press.

Perreault, J. & George, M. V. (1982). Growth of households and families in Canada in the 1980s and 1990s. *Canadian Statistical Review,* 15 (9).

Prince Edward Island. (1980). *Guidelines to the Regulations for Child Care Facilities Act.* Charlottetown: Child Care Facilities Board.

Quebec. (1983). Child day care act. *Gazette Officielle de Québec, 115* (44).

Roberts, A. F. B. (1972). A new view of the infant school movement. *British Journal of Educational Studies, 20,* 154–164.

Ruopp, R., Travers, J., Glantz, F. & Collen, C. (1979). *Children at the center* (final report of the National Day Care Study). Cambridge, Massachusetts: Abt Books.

Statistics Canada. (1979). *Canada's families.* Ottawa: Supply and Services.

Statistics Canada. (1981). *Canada's families.* Ottawa: Supply and Services.

Strickland, C. (1985). *Victorian domesticity: Families in the life and art of Louisa May Alcott.* University, Alabama: University of Alabama Press.

Yukon. (1980). *Yukon day care regulations.* Order in council.

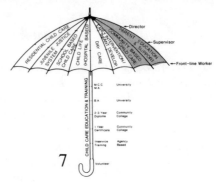

7

Infant Development Programs: Early Intervention in Delayed Development

DANA BRYNELSEN AND HELEN CUMMINGS[1]

INTRODUCTION

This chapter will provide a brief overview of infant development programs in Canada and the major social, political, and legal forces which contributed to their relatively rapid growth.[2] Infant development programs are one of many forms of health, education, or social services designed to provide early intervention for infants at risk for developmental problems or diagnosed as delayed or handicapped. Early intervention refers to those procedures which restructure the environment in order to facilitate the development of an infant or young child. Infant development programs in Canada, as described in this chapter, are primarily home-based and provide services to families with infants from newborns to three years old. It should be noted, however, that some populations of handicapped infants, such as visually impaired or hearing impaired, may be served by more specialized resources.

Like other human services in Canada, infant development programs vary considerably from province to province and from community to community. This wide variation in programs makes it impossible to provide a detailed description of these services. However, some similar and dissimilar features will be covered that relate to program objectives, population served, services provided, and parent involvement. This chapter will also provide an historical perspective of the development of services for handicapped or delayed infants and preschoolers, a description of the skills and knowledge base required by infant development program staff, and an outline of current trends in the field.

AN HISTORICAL PERSPECTIVE

Programs for delayed and handicapped infants and young children form part of the range of services for persons with handicaps in many parts of Canada. Some of these services have their roots in developments which took place in the nineteenth and early twentieth centuries. These included services for persons with visual and hearing impairment or mental handicaps. However, services for persons with handicaps developed largely after the Second World War; they reflect changes in society's perception of people with handicaps. Changing social values and attitudes toward persons with handicaps have led to increasing acceptance of and support for their right to participate as fully as possible in the communities in which they live.

These changes have been accompanied and strengthened by an advanced understanding of handicapping conditions and by the development of effective strategies for ameliorating the impact of a handicap. New concepts about the nature of intelligence and the potential contribution of facilitating environments toward intellectual development have also contributed to development of services; they represent significant departures from concepts held in the past.

Prior to the Second World War, intelligence was widely considered to be "fixed." It was thought that a person was destined at birth, by genetic endowment, to be either bright, normal, or slow. With few exceptions, professionals and the public alike did not consider environmental factors as having much influence on the development and growth of a child. This was particularly true of children with mental handicaps. Mental retardation was believed to be inherited, incurable, and irremedial (Blatt, 1971). It followed, therefore, that the professional advice given to families of children with severe mental handicaps was largely negative; families were encouraged to abdicate responsiblity for these children. Institutionalization was an accepted and common practice. Families who chose to keep a mentally handicapped son or daughter at home had little support. Children with severe mental handicaps were not eligible for school. Descriptions of the low level of functioning of institutionalized or isolated persons in the community perpetuated the myth that persons with mental handicaps were "ineducable" and were "threats" to society.

The Second World War and the period following brought many changes to North America. One major change was the awakening of North Americans to their prejudices and practices relating to minority groups. Although the civil rights movement had its roots in racial issues, it rapidly expanded to encompass discrimination of other groups, including persons with handicaps. In the late 1940s and early 1950s, parents of children with handicaps formed local, provincial or state, and national associations for the mentally handicapped. A primary goal of such parent groups was to create educational opportunities for their sons and daughters. In a direct challenge to professional beliefs, these parents believed that their children could learn and would benefit from an education. Families of significant political and social stature, such as the Kennedy family in the United States, joined this movement.

In 1961, President John F. Kennedy formed the President's Committee on Mental Retardation with a mandate to prepare a national plan to combat mental retardation. The President's Committee stressed the need for service in areas such as early diagnosis, home support, and early education. Services developed were to be comprehensive and community centered and were to provide a continuum of care. Within three years, major changes were made to American federal legislation, and comprehensive planning was underway in every American state (Kott, 1971).

Public interest and support for services for children with mental handicaps or those at risk for school failure was accompanied by a rapid growth of research in the field of child development. In 1961, the notion of "fixed" intelligence was challenged by the publication of Hunt's *Intelligence and Experience*. This was followed by a number of other landmark works which asserted that environmental experiences may alter the developmental course of infants and children (Skeels, 1966) and that early years were "critical" periods for such changes (Bloom, 1964). Although subsequent analysis of the earlier research (Clarke & Clarke, 1976) has resulted in a more temperate view of the importance of experience in infancy, the myth that mental retardation was inherited, incurable, and irremedial was shattered. As a result of these findings and in response to public pressure, the American federal government passed legislation in 1968 to fund model preschool programs, such as Headstart, for children with handicaps.

In some ways, Canadian interest and development of services paralleled the American experience. The parental movement in mental retardation spread as quickly in Canada as it did in the United States. Between 1948 and 1970, 320 local chapters of the Canadian Association for the Mentally Handicapped were created by local parent initiatives across Canada (National Institute on Mental Retardation, 1981). In 1964, three years after the creation of the President's Committee on Mental Retardation, Ottawa sponsored the first Canadian Federal/Provincial Conference on Mental Retardation in Canada. Judy LaMarsh, minister of national health and welfare, stated that "the main purpose of the conference was to indicate practical steps that might be taken to co-ordinate and improve services for mentally retarded persons'' (Mental Retardation in Canada, 1965, p. v). Throughout the proceedings, participants reiterated the need for early education, including home visiting programs staffed by trained persons to establish adaptive programs of home care early in the child's life.

Unlike the United States, however, the Canadian federal government has much less jurisdiction over the provinces in matters relating to health, education, or welfare. Therefore, nationwide reforms were much less evident in Canada. Nonetheless, by the mid-1970s parents and professionals in every Canadian province were discussing, planning, or implementing programs for infants and preschoolers with developmental problems. Canadian interest in this area was not generated solely by American research and social reform. Other major influences were the normalization movement, the reallocation of federal and provincial funds under the Canada Assistance Plan, and the support and influence of public health nurses.

The concept of normalization was first formulated in Denmark in 1959, when it was incorporated into Danish law governing services for persons with mental handicaps (Bank-Mikkelsen, 1969). One definition of normalization was: ''making available to the mentally retarded, patterns and conditions of everyday life which are as close as possible to the norms and patterns of the mainstream of society'' (Wolfensberger, 1972, p. 27). This concept spread throughout Europe and Canada and was adopted in principle in the early 1970s by the Canadian Association for the Mentally Retarded. The era of institutionalization of infants and young children was drawing to a close. Families were choosing to keep sons and daughters at home, and they looked to the community for support and education. In many communities, this support was developed by parent associations of the mentally handicapped; it involved group programs for preschool children and home visiting services for infants. A new cost-sharing federal/provincial formula under the Canadian Assistance Plan emerged in the early 1970s, and provincial governments had increased monies available to fund community-based programs for infants and preschoolers with handicaps. Public health nurses—strong advocates of service to families with children with developmental problems—were influential in many areas. Thus, parent interest, available government funds, and professional support from public health nurses were factors which contributed to the rapid growth of many services for infants and children with handicaps in the early 1970s. And among these services were infant development programs.

COMPONENTS OF INFANT DEVELOPMENT PROGRAMS

Infant development programs vary significantly across Canada (Shipe, 1985; U.B.C. Survey, 1985) for many reasons. At the time of writing (1986), there are over 130 infant development programs in Canada, employing over 400 staff. However, there is no legal mandate, federally or provincially, for the specific provisions of these services; therefore, no standard federal or provincial database exists. In the early years, many local programs developed before expert assistance was available (Sauer, 1975). This is still the case in some provinces. Only B.C. and Newfoundland have full-time provincial co-ordinators available to advise, train, and monitor local staff and encourage standard practices. Alberta and Saskatchewan have part-time provincial co-ordinators, and the Prince Edward Island co-ordinator is available only for programs serving mentally handicapped children (U.B.C. Survey, 1985).

Provincial guidelines for the operation of infant development programs have been drafted in British Columbia (B.C. Manual on Infant Development Programmes, in press), Alberta (Alberta Program Guidelines, 1980), Saskatchewan (Saskatchewan Association for the Mentally Retarded, 1985) and Ontario (Ramsden, 1977). However, one study (Ontario Provincial Guidelines, 1982) revealed that the guidelines were not followed by all programs and that some directors were not aware that guidelines existed. (It should be noted that Ontario has recently revised its guidelines [Ontario, 1986]). Programs to train staff adequately prior to employment are not yet available in Canada; only a few colleges and universities offer courses or programs that provide some of the necessary knowledge and skills required (U.B.C. Survey, 1985). At this time, only British Columbia and Ontario have established associations concerned with professional ethics and practices.

There is no legal mandate for this service, there are few provincial staff available for consultation, and pre-service training opportunities are inadequate. As a result, it is surprising that there are a number of inter- and intra-provincial similarities among programs. The fact that there are similarities may be explained in part by the high interest and excitement in this field which has encouraged informal but frequent information-sharing among parents and professionals. The following description will cover broad areas of service provided by most infant development programs in Canada.

Rationale for Infant Development Programs

Infant development programs in Canada are based on one or more of the following assumptions: 1) infancy is an important period of life; and delays in development during this period may have longterm, cumulative effects on the patterns of development of any child, as well as the patterns of interaction between the child and his or her family; 2) intervention for children with developmental problems may be most effective if begun as early in the child's life as possible; and 3) the family unit is the most crucial source of learning, developmental encouragement, and emotional support available to the child.

Program Objectives

The common objective for most programs, as described in the provincial guidelines from Ontario, Alberta, Saskatchewan, and British Columbia, is to encourage the development of the child. The following quotations illustrate how this objective may vary in focus and intent. In Ontario, "the major goal of the programs is to organize and enrich the infant's sensory experiences so that development in key areas is facilitated" (Ontario Provincial Guidelines, 1982, p. i). In Alberta, "this program aims at bringing professional support into the homes so that the family interaction with the child promotes a positive adaptation to the child's developmental delay and maximizes the child's potential" (Alberta Programme Guidelines, 1980, p. 3). In Saskatchewan, " the purpose is to provide a home-based intervention program for families who have children birth to five years of age . . . who are developmentally delayed or at risk for delay; to identify and implement realistic goals for their children" (Saskatchewan E.C.I.P. Provincial Council, 1985, p. 3). In British Columbia, "the aims of the programme are to help parents make optimal use of available services, to enlarge their knowledge of those factors pertinent to the overall growth and development of their child and to learn skills which will enable them to encourage the development of their child" (B.C. Manual on Infant Development Programmes, revised edition, in press).

If these stated objectives reflect the current program focus, differences would exist between programs in two major areas. Firstly, the primary "client" or "target" of intervention may differ and be viewed as the child, the parent, or the family. Secondly, the role of the staff vis-à-vis the parent may be perceived differently from one program to another.

Population Served

Infant development programs generally serve children from birth to three years or until they are eligible for pre-school (U.B.C. Survey, 1985). In some communities, preschool may be available for children aged two or two-and-a-half. In others, preschool may not be available and some children may be involved in an infant development program until age five or older (U.B.C. Survey, 1985). Children identified as handicapped, or developmentally delayed in one or more skill areas, or at significant risk of delay constitute the majority of children referred for service (U.B.C. Survey, 1985). Infants at risk for delay may be defined in a variety of ways, but they include children who have experienced adverse prenatal, neonatal, postnatal, or socioeconomic factors that are thought to contribute to developmental handicaps.

Most infant development program populations are cross-categorical and serve children representing a variety of developmental problems. However, the availability of a more specialized resource in a particular community—a home program for deaf children, for example—means that certain groups of children might not be served by such a program. Most provinces have special programs for children with visual and hearing impairments; these services include itinerant teachers, home visiting services and other resources. These are usually available from the time of diagnosis, but they vary considerably. A rural child with visual impairment, for example, may be involved in an infant development program because the worker for the Canadian National Institute for the Blind can visit only infrequently.

Participation in the infant development program is voluntary, although in some programs active parental involvement is required. The family generally remains in the program until the infant "catches up" to the norm for his or her age (as might be the case for a premature high risk infant) or becomes eligible for preschool. In some situations the families leave the infant development program if referred to a more specialized resource, such as a treatment center for children with multiple handicaps, or if the parent chooses to discontinue service.

Service Delivery

Administration.   With the exception of Nova Scotia, provincial governments provide funds to community sponsors which operate and staff the infant development programs (U.B.C. Survey, 1985). Sponsors include hospitals, health units, school boards, and private non-profit societies such as associations for mentally handicapped persons, preschool societies, or infant development program societies. One major provincial difference is the degree of professional and parental involvement in directing and monitoring the service.

In some provinces, such as B.C. and Saskatchewan, the provincial guidelines for the operation of this service specify that local programs be directed by committees comprised of parents involved in the infant development program and representatives from a range of professions and agencies. These representatives often include public health nurses, physicians, psychologists, social workers, therapists, and early child-hood educators. In other provinces, program administration may be the sole responsibility of an executive director for a sponsoring society, a physician, or a supervisor of a health unit.

Referrals. To encourage early referrals, many infant development pro-grams have an open referral policy in which a wide range of professionals and parents may refer. The majority of such referrals are from public health nurses, physicians, other community professionals, and parents. Such a policy may be established because most provinces do not have universal surveillance of the child population. Generally, a surveillance system involving regular developmental assessments of children an-nually or more frequently ensures early and appropriate referral to social, educational, or medical services. Without such a system, however, as-sessments and referrals are not the mandated responsibility of any indi-vidual or agency. Parents who have had concerns about their child's de-velopment have sometimes waited up to three years for confirmation of a problem and subsequent referral to a program (Robinson & Sheps, 1979).

Some parents have described the period between suspicion of a delay or handicap, confirmation, and referral to a program as being the most difficult period to cope with emotionally. The longer this period con-tinues, the more difficult it may be to help parents set realistic goals for their child. This may relate to how the parents perceive themselves in re-lation to the child. Studies have demonstrated that parents providing "optimal" home environments believe in their ability to influence their child's development (Tolleson, 1978). Parents with prolonged, unsuc-cessful caretaking experiences may feel unable to influence their child's development; these parents may withdraw more and more from normal parenting practices.

Delays in both diagnosis and assistance may play a significant role in decision-making at the time of diagnosis. Such delays have led parents to seek out-of-home care for their child (Brynelsen, 1983). Therefore, early referrals to infant programs are generally encouraged; an open referral policy that accepts referrals from parents and from a wide range of professionals may be of benefit.

Services provided.

HOME VISITS. Most infant development programs provide home visits to families on a regular basis. In some instances, families are visited for one or two hours weekly or bi-weekly. In some programs, the frequency and duration of visits is determined by the family. Workers who see families on that basis may be concerned that families have control over their involvement with the program and not become overly dependent on the staff. However, frequency of visits may also be determined by the number of families on the caseload; in situations where staff have a large service area, families may be seen less frequently than desired by either the staff or the parent.

ASSESSMENT AND PROGRAM PLANNING.   During the course of home visits, information is gathered that enables staff to determine the skills and needs of the infant and family, to develop a program plan, and to evaluate progress. Information may be gathered by one or more of the following methods: interviews with the parent and other involved professionals; observation of the child, home and family; and informal or formal testing of the child.

Most programs have a standard intake procedure. Information is collected on the child's growth and development, the parents' concerns and priorities for their child, and the results of previous assessments by other professionals. These might include family physicians, pediatricians, physiotherapists, psychologists, speech and language pathologists, child care workers, and social workers involved with the family.

Observation of the child and family during home visits provides a valuable source of information about the child's abilities, likes and dislikes, temperament, motivation, the home environment, interaction with the parent, and parenting styles. Although there are ongoing opportunities for unstructured observation during the course of visits, a number of assessment tools have been developed to measure some of the above areas. Familiarity with these tools enables staff to become more accurate and objective observers. In some instances, formal administration may be useful and required on a regular basis. Included in measures of this type are the Home Observation for Measurement of the Environment (HOME) (Caldwell & Snyder, 1978), and the Parent Behaviour Progression (Bromwich, 1983).

Another useful method of deriving information is by testing the child. There are many different tests in use in infant development programs in Canada. Norm-referenced tests compare an individual child's performance to a normative group of other children the same age. Ones in common use in Canada include the Bayley Scales of Infant Development (Bayley, 1969) and the Gesell Developmental Schedules (Knobloch, Stevens & Malone, 1980). The Bayley is designed to be administered by trained psychologists and is used more frequently in areas where staff are psychologists or have access to psychological assessments. Criterion-referenced tests compare a child's performance on an item to a sequence of skills. A Canadian test is the Vulpe Assessment Battery (Vulpe,

1977). The third type of test is curriculum-referenced. These tests provide teaching activities for each item included on the scale. Most infant development programs have a variety of curriculum-referenced tests available, such as the Portage Project (Bluma, Shearer, Froham & Hillard, 1976) or the Hawaii Early Learning Program (Furuno, O'Reilly, Hosaka, Inatsuka, Allman & Zeisloft, 1979). A useful description of the assessment and planning process is found in the text *Teaching Infants and Preschoolers with Handicaps* (Bailey & Wolery, 1984).

Assessment in an infant development program is a complex and ongoing process (Fewell, 1983). Information sources are varied; infants with diagnosed handicaps are often assessed by a range of professionals, and a number of test results must be taken into consideration in planning an education program. The tests used in infant development programs have serious limitations (Zelazo, 1982). Many are not standardized; those that are were standardized on a non-handicapped population. There is little research available to help staff select the most beneficial tests or to adapt a particular test to accommodate a child's handicap. Assessment data must also be constantly updated to reflect the current status of the child so that program objectives can be developed for the child and family. Infancy is characterized by rapid change, therefore the assessment process must be ongoing.

Consequently, developing a program of activities responsive to ongoing changes in the infant is a challenge. This challenge is more readily met when staff work in partnership with parents to set objectives and decide on teaching activities (Brynelsen, 1984; Honig, 1981; Mittler, 1983). If parents have access to assessment data and assistance in interpreting the data, they may be in a much better position than staff to make decisions. They know their infant better than staff in terms of what he or she is able and willing to do. They also know what important skills they want their infant to acquire. By involving parents there is also a greater chance that the infant's program will fit into the family routine and not be seen as an additional burden.

Parents are more likely to remain motivated if the activities they helped design are fun and are seen as part of "regular" family life. Visits by program staff will not result in significant developmental change in the infant. It is the parent's involvement with their child and the daily interactions and activities they provide that bring change, not only for the infant but also for themselves as parents.

GROUP ACTIVITIES. Most infant development programs emphasize home-based services. In terms of providing assistance and support to families of infants and young children, home-based programming offers real benefits. Parents are in their own territory; the infant is in his or her own world. Problems of generalizing information from another setting to the home are lessened. Other family members may be involved more readily. Patterns of behavior in a child which may not be observed in strange settings may be obvious at home. Assessments in familiar settings may help bring out the best abilities in children, which in turn can lead to more effective programming. However, many infant development programs also recognize the importance of providing group-based activities for infants and parents.

Homes can be isolating for parents of young children. There are advantages to some group activities in addition to home visits. These might include Mom and Tot groups, parent education workshops, or parent support groups. Groups can provide opportunities for parents to observe how other parents interact with their children, showing them alternative models of interaction which may help them with their child. Groups can also provide educational opportunities for infants and parents that are not accessible to them in the home. Therefore, an increasing number of infant development programs are offering parents a range of options and settings for involvement beyond the home program. Parents may then select from these options those that best meet their needs.

LIAISON WITH OTHER PROFESSIONALS. Staff in infant development programs generally work closely with other community professionals in providing services to families, in sharing skills and resources, and in keeping the community up-to-date on the program. Many children in infant development programs have been assessed by and are receiving services from other community professionals. Involvement in an infant development program may also lead to increased or new contacts with community professionals. It is important that involved professionals are informed that a family has been referred, are kept up to date on the progress of the infant, and are encouraged to work closely with the program staff in planning. Consulting professionals, such as physiotherapists or speech and language pathologists, may visit a child's home with staff to assess the child or to provide specialized input into the program. In other situations, infant development staff may accompany the parent and child to a clinic or hospital for specialized consultation. In some programs, infant development staff act as case co-ordinators to facilitate information sharing among the involved professionals and the family.

RESOURCE MATERIALS. Most infant development programs have a resource library of books, toys, and equipment. Parents can borrow children's books, books on normal development in infancy, and books relating to specific handicaps. Books written by parents who have a child with a handicap are also valuable resources for both parents and staff (Pivato, 1984; Schaefer, 1983). More specialized books also form part of the library and are used by staff to learn more about the impact a handicap may have on development.

The staff use toys to illustrate their value in encouraging the development of a particular skill or increasing exploration and manipulation in play. Equipment and aids to mobility may also be available through an infant development library.

REFERRAL TO PRESCHOOL. In many communities, preschools are available for children at age two or three. Infant development staff are involved in assisting parents to select an appropriate preschool for their child. Many communities have a range of preschool options available. These might include regular preschools, special needs preschools, and integrated preschools. The degree of parent involvement in preschools varies considerably, as do hours of operation and program goals. Provincial funds to support the education of children with delays or handicaps in preschools after they leave infant development programs are available in most provinces, but they are not available for preschool children on the comprehensive scale that they are available for schoolage children (U.B.C. Survey, 1985). In small communities or rural areas preschools may be few or non-existent.

Selecting an appropriate preschool may take several months; it can involve visits to preschools with the parents, assisting them in the transition, and following up with the preschool teacher and parent. Parents may find it difficult to leave an infant development program and the staff can do much to alleviate parental anxiety and make the transition productive.

INFANT DEVELOPMENT PROGRAM STAFF

The following describes the knowledge base, skills, attitudes, and personal characteristics which staff need in order to work effectively with infants, their families, and other community professionals.

Knowledge Base

Normal growth and development. It is essential for staff to understand the patterns of normal development in young children in order to plan with parents developmental programs for the child. Normal family development should also be covered and include patterns of family growth and change, parent-child interactions, and social systems as they relate to the family.

Learning theories. The current focus of infant development programs is to support and facilitate the growth of both parents and their children. It follows that staff must understand the principles of adult as well as child learning (Anastasiow, 1985). Learning theories include the bases of the relationship between experience and behavior, behavior principles, and problem-solving strategies.

Impact of a delay or handicap on child and family.   Knowledge of various significant handicapping conditions, current treatment, and therapeutic approaches is important. It is also important to understand the effects of stress on the family following the diagnosis of an infant with a handicap and the coping strategies which can be supported (Mitchell, in press). Cultural and value-related differences between families must also be understood so that families can be assisted to build on their strengths (Featherstone, 1981; Chud and Fahlman, 1985).

Assessment, program planning and evaluation.   The focus in this area should be on functional assessments and programming which recognizes the expressed needs of the family and the child.

Roles of other professionals and community resources.   The role of the infant development staff is that of "generalist," gathering information from a variety of sources and translating it into daily practical use for the family. Therefore, it is important to understand the specific skills and roles of other professionals involved in services to children and families and their potential contributions. An understanding of the function of various community resources available to children and families is essential to help the family use these services effectively.

Skills

Application of this knowledge requires the development of specific skills. Communication skills include the ability to listen, provide useful feedback, and recognize and respond to changing family interactions. Mastery of these communication skills requires the ability to summarize goals and activities in an understandable form, be it verbal or written. Teaching in the home requires skills in reassessing involvement with the family. The worker must also have skill and flexibility in carrying out assessments with the parent and planning relevant activities to encourage development. This involves using information and recommendations from the parent and from other professionals involved with the child and family in ways that each feels that his or her contribution is respected and valued (Mitchell, 1983).

Attitudes and Personal Characteristics

The attitudes and personal characteristics of staff are those required by other professionals working in the human service field. These include the ability to accept and respect the individuality of each family, to value each person no matter how severe his or her handicapping condition, and to believe that people have the ability to change and adapt when opportunities are provided. Flexibility, humor, and the ability to manage time are necessary, given the independent nature of the work. It is also a decided asset if staff are parents themselves and have firsthand knowledge of the challenges of parenting.

Training

Staff currently employed in infant development programs have backgrounds in a variety of fields related to early intervention. These include special education, early childhood education, nursing, psychology, therapy (occupational, physio and speech), social work, family studies, and child care. These areas may involve two to ten or more years of postsecondary education. Past experience in working with young children and families is generally requisite to employment.

Undergraduate and graduate course work, directly related to early intervention, is only now being developed. For example, the University of British Columbia Institute on Infant Development is in its third year. A part-time diploma program which will incorporate courses sponsored by the institute should be available at the University of British Columbia soon. However, on the job training remains the major vehicle for education of infant development staff in Canada (U.B.C. Survey, 1985).

Professional Literature

At present, newsletters of a regional or provincial nature share information about new activities in the field, current staff training opportunities, and new resource books and materials available. Two provinces, British Columbia and Ontario, have registered societies representing professionals employed as staff in infant development programs. No Canadian journals directed specifically to infant development programs exist. American journals of interest to staff include *Topics in Early Childhood Special Education* and *Infant Mental Health Journal*. Given the multidisciplinary nature of the field, staff must keep up with new developments published in other professional journals including medicine, nursing, therapy, education, and psychology.

CURRENT TRENDS

Many infant development programs are changing in direction and focus in response to current trends in the field, trends suported by recent research findings. Foremost among these are new views of both the infant and the parent or primary caregiver. Once considered passive recipients of professional stimulation, capable of reacting but not initiating, both the child and the parent are increasingly viewed as active and interactive participants. The focus is now shifting from instructing parents on how to stimulate their babies to a much broader and more important goal of encouraging "mutually satisfying parent/infant interactions" (Bromwich, 1977, p. 78).

A better understanding of social systems and ecological theory is also bringing changes (Bronfenbrenner, 1975; Dunst, in preparation). Parents and infants are no longer seen as isolated units but as part of larger social networks. Research demonstrates that families with strong supportive social networks, which include nuclear and extended family members, friends, neighbors, and community agencies such as churches, are often associated with those families who are better able to interact positively with their own children (Dunst, 1983). Infant development programs are beginning to help parents forge stronger links among these groups by providing opportunities for involvement (Wilson, 1984). The ability of staff to co-ordinate or mediate social networks on behalf of families may have a greater impact on how a family manages than previous narrowly focused interventions. This is also reinforced by normalization ideology, which stresses the importance of normal life experiences in terms of growth and development for infant and family.

As the program focus changes so does the role of infant development staff. Staff are attempting to bridge the authority-layman gap, which traditionally characterizes professional-parent encounters (Heifetz, 1980). Increasingly, staff view themselves as working in partnership with parents. This partnership is based on mutual respect and joint decision-making and requires staff to relinquish certain powers to enable parents to become increasingly independent and in control of their and their children's lives (Brynelsen, 1984). Staff accept that there is no best way for parents to help a child. Instead, each family is assisted to "discover which solution is best for them and their needs at a particular time" (Bromwich, 1981, p. ix).

RESEARCH

Although there is a growing body of research relevant to early intervention, there are a number of problems associated with the translation of this research to practice in infant development programs. Firstly, existing research comes from a multitude of disciplines, from pediatric neurology to adult education. Locating relevant research and translating it into practical application is often difficult for individual practitioners. Few staff employed in infant development programs have the training and resources to access and interpret such research easily.

Secondly, much of the existing data derived from the evaluation of early intervention efforts is subject to serious methodological and design flaws. The field is new and the problems associated with the evaluation of programs for infants and their families are many (Bricker, 1985; Marfo & Kysela, 1985). These problems include small sample sizes, population differences, inadequate tools to measure change, and insufficient funds for research. The field is also characterized by conflicting theories of human development and learning which lead to controversies about which aspects of child and family development are relevant.

Lastly, with few exceptions, staff in Canadian infant development programs are dependent on research findings, evaluation tools, and curricula developed in the United States. Significant differences exist between American and Canadian cultures and their respective education, social, and health care systems. Little research is available to assist staff in infant development programs to choose, modify, or assess findings in view of cultural variations.

These problems and others present significant challenges to staff in infant development programs in Canada. Recognition of these problems and attempts to solve them are leading to increased efforts by staff to develop better training opportunities. Information-sharing via newsletters and the formation of professional associations in B.C. and Ontario are also examples of strategies that help bridge the gap between existing research and practice in the field. It is hoped that these initial efforts will be followed by the development of standards and guidelines, based on current research, for the training of personnel and the operation of infant development programs (Mitchell, in preparation).

SUMMARY

The intent of this chapter has been to provide a brief overview of infant development programs in Canada. Since the inception of the first programs in the mid-1970s, there has been a relatively rapid expansion of this service throughout Canada. As mentioned earlier, there are currently over 130 programs in operation employing over 400 staff. Many programs, once isolated pilot projects, are now part of larger human service networks and are increasingly viewed as accepted services in their communities. However, their rapid growth has not been accompanied by the development of regional or provincial resources sufficient to meet staff training needs or to provide expert consultation on program direction. Hopefully, the next ten years will see continued growth of this new field accompanied by the development of support, information, and evaluation services to help staff meet the needs of the infants and families they serve.

NOTES

1. The authors are grateful to Dr. D. R. Mitchell for his review of this chapter and helpful comments.
2. Infant development programs are also called infant stimulation programs or early intervention programs, but throughout this chapter they will be referred to as infant development programs.

REFERENCES

Alberta Program Guidelines (1980). *Early intervention program for families with developmentally delayed children.* Alberta: Social Services and Community Health.

Anastasiow, N. J. (1985). Parent training as adult development. In S. Harel & N. J. Anastasiow (Eds.) *The at-risk infant. Psycho/socio/medical aspects* (pp. 5–12). Baltimore: Paul H. Brookes.

Bailey, D. B. & Wolery, M. (1984). *Teaching infants and preschoolers with handicaps.* Columbus, Ohio: Charles E. Merrill.

Bank-Mikkelsen, N. E. (1969). A metropolitan area in Denmark: Copenhagen. In R. Kugel & W. Wolfensberger (Eds.) *Changing patterns in residential services for the mentally retarded.* Washington, DC: President's Committee on Mental Retardation.

Bayley, N. (1969). *Bayley scales of infant development.* New York: Psychological Corporation.

Blatt, B. (1971). Some persistently recurring assumptions concerning education of the mentally retarded. In J. H. Rothstein (Ed.) *Mental retardation. Readings and resources* (pp. 36–46). San Francisco: Holt, Rinehart & Winston.

Bloom, B. S. (1964). *Stability and change in human characteristics.* New York: Wiley.

Bluma, S. M., Shearer, M. S., Frohan, A. H. & Hillard, J. M. (1976). *Portage guide to early education.* Portage, Wisconsin: Cooperative Educational Agency.

Bricker, D. (1984). An analysis of early intervention programs: Attendant issues and future directions. In B. Blatt & R. Morris (Eds.) *Perspectives in special education.* New York: Scott, Foresman Publishing Co.

British Columbia. (in press). *B.C. manual on infant development programmes.* (revised) Victoria.

Bromwich, R. (1977). Stimulation in the first year of life? A perspective on infant development. *Young Children, 32* (2), 71–82.

Bromwich, R. (1981). *Working with parents of infants: An interactional approach.* Baltimore: University Park Press.

Bromwich, R. (1983). *Manual for the parent behavior progression (PBP).* California State University, Department of Educational Psychology.

Bronfenbrenner, U. (1975). Is early intervention effective? In B. Friedlander, G. Sterritt & G. Kirk (Eds.) *Exceptional Infant,* vol. 3.

Brynelsen, D. (1983). Problems experienced by line staff in management of children with multiple handicaps. In G. Schwartz (Ed.) *Advances in research and services for children with special needs.* Vancouver: University of British Columbia Press.

Brynelsen, D. (Ed.) (1984). *Working together.* Vancouver: National Institute on Mental Retardation and British Columbians for Mentally Handicapped People.

Caldwell, B. & Snyder, C. (1978). *Home observation for measurement of the environment.* Little Rock, Arkansas: Center for Child Development and Education, University of Arkansas.

Chud, G. & Fahlman, R. (1985). *Early childhood education for a multicultural society.* Vancouver: Western Education Development Group, Faculty of Education, University of British Columbia.

Clarke, A. M. & Clarke, A. D. B. (1976). *Early experience: Myth and evidence.* New York: Macmillan.

Dunst, C. J. (1982). Theoretical bases and pragmatic considerations in infant curriculum construction. In J. Anderson (Ed.) *Curricula for high-risk and handicapped infants*. Chapel Hill, North Carolina: Technical Assistance Development System.

Dunst, C. J. (1983). *A systems-level, family-focused approach to assessment and intervention with profoundly handicapped children*. Paper presented at Handicapped Children's Early Education Program Conference, Washington, DC.

Dunst, C. J. (in preparation). Rethinking early intervention. *Analysis and intervention in development disabilities*.

Featherstone, H. (1981). *A difference in the family. Living with a disabled child*. Middlesex, England: Penguin Books.

Fewell, R. R. (1983). Assessing handicapped infants. In S. G. Garwood and R. R. Fewell (Eds.) *Educating handicapped infants* (pp. 257–297). Rockville, Maryland: Aspen Systems Corporation.

Furuno, S., O'Reilly, K. A., Hosaka, C. M., Inatsuka, T. T., Allman, T. L. & Zeisloft, B. (1979). *Hawaii early learning profile*. Palo Alto, California: VORT.

Heifitz, L. J. (1980). From consumer to middleman: Emerging roles for parents in the network of services for retarded children. In R. R. Abidin (Ed.) *Parent education and intervention handbook* (pp. 349–383). Springfield, Illinois: Charles C. Thomas.

Honig, A. S. (1981). *Working in partnership with parents of handicapped infants*. Paper presented at Johns Hopkins University Infant Symposium, Baltimore, Maryland.

Hunt, J. (1961) *Intelligence and experience*. New York: Ronal Press.

Knobloch, H., Stevens, F. & Malone, A. F. (1980). *Manual of developmental diagnosis*. Hagerstown, Maryland: Harper & Row.

Kott, M. G. (1971). The history of mental retardation. In J. H. Rothstein (Ed.) *Mental retardation: Readings and resources*. (pp. 24–35). San Francisco: Holt, Rinehart & Winston.

LaMarsh, J. (1965). Opening remarks. *Mental retardation in Canada*. Ottawa: Federal-provincial conference, Queen's Printer.

Marfo, K. & Kysela, G. (1985). Early intervention with mentally handicapped children: A critical appraisal of applied research. *Journal of Pediatric Psychology, 10,* 305–324.

Mitchell, D. R. (1983). International trends in special education. *Canadian Journal of Mental Retardation, 33,* 6–13.

Mitchell, D. R. (in press). A developmental systems approach to planning and evaluating services for persons with handicaps. In R. I. Brown (Ed.) *Rehabilitation and education, volume 2: Management and administration in rehabilitation: Impact on programmes and personnel*. Beckenham, Kent: Croom Helm.

Mitchell, D. R. (in preparation). Waikato scale for evaluating early intervention programmes. Hamilton, New Zealand, University of Waikato.

Mittler, P. & Mittler, H. (1983). Partnership with parents: An overview. In Peter Mittler & Helen McConachie (Eds.) *Parents, professionals and mentally handicapped people* (pp. 8–43). London: Croom Helm.

National Institute on Mental Retardation (1981). Historical perspectives on mental retardation. *Orientation manual on mental retardation* (pp. 1–24). Toronto.

Ontario. (1986). *Consultation paper on proposed guidelines for infant development services.* Toronto: Community Services Division, Ministry of Community and Social Services.

Ontario Provincial Guidelines (1982). *Survey of infant stimulation programs in Ontario.* Toronto: Queen's Printer.

Pivato, E. (Ed.) (1984). *Different hopes, different dreams.* Edmonton: Academic Printing and Publishing.

Ramsden, M. (1977). *Ministry guidelines for infant stimulation programmes.* Toronto: Ontario Ministry of Community and Social Services.

Robinson, G. & Sheps, S. (1979). *Children with developmental handicaps: Is there a gap between suspicion and referral?* Vancouver, BC: University of British Columbia, Department of Pediatrics.

Saskatchewan E.C.I.P. Provincial Council. (1985). *Saskatchewan's early childhood home based intervention program: Standards and guidelines.* Saskatoon: Saskatchewan Association for the Mentally Retarded.

Sauer, D. (1975). Infant home care programme. *Deficience mentale/ Mental retardation: Canadian association for the mentally retarded, 25* (3), 26–29.

Schaefer, N. (1983). *Does she know she's there?* Toronto: Fitzhenry and Whiteside.

Shipe, D. (1985). Early intervention. In N. Marlette & B. Gall (Eds.). *Dialogue on disability* (pp. 39–60). Calgary: University of Calgary Press.

Skeels, H. M. (1966). Adult status of children with contrasting early life experiences. *Monographs of the society for research in child development, 31* (3).

Tolleson, L. (1978). *Parents' beliefs, attitudes and values and their relationship to home environment provided for developmentally delayed infants involved in a home-based intervention programme.* Unpublished master's thesis, University of British Columbia, Vancouver.

University of British Columbia (1985). *U.B.C. survey of infant development programmes in Canada.* Vancouver: University of British Columbia, Faculty of Education.

Vulpe, S. G. (1977). *Vulpe assessment battery.* Toronto: National Institute on Mental Retardation.

Wilson, R. (1984). Dads only. *Infant development programme of B.C.: Provincial newsjournal, 2* (3), 7.

Wolfensberger, W. (1972). *The principle of normalization in human services.* Toronto: National Institute on Mental Retardation.

Zelazo, P. R. (1982). Alternative assessment procedures for handicapped infants and toddlers: Theoretical and practical issues. In D. D. Bricker (Ed.) *Intervention with at-risk and handicapped infants.* (pp 107–128). Baltimore: University Park Press.

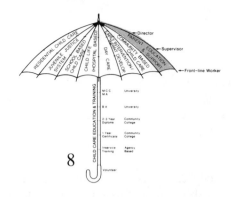

8

Community-Based Child Care

PETER A. GABOR

THE DEVELOPMENT OF COMMUNITY PROGRAMS

During the last fifteen years, the focus of child care practice has moved from an almost exclusively institutional base to one that includes community-based practice. Today, community-based child care is expanding rapidly, with excellent prospects for future growth. The movement toward community-based practice is a reflection of a number of separate developments, each representing a major trend in child care.

A key development leading to increased involvement of child care workers in the community was the realization that the post-discharge environment is perhaps the key determinant of successful adaptation after institutional placement (Allerhand, Weber & Haug, 1966; Taylor & Alpert, 1973). Outcome research suggests that regardless of success during residential placement, what happens after placement will determine whether gains will be maintained or existing problems overcome. In the light of these findings, institutional programs began to develop aftercare components designed to make the post-discharge environment more supportive to the youngster. Child care workers were frequently involved in aftercare programs, continuing their involvement with children individually and in groups and offering their services to parents, especially in the area of child management. The involvement of child care workers in aftercare services was a logical expansion of their role, as it built on the relationship formed during the youngster's stay in residential care and took advantage of worker's expertise in child management.

A related development has seen the helping professions increasingly favor ecological, rather than child-centered, approaches. Recognition of the potential hazards of institutional care (Shyne, 1973) and the related prominence of the normalization movement (Wolfensberger, 1972) have also been factors in this trend. As a consequence, services have been moved closer to the child's natural environment (Whittaker, 1977), thereby increasing the opportunity for influencing key systems such as the family, school, and peer group.

Undoubtedly, these professional trends have also influenced legislative and policy developments. In 1978, the Family Support Worker Program was established in British Columbia primarily as a means of reducing the need for specialized forms of services (Ministry of Human Resources, 1978). Subsequently, in Ontario a consultation paper issued by the government prior to the drafting of the current Children's Act (Ministry of Community and Social Services, 1982) declared that one of the principles of the new act would be that: "services to children should support, enhance, and supplement the family, whenever possible, rather than compete with the family by providing alternative care and supervision." The recently passed Child Welfare Act (Government of the Province of Alberta, 1984) in Alberta also states that community measures should be tried first:

> If it is not inconsistent with the protection of a child who may be in need of protective services, the child's family should be referred to community resources for services that would support and preserve the family and prevent the need for any other intervention under this Act.

Provisions such as these have had a major impact on child care, legitimizing and encouraging family-oriented and community-based programming.

In the child care field, this move toward the community has resulted in two types of program changes. First, institutional programs, which tend to be relatively isolated, have increasingly given way to group home programs. In Ontario, for example, the number of children in institutional placement declined by over 27 per cent between 1970 and 1980 (Ministry of Community and Social Services, 1983). Secondly and perhaps more profoundly, a new class of programs, community-based child care programs, have developed to take their place beside the more familiar group care programs, in some cases as adjuncts and in others as alternatives to group care programs. For example, the move to group homes has meant that children were more likely to attend schools in the community rather than remain in in-house school programs. This change has prompted the creation of school liaison programs, which help children adjust to the community and, in turn, assist the community to improve services for children with special needs. Similarly, life skills and community activity programs have been developed to help children function more effectively in the community while continuing to live at home; these programs also increase the resources the neighborhood can offer youngsters who might otherwise need group care placements.

In the late 1960s, more and more adolescents left their homes, and most sizeable cities in Canada have seen the establishment of a permanent core of youngsters living on their own with marginal resources. Many of these children have left behind unsatisfying home situations; they are often unprepared to make constructive use of their independence. Consequently, they are not only vulnerable to such dangers as prostitution, drug and substance abuse, and delinquency, but they also tend to miss out on their education and on developing appropriate work, social, and life skills. A high proportion of these children are in need of social services; a range of community programs offering both emergency and longterm services has developed in response to the need. The people who staff such programs are not always clearly aligned or identified with any recognizable professional group, but many staff members have been designated as child care workers. These programs include runaway and street worker programs, life skills training programs, and outreach.

Another trend which has had a strong impact on the delivery of child care services has been the increasing focus on the prevention of problems, a distinct shift from the earlier preoccupation with cure and treatment. Associated with this trend are efforts aimed at encouraging appropriate development and enhancing well-being and competence, an outlook characteristic of holistic approaches.

Institutional and other group care approaches concern themselves primarily with reducing the seriousness and impact of already identified problems, referred to in the public health field as a tertiary prevention approach. More preventive approaches involve interventions in the environmental systems in which people live. Such interventions may involve identifying problems early in order to minimize consequences, or they may focus on working with high-risk groups to prevent the occurrence of problems in the first place. In public health these approaches would be considered secondary and primary prevention, respectively. These efforts normally take place in the community and aim to help people make more effective use of their social environment. Increasingly, there is also an emphasis on making social environments more responsive to people's needs, as illustrated by helping models such as the *mediating model* (Shulman, 1984). Community child care programs can in many instances be viewed as operating on the secondary and primary prevention levels.

Contract workers and runaway services are examples of secondary prevention programs, and street worker and community activity programs serve primary prevention purposes.

Finally, child care work has been affected, no less than other social services, by the increased cost consciousness which has accompanied the recent troubled economic times. More and more, funders scrutinize the costs of services and seek less expensive alternatives. And group care programs tend to be relatively costly because of the need to staff around the clock. Funders, hoping to realize savings, have therefore increasingly favored the community child care model. While community programs are usually less expensive than group care programs, it is important to recognize that not all community programs can be viewed as alternatives to group care. In fact, community projects come in many different forms and vary greatly in costs, ranging from relatively inexpensive recreation programs to highly sophisticated ventures providing intensive services. It may be legitimate to compare these various programs to group care, but a comparison of costs will often reveal that the community alternative, while less expensive, is still a relatively costly operation. Thus, while economics have favored the development of community child care, the arguments and comparisons have often been simplistic, comparing the costs of different programs providing different services. Funders have often opted for the less expensive alternatives. As a result, the continuum of child welfare resources often has gaps in the area of more intensive, treatment-oriented programs and a proliferation of less expensive programs.

THE RANGE AND VARIETY OF COMMUNITY CHILD CARE

The growth of community child care has seen the development of numerous innovative programs across Canada. A number of such programs will be described to illustrate the rich variety of community-based services which are now available to young people.[1]

Programs Supporting Young People in their Homes

Recognizing that for most young people the best possible placement available remains their own home, programs supporting children and families are now commonly available. Family support programs such as the one operated by Huntley Youth Services in Toronto attempt to strengthen the ability of families to care for children with special needs (Huntley Youth Services, n.d.). Other programs aim to relate primarily to the young person, helping with school, social functioning, peer relations, and work. The *Contract Worker* program offered by Central Toronto Youth Services is one example of this approach. This agency lists the following responsibilities of contract workers (Central Toronto Youth Services, n.d.):

1. Active intervention aimed at solving specific problems;
2. Developing behavioral control, life and social skills, and job related skills;
3. Counseling to increase the ability to deal with frustration and to increase self-awareness;
4. Befriending and role modeling.

Supporting the Child in School

Young people experiencing problems at school often develop difficulties in other areas of their lives as well. Because schools are often unable or unwilling to work with young people who have special needs, child care approaches have been developed to help children succeed at school. Programs developed by the St. Leonard Society of Burnaby, B.C. provide examples of such approaches. Three programs have been established and all utilize teams of child care workers and teachers. *The Armstrong Special Program,* for example, serves elementary school children with behavioral problems and provides "one-to-one, group and family counseling . . . [to enable children] to return to their home school within a reasonable period of time" (Lower Mainland St. Leonard's Society, n.d.).

Other programs, often referred to as life skills programs, supplement the efforts of schools and caregivers by teaching practical skills required in daily life. The *Calgary Life Skills Program* attempts to teach skills needed in the "management of personal affairs in five areas: self, leisure, job, community, and family" (Alberta Social Services and Community Health, 1982).

There are a variety of other child care opportunities in schools. In Ontario, many child care workers are employed as Home-School Liaison Workers or as Adolescent Care Workers. The former work primarily in elementary schools and help the family resolve school problems. Adolescent care workers are involved with older youngsters who are not attending regularly; they attempt to help such young people become constructively involved with school. In other Ontario programs, child care workers are assigned to work on an individual basis with children who have special needs, thereby allowing them to remain in a regular classroom setting. Such workers have assisted many children, including hearing and visually impaired students and behaviorally disruptive youngsters.

Community Aspects of Group Care

During the past few years, community dimensions have been added to many residential programs. Child care workers are now commonly involved in family work while the child is in residential care. For example, family work is listed as an important component of almost every residential program described in the program catalog published by Youth Horizons, a large residential agency in Montreal (Youth Horizons, n.d.). Child care workers are often involved in aspects of family work, with responsibilities such as arranging and supervising visits and offering advice and support to parents.

Many residential programs have also developed aftercare programs aimed at helping children and families with the transition from residential placement. Child care workers are the key aftercare personnel, offering help, support, and information.

Some community programs resemble residential care and are clearly the result of the evolution of group care. Day treatment for children with behavioral and emotional problems, as offered in the *Contact* program of Youth Horizons, is one example of such a development (Youth Horizons, n.d.); another is *Training Apartments* for mentally handicapped people, operated by Taylor-Thibodeau Centre in Montreal (Le Centre D'Acceuil les Promotions Sociales Taylor-Thibodeau, n.d.). Because of the design of both these programs, extensive community contact is provided for the client. These descriptions indicate that community child care has gained a foothold even in group care.

Street Programs

Some of the most innovative community child care work takes place in street programs. Because these projects tend to work with young people before problems have arisen or have been recognized by formal helping systems, these operations have the clearest preventive orientation.

Street programs often attempt to engage young people through the use of outreach techniques. In the communities of the South Shore of Montreal, where high delinquency rates are a problem, a range of programs have been organized to provide young people with constructive alternatives (Comité de Prévention de Crime de la Rive-Sud de Montréal, n.d.). These programs reach into the schools and provide life skills and job search training, sex education, counseling, and activity centers.

Whereas these programs are aimed at the entire population of adolescents, other outreach programs, such as the *Inner City Youth Programme* in Toronto (Huntley Youth Services, n.d.) attempt to contact young people in high-risk situations. This latter program offers counseling, information, and skill training to young people who spend their time on the Yonge Street strip.

Street programs are often the only means of contacting young people who are alienated from traditional community structures and are therefore shut off from help and support. As social pressures and youth unemployment continue to increase, it can be expected that the numbers of young people who become isolated and estranged will grow, increasing the need for street programs.

IMPLICATIONS FOR CHILD CARE PRACTICE

Definition of Community Child Care

The move of child care into the community has altered the nature of the profession; workers are now involved in a wide range of tasks, many of which are radically different from those responsibilities traditionally associated with residential child care work. In turn, additional knowledge and skills, as well as different attitudes and a new perspective, are now required of workers.

Community child care modifies and expands the role developed in group care. The distinctive feature of residential child care is the constant contact provided in the life space of the client. The aim of the work is to integrate the "child's total experience in residence—his specialized treatment requirements with his normative requirements for social, educational, work, and recreational experiences" (Barnes, 1980). The work has a dual purpose: the provision of basic care, and the remediation of difficulties or problems experienced by the child or those around him. Both care and remediation are provided through skillful management of the living situation, using the events and interactions of the child's life to further his emotional, social, and instrumental competence (Trieschman, Whittaker & Brendtro, 1969).

Community child care work has similar purposes. Although the provision of basic care is not, by definition, the mandate of community child care, the enhancement of development is a more explicit focus of the work. Because the child continues to live in the community, child care work increasingly involves contact with the child's family, friends, substitute caregivers, teachers, and others. As the child continues to be involved with the community, child care interventions must be undertaken with due regard to the influence and impact of key people and systems in the child's life. Indeed, at times, these people and systems become the focus of child care work. In brief, child care workers have had to add to their initial core knowledge and skills; they have had to develop an ability to work with adults and adopt a new perspective, shifting from what was previously a child-centered orientation to one that recognizes the importance of the social environment to the development of the child (Garbarino, 1982). Moreover, work in the community may inadvertently or deliberately lead to the worker's involvement in local politics. Thus community child care workers need to develop an understanding of, and sensitivity to, political processes, as well as the skills to effectively participate at the political level.

VanderVen (1981) has analyzed the nature of child care work utilizing Bronfenbrenner's hierarchical levels in the ecological system. This analysis helps to elaborate the differences between community and residential child care work and clarifies the contexts within which community child care is practised. Level 1 of the environment is the *microsystem,* that is, the immediate environment containing the child. Work at this level is directly with children. Level 2 of the environment is the *mesosystem,* which is a system of direct settings within which the child is involved. Practice at this level involves working *through* those people responsible for the various settings: facilitating, encouraging, enabling, and co-ordinating. Work at this level involves indirect contact with children. In applying this schema to the case of child care, it appears that much of child care work, both residential and in the community, is performed at Level 1, but some aspects of the work fit the criteria for Level 2.

Consider, for example, the case of the child care worker in group care who works directly with the children, that is, at Level 1 of the environment. At the same time, this worker may have the opportunity to work with the child's parents and teachers, or to advocate on behalf of the child within the residential program itself. These are all examples of work which takes place at Level 2. The community child care worker may also be involved in work at both levels. Leading a recreational program, teaching job search skills, and managing an emergency program for runaways could be considered examples of work at Level 1, while supporting a child within the family, at work, or in school may involve considerable work with parents, foster parents, employers, teachers, and other adults, that is, at Level 2. The respective proportions of work at the two levels vary depending on the design of a particular program and the job description of the worker. Nevertheless, in considering the nature of residential and community work, it appears that, on the whole, much of residential work involves direct work with children and can therefore be characterized as being performed at Level 1, while community child care seems to involve more frequent contact with key people in the child's life and thus operates at Level 2 as well as Level 1.

VanderVen indicates that work at Level 1 requires identification with children, while work at Level 2 must combine identification with both children and their parents. In considering the respective demands of residential and community child care, it seems that this analysis is applicable. Residential workers, who work primarily with children, tend to have a strong identification with their charges, at times to the extent that they seem almost anti-adult (VanderVen, 1979). To be effective, community workers must be able to identify with adults as well. VanderVen indicates that such a shift in orientation occurs quite naturally as people grow from late adolescence to adulthood. This suggests that community child care work is suited more to the older, experienced child care practitioner than to the younger worker just beginning a career in the field.

As child care workers move into the community, their practice may at times resemble that of other professionals based in the community. There are a number of similarities between community child care and the practices of other professions, but for child care, struggling with obtaining professional recognition and acceptance, it is vital to demonstrate that its community-based practice is not a duplication of the work of existing professions. Community child care needs to be clear about its underlying philosophy, focus, and approaches, to be able to show convincingly that it can make a unique contribution to existing services.

While many aspects of child care work are shared with other professions, child care is unique because of the context within which it is practiced and because of the particular combination of values and approaches which characterize it. The context of practice is, of course, the child's everyday living environment. Child care workers involve themselves for several hours at a time in the events and activities of their client's day. The practice is holistic: oriented toward growth, development, and the enhancement of human functioning. The underlying philosophy is essentially humanistic: there is a belief in the potential of people to live effectively, given the right kind of experiences, supports, and opportunities. Child care practice is action-oriented, practical, and informal, three characteristics which enhance the ability of child care workers to relate to their clients—often young people who are not receptive to more formal, clinically oriented professionals. It should be emphasized, however, that although child care is less formal than other professions, child care workers often make use of powerful and sophisticated interventions. The practice is eclectic, drawing on skills from other disciplines and blending these with the approaches developed in child care. Finally, child care practice tends to be interdisciplinary, and child care workers are often responsible for co-ordinating and interpreting the efforts of other professionals.

Barnes's (1980) description of the European *educateur* describes well the distinctive aspects of community—and residential—child care:

> Thus, the educateur, a specialist in working with youth as a "constant contact practitioner" or generalist, engages with his clients in the thick of whatever they are doing. He can relate purposefully during a wide range of life space incidents or program events, and it is his expertise to structure the nature and operation of these events so that they are therapeutic and growth-inducing for the youngsters involved. The skill of the educateur is in relating directly to children and youth and helping them over the total range of their experience. Through making conscious use of the available milieux, individual and peer relationships, his own personality, and appropriate outside resources, the educateur transforms the whole experience of everyday life, whether in community or residential programs, into an educational and rehabilitative program.

Comparison of Community and Residential Child Care

Much of the same knowledge and many similar skills are required for the effective practice of both residential and community child care. Workers in both settings must relate effectively to children and need skills in counseling, advocacy, teaching, group leadership, crisis intervention, activity programming, and behavioral management. In residential practice, these skills are used within the context of the group living situation; interventions are usually directed towards the children. In community child care, many of the same skills are required, but in different contexts: within families, groups, and organizations. Consequently, child care workers are often called upon to work with adults as well as children. Thus, the community worker must be able to relate to adults, families, and organizations.

A recent study examining the job functions of child care workers in British Columbia provides useful data for comparing community and residential child care (Anglin, 1983). This study describes the job functions of child care workers in various settings and concludes that family support work, a form of community child care, has the highest job complexity, according to the definition used. Residential child care is of a lower level of complexity. While the author of this study points out that specific workers in less complex settings may be performing highly complex work, the results can nevertheless be viewed as one measure of the level of complexity in various child care settings. It is also shown that there are many job functions common to all forms of child care. This study suggests that the essential nature of the work is similar in both group and community care, but some community work is more varied and complex.

Professional Identity

Because community child care is new, neither the field nor the discipline are as yet clearly defined. Community child care is practiced in settings as varied as youth recreational programs, drop-in centers, schools, and homes, with the result that child care workers are at times confused with recreational leaders, lay counselors, teacher's aides, social workers, or others (Ricks & Charlesworth, 1982). Indeed, there is no widely accepted definition of community child care work which could help define the profession or at least indicate what lies within and outside its boundaries. There is not even an unequivocal understanding about the relationship between community and residential child care; certainly a clear consensus that residential and community child care are branches of the same profession is still in a formative stage.

From time to time, community workers have attempted to form their own associations, as did Community Youth Workers in Alberta just before the turn of the decade. The attempt failed and it had the effect of retarding the growth of the Child Care Workers' Association of Alberta for a number of years. In the current troubled economic times, even a unified field of child care is facing an uphill battle in its efforts to gain professional recognition; the task may be impossible if the two branches of child care are contenders for scarce resources. To the degree that community child care tries to go separately, it is distancing itself from roots which can help provide a clearcut identity and develop its knowledge base and technology. Correspondingly, this distancing can deprive the profession of one of its most vigorous and energetic branches.

The claim to professional recognition is significantly strengthened if child care can define itself to include both community and residential practice. Increasingly, child welfare agencies are developing both residential and community components. A unified field of child care is ideally positioned to play a key role, having expertise in both group care and community services. A close association of the two branches will make it possible for residential and community child care to draw on each other, thereby enhancing the effectiveness of child care practice generally. Many approaches and techniques perfected in group care—activity program leadership and behavioral management, for example—can be very useful in community work, while community child care can offer a more ecologically oriented perspective as well as concrete approaches to involving families in group care services.

Finally, a united field significantly improves career opportunities in child care. Lack of career opportunities and a lack of variety in the work are two reasons for the high turnover in the profession (Gabor, 1975). With the field encompassing both community and residential work, more varied and complex career patterns might be possible. For example, a worker might begin in residential work, move to community work after a few years, then return to group care in a supervisory capacity. The advantages to this type of career progression are twofold: The individual is afforded the opportunity to try a variety of assignments which can enhance practice skills as well as prepare the worker for advancement. At the same time, community child care benefits from acquiring a worker with well-developed skills, and group care benefits from acquiring a supervisor who can bring a community perspective to the work.

Education and Career Development

The foregoing discussion leads to a number of considerations in child care education and career development. While little data exists on career patterns in child care, many workers in community programs seem to have worked before in a position which involved direct practice with children. Possibly there is a self-selection in operation, since after a few years of working directly with children, people begin to look for new challenges and variety and they move on to community work. Increasingly, people also express an interest in community work from the beginning of their careers, and it is likely that over the next several years, more and more people will enter community work without previous group care experience.

Educational programs which train people for entry into the field have traditionally emphasized work directly with children. A perusal of the announcements of community college training programs indicates that most of the content is designed to provide direct practice skills. Thus courses like "Observation and Assessment," "Therapeutic Activities," and "Group Dynamics" constitute the largest part of the curricula, preparing people for working with children alone or in groups. Many programs now provide at least an exposure to topics which are relevant for community work. Accordingly, courses with titles like "The Role of the

Child Care Worker in the Family, School, and Community" and "Family Support and Intervention" are also offered. Such courses attend to the theme of working with adults as well as children, in family and in community systems. Although the emphasis on such course content may now be increasing, it would be appropriate for child care education to give more emphasis to this theme (Beker & Maier, 1981).

From a pedagogic point of view, it is sensible that skills and knowledge relating to direct practice be taught first. However, because training is aimed at the direct practice level, it is important to recognize the needs of experienced child care workers who are ready to move into community work. Courses leading to advanced diplomas could be offered by existing child care training programs, with scheduling to accommodate part-time study. Similarly, agencies should provide for this need through in-service events and should be prepared to support the efforts of beginning community workers through supervision. At present there are few such supports, resulting in ill-prepared workers undertaking tasks too complex for their skills.

CURRENT ISSUES IN COMMUNITY CHILD CARE

The rapid growth of community child care has resulted in problems as well as opportunities. Some of the concerns relate to the profession itself and some to the way services and organizations are structured in the field. Because community child care is a relatively new field, there is little to guide future developments. In this section, some of the key issues facing the field today will be discussed.

Standards for Programs and Practitioners

Community programs have experienced unprecedented growth in recent years. Although community programs were a major resource in British Columbia by the late 1970s, in many other jurisdictions they are a relatively recent innovation. It was not until 1982, for example, that community programs were acknowledged as a distinct program category in Alberta, with forty-eight community programs listed in the provincial program guide (Alberta Social Services and Community Health, 1982). The proliferation of these programs was undoubtedly accelerated by economic considerations, legislative trends, and professional developments. However, it can be argued that the quickly growing demand for such programs did not leave a sufficient opportunity for adequate preparation and orderly growth. Although community programs were quite prominent in

Alberta by 1982, there is no mention made of community programs in the applicable standard-setting document, *Standards for Child Care* (Alberta Association of Child Care Centers, 1981; the topic will be covered in the planned third edition). Under such circumstances, it is hardly surprising that program standards are a key issue needing to be addressed.

A related concern is the matter of standards for community workers. Child care has long been a field where standard credentials have been lacking, leaving agencies with the power to decide who is and who is not a child care worker through their hiring process (Austin, 1981). For example, the Alberta government exercised just such discretion when, through its funding process, it declared that direct service positions in community programs would be regarded and funded as child care positions. This decision created hundreds of community child care positions; the profession faced great potential growth within the province. However, many of the people filling these positions have neither child care training nor child care experience and consequently, at a time when residential child care seems to be making headway in upgrading staff qualifications, community child care can still be practiced by anyone who manages to get a job. And there is a related concern, even when qualified people are employed in community programs. Because child care training programs tend to emphasize work in group care, and because few workers in residential programs have much experience in community work, even trained and experienced child care workers do not always have preparation appropriate to community work.

The development and implementation of appropriate standards is complicated by current political and economic trends. The political goals of "less government" and "privatization" throughout the country have resulted in less direct government delivery of and funding for human services. For child care, this development has led to an increased reliance on *contracted services,* an arrangement under which child care services are purchased by the government for its clients, on a case-by-case basis. Often the scope of service is narrowly defined, and the fees paid cover only a minimum wage with no provision for benefits. This type of service arrangement is increasing across Canada; in British Columbia the practice is widespread.

While contracted services offer employment opportunities and possibilities for creative service design, it appears, judging from the British Columbia experience, that governments are more likely to exploit these arrangements for their cost-saving potential, while being less concerned about the quality of contracted services. Because fees are low and benefits are not provided, and because there is no assurance of continued employment beyond the current contract, career opportunities are limited. Thus, experienced workers are not usually attracted to contract work. Moreover, there is constant worker turnover as people leave contract work to take more traditional and stable jobs. The result is that the least experienced or trained people perform the majority of contract work. Yet, because of the complexity of the tasks and the need for the ability to work with minimum supervision and supports, contract work is best suited to the most able and experienced child care workers.

The present lack of standards for programs as well as practitioners leaves the field in a very vulnerable position. This is a situation which must be urgently addressed to ensure the quality of the services provided.

Impact on Families

The growing prominence of community child care represents a promising development for families in need of child welfare services. In effect, community child care brings services to families, lessening the chance that children are served in isolation removed from their family and community. At the same time, community child care workers are in a position to involve family members in the child's treatment. There is considerable evidence now that chances of favorable outcomes in child welfare services are increased if the child and the family can both be involved in the effort to change (Maluccio & Sinanoglu, 1981).

Community programs appear to be less bureaucratic in their organization and structures than many child welfare programs and more flexible and responsive in delivering their services. This is of considerable advantage in providing services and designing programs according to the unique needs of individual families. Thus, services can be provided at various times of the week, including weekends; the child or the family or some combination of the two can be the focus of service; and the services can be provided in-home or outside the home. Moreover, there is an informality about community child care that is attractive to some families. These qualities make community child care programs more accessible, again increasing the possibility that the family will join in the child's treatment.

As well, community child care services are sufficiently flexible that they can be offered at various points of need. Services can be offered to high risk individuals and families in the hope that problems can be prevented. Early service can be provided before a problem has grown too large and complex. Some community services can be designed to take the place of or shorten residential placement. This in turn maximizes the chances that the family can be kept united or can be successfully reunited. Finally, services can be offered after placement in order to help the family to accommodate the return of the child and help support the child's various community involvements.

Overall, community child care work appears to be an ideal medium for delivering family-oriented child welfare programs. Hopefully, community programs can maintain their present flexibility and client orientation. To the degree they are successful in doing this, community child care promises to be influential in increasing the family orientation of child welfare services.

The Need for Research

Although, as the trends and developments described above indicate, community child care is becoming an ever more significant branch of the profession, very little empirical research has been conducted on the topic of community-based programs and practice. It is not surprising, therefore, that as yet there is an almost nonexistent literature in the area of community child care practice, although there are an increasing number of descriptive studies about community programs. In this respect community child care is not too different from group care, which for many years lacked a research base (Powell, 1982) and is just now beginning to acquire adequate literature. From time to time the field of child care is urged to devote more effort into research endeavors (Beker, 1979). Community child care needs to take such exhortations seriously if it is to develop a solid professional base.

One part of the research agenda for community child care relates to two issues discussed earlier: 1) adequate educational preparation for child care workers, and 2) unclear boundaries for community child care. Studies aimed at describing and analyzing what child care workers do in the community would be helpful in determining the education required by community workers and would help define community child care and its relationship to other professions. Research is also needed to demonstrate the effectiveness and efficiency of community child care. Presumably such studies could elaborate on when, for whom, and in what circumstances community child care services are most appropriate.

Answers to such questions are by no means predictable. To date, community child care practice is based on accumulated wisdom, not on an empirical base. It is not being suggested that practice should develop only from an empirical base but rather that more empirical research would be desirable. As more research results become available, there may be some surprises which will lead to the re-examination of widely accepted practices. For example, Stein (1981) reports on the results of a demonstration study which attempted to provide community services to prevent residential placement. This study found that parents of children who were maintained in the community were *less* favorable about results than were parents whose children received more traditional residential services. Undoubtedly such results may be interpreted in different ways, but they serve to underline the importance of research.

Undoubtedly, community child care will attract increased research activity in the future because funders will be interested in determining whether increased reliance on community child care is warranted. This type of research provides a starting point, but it tends to be too narrowly focussed to provide the information required for the continued development of the profession. If the questions posed above are to be answered, community child care will need to generate its own research activities. To ensure that this happens and that the research is practical and useful, those who have the greatest stake in the development of the field—child care workers—must take an interest in this area (Kreuger, 1982).

SUMMARY AND CONCLUSIONS

Over the past several years, child care work has changed significantly. Fifteen years ago child care was almost always practiced in group care situations; today there are numerous community agencies which employ child care workers. The development of child care has been accelerated by a number of trends in the helping professions, most notably ecological concepts and a growing preference for family- and community-based services. As well, increased cost consciousness on the part of funders has helped community child care.

The practice of community child care takes place within a wide variety of settings, ranging from street corners to day treatment programs, and including schools, homes, and crisis centers. As a result, the definition of the field is unclear and boundaries are ill-defined. As the field struggles to define itself more clearly, it may be tempting to cast a wide net and include all things within the definition of community child care. But the profession would be better served by defining itself in a way congruent with its beginnings. Community child care should build on child care's humanistic philosophical base, its holistic orientation, and on the traditional ability of its practitioners to engage and relate to people effectively. Child care should remain a constant contact practice and should continue to emphasize the goal of helping people transform the events of daily living into growth-promoting experiences.

At the same time, it is important to recognize that community child care is different from group care in two important respects: 1) the context of the practice is the community, and 2) interventions often involve the child's family or others in the community. This suggests that additional skills and knowledge are required for the practice of community child care, and also that the work requires a shift from a primarily child-centered orientation to one that can include parents and other adults.

There are several key issues facing the field at this time. Perhaps the most important is that few standards exist either for community programs or for practitioners. Compounding the problem is the fact that, as yet, few educational programs prepare people for community child care work. Consequently, agencies can designate who is a community worker through their hiring process. Too often underqualified people are hired, leaving the profession in a very precarious position.

In spite of these concerns and issues, the growth of community child care is an exciting development for the field. This field of practice is well situated to play a key part in the ecologically oriented approaches to children's services which are so prominent today.

NOTE

1. The programs described were selected solely on the basis that they illustrate a cross-section of program types. There are, of course, many programs across the country providing similar services. No evaluative comment is implied, either on the programs included or on those omitted.

REFERENCES

Alberta. *Child Welfare Act.* (1984). Statutes of Alberta, Chapter C8.1.
Alberta Association of Child Care Centres. (1981). *Standards for child care.* Edmonton.
Alberta Social Services and Community Health. (1982). *Guide to community and residential resources.* Edmonton.
Allerhand, M. E., Weber, R. E. & Haug, M. (1966). *Adaptation and*

adaptability: The Bellefaire followup study. New York: Child Welfare League of America.

Anglin, J. P. (1983). Setting the sights: An assessment of child care job functions and training needs in British Columbia. In C. Denholm, A. Pence & R. Ferguson (Eds.) *The scope of child care in British Columbia.* (pp. 7–24). Victoria: The University of Victoria.

Austin, D. (1981). Formal educational preparation: The structural prerequisite to the professional status of the child care worker. *Child Care Quarterly, 10* (3), 250–260.

Barnes, F. H. (1980). *The child care worker: A conceptual approach.* A paper prepared for the Conference-Research Sequence in Child Care Education, Pittsburgh, Pennsylvania.

Beker, J. (1979). Editorial: Child care education and trainers. *Child Care Quarterly, 8* (1), 161–162.

Beker, J. & Maier, H. W. (1981). Emerging issues in child care education: A platform for planning. *Child Care Quarterly, 10* (3), 200–209.

Central Toronto Youth Services. (N.D.) *Outreach treatment programming: Theory and practice of contract work for troubled adolescents.* Toronto.

Comité de Prévention de Crime de la Rive-Sude de Montréal. (1983). *Répertoire des interventions préventives en matiére "jeunesse."* Montreal.

Gabor, P. A. (1975). *A theoretical exploration of the child care worker position in the treatment institution.* Unpublished master's thesis, McGill University, Montreal.

Garbarino, J. (1982). *Children and families in the social environment.* New York: Aldine.

Huntley Youth Services. (N.D.) *Programs of Huntley Youth Services Sponsored by Big Sisters Association.* Toronto.

Kreuger, M. A. (1982). Child care worker involvement in research. *Journal of Child Care, 1* (1), 59–65.

Le Centre d'Acceuil des Promotions Sociales Taylor-Thibodeau. (N.D.) *Resource development plan.* Montreal.

Lower Mainland St. Leonard's Society. (N.D.) Untitled document summarizing agency programs. South Burnaby, BC.

Maluccio, A. & Sinanogul, P. A. (Eds.) (1981). *The challenge of partnership: Working with parents of children in foster care.* New York: Child Welfare League of America.

Ministry of Community and Social Services. (1982). *The children's act: A consultation paper.* Toronto.

Ministry of Community and Social Services. (1983). *Three decades of*

change: The evolution of residential care and community alternatives in children's services. Toronto.

Ministry of Human Resources. (1978). *The family and children's services policy manual.* Victoria.

Powell, D. R. (1982). The role of research in the development of the
child care profession. *Child Care Quarterly, 11* (1), 4–11.

Ricks, F. & Charlesworth, J. (1982). Role and functions of child care
workers. *Journal of Child Care, 1* (1), 35–43.

Shulman, L. (1984). *The skills of helping.* Itasca, Illinois: F. E.
Peacock.

Shyne, A. W. (1973). Research on child-caring institutions. In D. M.
Pappenfort, D. M. Kilpatrick & R. W. Roberts (Eds.) *Child
caring: Social policy and the institution.* Chicago: Aldine.

Stein, T. J. (1981). *Social work practice in child welfare.* Englewood
Cliffs: Prentice-Hall.

Taylor, D. A. & Alpert, S. W. (1973). *Community and support following residential treatment.* New York: Child Welfare League of
America.

Trieschman, A. E., Whittaker, J. K. & Brendtro, L. K. (1969). *The
other twenty-three hours: Child care work in a therapeutic
milieu.* Chicago: Aldine.

VanderVen, K. D. (1979). Developmental characteristics of child care
workers and design of training programs. *Child Care Quarterly,
8* (2), 100–112.

VanderVen, K. D. (1981). Patterns of career development in group care.
In F. Ainsworth & L. C. Fulcher (Eds.) *Group care for children.* London: Tavistock.

Whittaker, J. K. (1977). Child welfare: Residential treatment. In
Encyclopedia of Social Work. Washington, DC: National Association of Social Workers.

Wolfensberger, W. (1972). *Normalization.* New York: National Institute
on Mental Retardation.

Youth Horizons. (1984). *Program description summaries.* Montreal.

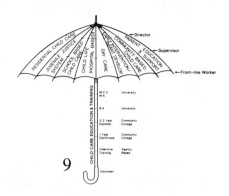

9

Parent Education and Support:
An Emerging Field for Child Care Work

JAMES ANGLIN AND ROBERT GLOSSOP

In this chapter, we will explore the role of parent education and support in the development of the child care profession. Several key terms are critical to this discussion. *Parent education,* as used here, refers to a broad range of programs and strategies designed to assist parents, or parents-to-be, in fulfilling their childbearing and childrearing responsibilities through the enhancement of their knowledge or skills. Included within this term are individual, group, and mass media approaches which focus on information giving, skill development, and problem-solving. Such approaches are usually designed and delivered by professionals. *Parent support,* on the other hand, encompasses formal and informal initiatives intended primarily to strengthen parents' emotional, social, or material resources. A wide spectrum of programs from mutual-aid groups to professional counseling share a common element in serving to provide a supportive environment for parents. Finally, *family support programs* are programs providing direct services to families which have a preventive orientation. Such programs may involve parent education or parent support approaches or may focus on other modes of family-oriented intervention. Weiss (1983) has identified eight types of family support programs which deal with:

1) Prenatal and infant development
2) Child abuse and neglect prevention
3) Early childhood education
4) Parent education and support
5) Home, school, and community linkages
6) Families with special needs

7)   Neighborhood-based mutual help and informal support
8)   Family-oriented day care

Child care workers, although currently involved in a variety of family support programs, have not traditionally been employed in the provision of parent education and support. Prior to presenting some recent innovative programs involving child care workers directly in parent education and support, several important themes evident in the current family support literature will be reviewed.

CHANGING UNDERSTANDINGS OF FAMILY LIFE

In recent years it has become obvious that the contemporary family takes many forms: nuclear, extended, childless, single parent, blended, separated, communal, dual-residence, gay, tribal, and so on. In fact, at any moment, the number of Canadians living in the stereotypic model of "mum at home, dad at work, and their own two biological children" represents the family reality of only 7 per cent of the population (Anglin, 1983a). Even if this stereotypic family model is expanded to encompass *any* style or combination of two parents and two children, it represents the actual living situation of only one Canadian in five. It is clear that we need to talk and think about different *families,* rather than *the* family as if it were a single, monolithic entity. We must look beyond structure and form if we are truly to understand both the unique experiences and preferences as well as the common needs and aspirations of diverse family forms. In her book *Families in Canada Today* (1983), Eichler suggests the need for a dimensional view of family to replace the traditional, monolithic view. Specifically, Eichler identifies six dimensions: "the procreative dimension; the socialization dimension; the sexual dimension; the residential dimension; the economic dimension; and the emotional dimension" (1983, p. 6). As she observes,

If we free ourselves from the monolithic notion that families have a particular structure and instead operate on the assumption that the structure of families is (and always has been) fluid, there is no reason to concern ourselves with the thought of the "death of the family".... In short, then, families are currently in a process of transition that can be expected to continue for another generation since many of these changes at present involve the middle aged, and patterns of familial interactions for the young are still in the process of emerging. These changes are touching the very basis of our definitions of self and others. We have neither fully understood what the changes are, nor have we sufficiently tried to describe and analyse them and to try to look at some of their implications for individual members of families and policy makers (pp. 25–26).

The implication for child care workers is the necessity to remain open to learn from families themselves about what their family life is like, what it is becoming, and what they would like it to be.

THE SOCIAL ECOLOGICAL PERSPECTIVE

An evolving awareness of the ecology of our social life (paralleling the concern with the ecology of our natural environment) has begun to sensitize human service professionals to the many and varied domains and levels of family functioning. It is no longer sufficient merely to view a family as a system. Each family, in a very real and significant way, is one system embedded in a series of overlapping systems. This realization of the complexity of family interactions within society requires a new set of conceptual categories to assist us to describe, analyze and understand it. The father of the current movement in social ecology is Urie Bronfenbrenner, whose book *The Ecology of Human Development* (1979) has radically altered the direction of thinking, research, and practice in the fields of child development, social services, and social policy.

In Bronfenbrenner's terminology, the complex inter-relations of persons within their immediate, face-to-face settings is referred to as the *microsystem*. The microsystem is the set of immediate, face-to-face relationships fanning out from a given individual in his or her immediate settings, such as family, school, church, peer group, and neighborhood. One can then analyze a child's or parent's environment in terms of the range of microsystems in which he or she participates. The next level, the *mesosystem*, consists of the inter-relationships between microsystems. Some important mesosystems for families include home-school, home-work, and home-neighborhood. The extent and nature of a family's mesosystems constitute important variables affecting the functioning of family members.

Beyond the mesosystem lie the settings within which the person or family do not participate directly, but which have an impact on their lives: these settings form the *exosystem*. It is important to recognize that what may be an exosystem for one person may be a microsystem for another. A social ecological "map" can be projected out from the particular person who is the focus of attention. Thus the father's workplace may be an exosystem for the child while being a microsystem for the parent.

Lastly, the broad sociocultural and institutional patterns characteristic of a social group, or society at large, constitute the *macrosystem*. This level encompasses the basic assumptions and organizing frameworks that form the societal blueprints for how things work. Different views of human nature, an individualistic versus co-operative ethic, democracy versus totalitarianism all represent phenomena at the macrosystem level of society.

The social ecological perspective, once its "high tech" sounding terminology is mastered, can provide important conceptual tools which can help make sense of what James Garbarino calls "these swirling social forces" (1983, p. 11) that surround all of us. For child care workers to respond effectively to the needs of children, parents, and families, they must be able to understand and be comfortable in assessing and intervening within all four of these ecological levels. Although an individual worker may be engaged primarily at the microsystem and mesosystem levels of a client's life, it is increasingly apparent that effective child care practice requires a number of child care workers to enter into the exosystems of their client's worlds, and that the child care professional associations address themselves to issues at the macrosystem level of society (Ferguson & Anglin, 1985).

INFORMAL AND FORMAL HELPING

Our understanding of the social ecology of family life is still in its infancy, however one of our earliest discoveries has been the daily fabric of family functioning relating to help-seeking and help-giving. A survey of helping relationships at the family level exposes a network of interwoven threads of helping, cutting across both informal forms of helping (helping provided by family members, friends, neighbors, and acquaintances) and formal helping (professional services). The range of helping sectors constituting the informal and formal domains are depicted in Figure 1.

Families

Different forms of informational, social, emotional, and material resources are sought, provided, and exchanged in each of these sectors. For example, in the most informal sector, families, both nuclear and extended family members assist each other in a myriad of ways through exchanging goods and services (for example, purchasing of food and meal preparations), sharing experiences and advice (parent-child, parent-

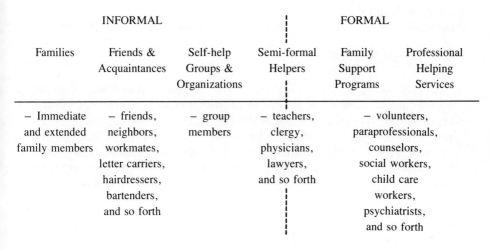

FIGURE 1. Spectrum of Informal and Formal Support

grandparent, and so on), gift-giving (birthdays, special events, spontaneously), and so forth.

Friends and Acquaintances

The web of personal relationships with friends and acquaintances that envelops families often provides important feedback and support to family members across a wide range of approaches to helping. When this network is weak, or largely non-existent, any family, no matter what its personal and economic resources, is more at risk of succumbing to stresses and strains that can spiral without such support.

Self-help Groups

Increasingly, as a response to many of the changes in family life alluded to earlier, family members are moving beyond the sometimes fragile and limited sources of naturally occurring support networks and joining with others sharing a common need or situation. Self-help groups represent one of the most powerful sources of experiential learning and social support available beyond the confines of the family itself (Katz & Bender, 1976). Self-help groups consist of persons who intentionally, and without being controlled by a professional organization, come together to help each other to achieve a common purpose, whether it be of a personal, social, emotional, medical, intellectual, or political nature.

Semi-formal Helpers

Beyond self-help groups and organizations can be found an important sector consisting of what we call semi-formal helpers. These helpers include professionals such as doctors, lawyers, clergy, police, and teachers who have occasion to contact, or be contacted by, families at times of developmental or situational stress. As a secondary function of their work, they may be involved in a significant amount of counseling and referral to formal helping services. Being situated on the boundary between the informal and formal helping sectors provides such professionals with unique opportunities and responsibilities to facilitate the matching of families with various resources of the formal and informal helping sectors.

Family Support Programs

As was noted in the introduction to this chapter, there exists a range of family support programs which have emerged over the past twenty years in North America. Although these programs differ widely in terms of their specific target groups, objectives, auspices, and modes of operation, they tend to be characterized by a preventive orientation which often incorporates principles of networking, peer support, and the empoempowerment of parents. Some of the most innovative parent education and support programs can be included in this category. As noted by Weiss (1983), such programs tend to be based on an awareness of the ecology of family functioning and a respect for informal and formal helping networks.

> One of the most striking things about the recent evolution of these programs is their emphasis on a more ecological approach. This approach is based on the ecological principle that while the family is the primary institution that determines a child's development, other institutions impinge on it and affect the family's capacity to nurture its children. . . . The movement towards more ecological intervention strategies is reflected in the shift from the focus on individuals, usually the child, to an emphasis on the relationship and interaction between the parent and child, and increasingly, on the relationship between the family and formal and informal sources of support for them within the community (p. 3).

Professional Helping Services

Lastly we turn to the domain of the professional helping services. This sector includes all professionals primarily providing personal and family-oriented services, including counseling and therapeutic services as well as statutory interventions mandated by government legislation. These services can be provided under the auspices of public or private agencies and are increasingly focussed on crisis-oriented forms of intervention. The role of professional helping services is currently being questioned by governments throughout the western world; both the federal government and the various provincial governments across Canada are no exception. It is unlikely that we will witness further expansion of these services at anything like the rate experienced in the 1960s and 1970s. In the words of James Whittaker:

> Draconian budget cuts in child and family services, the continuing shortage of professionally trained child welfare staff, and the limits posed by energy shortages and by inflation all argue for the elevation of informal helping strategies to a first-order priority in child welfare ... it means adopting a state of mind that views strengthening the family and identifying social support networks as the primary goals and providing direct professional help as the secondary goal in service provision (1983, pp. 179–180).

Professional child care has come to be viewed as a temporary support service for the family, even when it involves placement in residential treatment centers (Maier, 1981, p. 59). Whatever the care or treatment modality, the guiding principle is to optimize the development of the child within the context of the family and community while seeking to minimize the intrusiveness and disruptiveness of the child care service.

With the preceding backdrop of discussion relating to contemporary family life, social ecology, and informal and formal helping networks, we will turn our attention briefly to a consideration of parenting in today's society.

A PERSPECTIVE ON PARENTING

In line with the recent reappreciation of family life and the nature of helping, a comprehensive study was undertaken by Rhona and Robert Rapoport and Ziona Strelitz (1980) which integrated findings from contemporary research in a variety of fields of inquiry. The study formulated a set of propositions that the researchers feel should guide our understanding of parenthood today. These propositions can assist child care workers in assessing their responses to the needs and realities of parents with whom they work. These propositions include:

1. Parents are people.

Just as parents need to be reminded that their children are persons (Chess, Thomas & Birch, 1976), so do professionals need to be reminded that parents are persons too! As such, parents have a wide range of needs—emotional, intellectual, physical, financial, relational, familial and spiritual—that require recognition and respect. A narrow focus solely on the needs and experiences of children, or even on the parent-child relationship, will ignore a large set of parenting issues equally important for the positive functioning of the child.

2. There should be a balance of fulfillment within families and between family and other involvements.

Parenthood involves responding to a continuous set of challenges which demand a balancing of the demands of friendships, work, leisure, community involvements and, frequently, spouse, as well as relations with children. One of the most difficult stresses on parents today results from changes to many traditional patterns in virtually all areas of family life, including sex roles, the division of labor, and child care. Each family is faced with the need to create and negotiate arrangements appropriate to itself and its members. It can draw from a wide range of socially acceptable alternatives. As such, there are no fixed formulas for today's parents or for child care professionals regarding what will be best for any particular family.

3. Parents' needs and childrens' needs are not always coterminous.

Although parents' and childrens' needs sometimes coincide, compromises frequently must be worked out, preferably through arrangements of mutual accommmodation rather than by unilateral use of force. Neither the total gratification of children nor the martyrdom of parents is realistic or desirable.

4. Families vary in structure and culture.

The pluralistic nature of society as a whole requires that professionals become sensitive to a range of values, beliefs, preferences, and customs.

As noted earlier, the wide spectrum of contemporary family forms and structures calls for an appreciation of the dimensions of family life and the variety of ways in which these can be addressed.

5. Biological parents are not the only people involved in parenting functions—nor should they be.

In Canada, there is an ongoing debate concerning the proper role of government in relation to the care of children, particularly the care of young children of employed parents. The issue of the impact of a variety of caregiving arrangements, from family day care to longterm residential care, must be addressed by child care workers if their expertise and experience are to play a significant part in the formation and evolution of public and institutional policies on parenting and child care.

6. There is no "right" way to parent: there are many ways to be a "good parent."

The rich and complex interplay of such factors as parental character and style, children's needs and abilities, the family's stage of development, and community opportunities (to name but a few) provides a formidable challenge to child care workers seeking to assist families. It would appear that we know much more about what goes wrong in parenting than we do about creating conditions that are positive for particular families.

7. Parents learn about themselves through parenting.

Parenthood is now being seen as an important phase in adult development (Galinsky, 1981). Child care workers who are parents will well remember the dramatic changes in their perspectives on children, child care, and just about everything else, that took place following the birth of their first child. Parenthood is a transforming experience which must be understood not only in terms of the impact on the child's development, but also in terms of the impact on the development of the parent.

Following this consideration of parenting, and informed by the previous discussions of family life, social ecology and helping networks, it is now possible to set forth a framework for viewing the territory of parenting. Figure 2 outlines in graphic form the range of parenting concerns utilizing the ecological levels as outlined by Bronfenbrenner which were highlighted previously.

At the center of the figure we have placed the parent, indicating that the parent has a variety of personal needs. Moving beyond the sphere of

FIGURE 2. The Ecology of Parent Functioning

the parent as an individual person, we find a range of people in various settings which constitute the parent's microsystem. Members characteristically include spouse or ex-spouse, children, relatives, teachers, friends, workmates, neighbors, human service workers (such as doctors or social workers), and local merchants and decision-makers. Included as well, recognizing their important roles, are community groups (such as church, recreation, and social groups) and local media outlets (including radio, television, and newspapers). As we have noted earlier, it is the relationships between the persons in various microsystem settings that constitute the parent's mesosystem. Different parents, of course, will be characterized by both different microsystem and mesosystem networks.

Beyond the circle of immediate personal contacts are depicted the broader exosystems which extend beyond the microsystem level of the parent's direct experience. For example, there will likely be levels in the parent's work system (agency, company, corporation, and so forth) that lie beyond the parent's direct involvement. However, it is important to understand that the impact of decisions and organizational procedures at the exosystem level is continuously, and sometimes dramatically, experienced in the daily lives of parents and their families. Often this level of impact is not clearly acknowledged by families, and family members can blame themselves for the negative impact of the exosystem.

Finally, encompassing all of these subsystems—the individual parent, the microsystem, the mesosystem, and the exosystem—is the macrosystem, consisting of the overarching and all-pervasive ideological, cultural, and institutional patterns of our society as a whole. Fundamental beliefs and patterns related to childhood, childrearing, normal family functioning and effective parenting differ considerably across cultures and throughout history within cultures.

With this understanding of the world of parenting, we will now turn to a consideration of some exciting and highly innovative responses to parents' needs for education and support involving child care workers.

PARENT EDUCATION AND SUPPORT: THE CHILD CARE RESPONSE

As a basis for reviewing several programs in which child care workers have addressed the needs of parents (as opposed to their children), a continuum of parent education needs and related professional responses, adapted from the work of Dokecki (Powell, 1984), can provide a useful guide. The continuum consists of four levels which are dynamic and overlapping. That is, most parent education or support programs will address more than one level of need or response.

This continuum identifies parent needs (from the need to anticipate future developments to the need for protection of the child) and professional responses (from provision of information to direct intervention). As the needs of the parents become more acute, professional services become more intensive.

Four program approaches involving child care workers in addressing different dimensions of the continuum of parent needs will be described.

Level/Type of Need		Worker Response
Level I:	Parents provide well for their children on a day-to-day basis and evidence no obvious parent education needs	Prospective mode: worker provides anticipatory guidance relating to future developmental needs
Level II:	Parents manage well most of the time, but are somewhat uneasy about specific childrearing skills; they unknowingly engage in certain childrearing practices likely to lead to difficulties in the future	Resource mode: worker is available to parents who inquire about specific childrearing matters
Level III:	Parents' children have difficulty relating to others, including their parents; parents may be doing many things well, and have not abdicated the parent role	Collaborative mode: worker and parents work together to identify possible solutions to problems causing difficulty for the child
Level IV:	Parents' social, emotional and material resources are not sufficient to provide for the growth and development needs of their children	Protective mode: worker may need to monitor parent-child situation closely; ultimately the child or parent may need to be removed from the home

FIGURE 3. Continuum of Parent Needs and Worker Responses

The Primary Prevention Project

A notable program developed by child care workers, which addresses the prospective and resource needs of parents, is the Primary Prevention Project carried out under the auspices of the Canadian Mental Health Association, Ontario Division. The project involved ten child care workers in preparatory work with parents on the development of course content, with close collaboration by other professionals, including educators, psychiatrists, psychologists, and social workers. The project, true to the best principles of child care work, went directly to the clients (in this case parents) to ascertain their needs. Feedback from over one thousand parents in more than eighteen cities in Ontario confirmed that parents had two fundamental needs: "first, support in their role as parents and second, techniques that help them in their task" (Canadian Mental Health Association, 1982, p. 6).

The authors stress in the Project Instructors Manual that:

> Certain qualities aid the development of good parenting skills . . . parents who *understand* the importance of nurturing children, who have the ability to *communicate effectively* with their children, explore *flexible responses, empathize,* and who have acquired *insight* into their child's needs and their own behaviour, tend to parent well (CMHA, 1982, p. 6, emphasis in original).

The delivery format for the program consists of weekly sessions held over a ten-week period facilitated by trained leaders who have, according to the Ontario college DACUM classification, "Child Care Worker Level III minimum or equivalency" (CMHA, 1982, p. 7), and: "a) demonstrated teaching ability with parents; b) broad knowledge of basic child care skills; c) broad knowledge of normal growth and development of children and adolescents; d) familiarity with community resources." Others with three years of direct experience with children and a wide range of demonstrated abilities in group work, child care skills, sensitivity to parental values and roles, knowledge of community resources, and respect for confidentiality could also be selected for leadership training in the project.

Parents are asked to examine their own feelings and experiences in relation to situations and to participate in role plays. Situations are structured in order to provide an experiential basis ("grounding") not found in more traditional discussion formats. In addition to sessions, parents are provided with practice-oriented homework. Specific content includes: communication techniques; food (nutritional and emotional aspects); family routines; establishing limits and appropriate consequences; anchor points (aspects of the daily routine that represent primary interaction between the parent and child); play and family togetherness; the child, family, and school; and the child and the community.

Such features as the initial and extensive assessment of parents' needs, the emphasis on grounding, and the practical orientation to daily routines and interactions provide a strong flavor of child care work and serve to make this approach a flexible alternative to the more traditional and highly structured programs.

The ABC Project

A second approach, addressing parent needs primarily through the collaborative mode, was developed at the Clarke Institute for Psychiatry in Toronto. Developing out of a day-treatment, operant conditioning program for autistic children, the ABC (A for Analysis; B for Behavior; and C for Change) Project involves child care workers in the provision of assessment and intervention services for families in the context of their own homes and community (Webster, Somjen, Sloman, Bradley, Mooney & Mack, 1979).

This project places a heavy emphasis on modeling and teaching behavioral techniques and involving parents as crucial members of the planning team. In conjunction with the home-based program, a Parent Education and Discussion (PED) program is also carried out. As the authors note, "after some experimentation with 'dynamic' approaches, we adopted a fairly didactic format in which one member more-or-less lectured for 40 minutes and then led the group in discussion around the specific theme which had been introduced earlier" (Webster et al., 1979, p. 16). The authors also observe that more personal matters generally emerge in the discussion, and that parents can sometimes make more effective presentations than the child care workers or other professionals. As well, the experience indicates that "while family-centered child care work can offer plenty of satisfaction, it . . . can be very wearing" (p. 17). The support of concerned and knowledgeable colleagues is deemed to be essential for the child care workers involved in such intense and relatively autonomous functioning.

The authors conclude by recommending that "child care training programs should teach students the skills needed for success in this kind of work since more child care programs will likely be centered on the family in future years" (p. 17). Prior to considering issues of education and training for parent education and support, two types of programs addressing parent needs through the protective mode will round out our discussion of child care program examples.

The Special Services for Children Program

A recent development in the child care field has been the advent of community-based family support programs which assign responsibility to child care workers for providing intensive parent education and support in various forms where a child is at risk. In British Columbia, for example, the Ministry of Social Services and Housing contracts on a yearly basis with private societies under the Special Services for Children program to provide child care workers to families identified by the ministry in an attempt to reduce the risk that a child may need to be taken into care. The Special Services society, in turn, contracts with individual child care workers to provide an agreed-upon number of hours of service to the family. Characteristically, this entails about five hours per week; contracts generally run for a three-month period with the option of being renewed should circumstances warrant. Current contracting procedures and policies do not allow for parent groups to be provided on this basis, but some societies see the value of such a service and would be eager to develop group programs were funding available. Such contract services can provide education and support for families requiring a protective orientation when removal of the child is not yet the intervention of choice.

Groups for Parents of Children in Residential Care

Traditionally, child care intervention involved the removal of the child from the home and the provision of substitute care in a foster residence or institution. In recent years, even this extreme response to inadequate family situations has come to be viewed as a temporary supplementary service which needs to maintain ties with parents both to enhance the effectiveness of treatment while the child is in care and to prepare for the child's return home. Such strategies as home visits, brief and extended visits of family members to the program, and family counseling have been common elements in residential child care work for some time (Littauer, 1980). However, the development of parent groups offering education and support for parents of children in care does not appear to have been widely adopted as a key aspect of family involvement.

As has been demonstrated by a number of studies (Coates, 1981; Mahoney, 1981; Whittaker & Garbarino, 1983), family support is both one of the best predictors of a child's success in residential treatment and the most important single factor in determining the child's postdischarge adaptation. Anglin (1985), in providing a framework for the development of education and support groups for parents of children in residential care, suggests a continuum of parent groups which can complement the treatment program at all stages. At, or prior to, intake, parents could be invited to an orientation session which could serve as a non-threatening introduction to the staff, program, and facilities. Such a session could set a tone for future involvement and initiate a supportive group process. During the child's stay in the residence, child care workers could offer focussed sessions relating to areas of strong parental concern, such as establishing routines, limit-setting, and discipline without force. These sessions could be didactic and minimally threatening in the early stages until parents are ready to share in a more personal manner, similar to the Parent Education and Discussion Program (PED). Following discharge of the child, sessions could be offered relating to the particular concerns of families with a returning child, such as school adjustment, the use of community resources, communicating with friends and extended family, and re-establishing some form of family equilibrium. For those willing and able to make use of an ongoing support group, child care workers could facilitate the initiation of such a group or refer parents to such groups in the community.

ASSESSING THE NEED FOR EDUCATION AND TRAINING

Although there is no comprehensive information on the types of programs involving child care workers in parent education and support across Canada, data have been gathered in British Columbia on the extent to which child care workers in four types of programs are involved in "parenting skills training" (Anglin, 1983b). Parenting skills training was defined as "assisting parents to learn and develop child-related skills." Responses were gathered in structured interviews with 46 employers of child care workers throughout the province, who as a group employed 576 workers. The two major urban centers (Vancouver and Victoria) and the northern and interior regions were sampled across four types of child care programs: residential care (225 workers); educational (64 workers); family support[1] (government employed, community-based workers—127 workers); and special services (private agency, community-based contract workers—160 workers). The family support workers were most frequently involved in parenting skills training (93.7 per cent of workers), residential care workers, perhaps surprisingly, were next (69.3 per cent), with the other two groups—educational and special services—the least involved (56.3 and 55 per cent). The overall percentage of child care workers involved in parenting skills training was 68.6 per cent, which placed this job function in twelfth place in a ranking of all twenty-one direct service job functions. In terms of workers with a significant need for further education and training, parenting skills training was ranked seventh by employers, with 63.9 per cent of workers in need. Interestingly, when asked directly, 81.6 per cent of workers indicated they had a high interest or need for further education and training in this area, representing a ranking of fourth in relation to all twenty-one job functions. Thus, this area of child care work was identified in the survey findings as a likely "growth area" in terms of future education and training.

Following completion of the survey, one of the authors offered workshops on parent education at regional and national child care conferences and through community college extension programs. A strong response, indicated by both the number and enthusiasm of participants, appeared to confirm the high relevance of this area for child care workers in general. As an elective in the School of Child Care at the University of Victoria, a course combining an introduction to normative family development with a review of parent education and support approaches has been offered since 1982.

STRENGTHS AND LIMITATIONS OF CHILD CARE WORKERS

As more child care workers are becoming involved in various approaches to parent education and support, a number of characteristic strengths and limitations are becoming apparent. Probably the greatest strength lies in the child care workers' direct experience of a variety of children with a range of needs across a number of settings. No other professional has such a broad perspective of the day-to-day functioning of children. Secondly, child care workers characteristically possess a developmental (as opposed to pathological) orientation to child functioning. Parents, as much as professional workers, need such an understanding of normative child development. And thirdly, child care workers are generally able, as a result of their mandate and style of work, to participate with parents and children in their natural environments of home, school, and community. As such, they are in an excellent positon both to observe and provide feedback on daily routines and behaviors which form the essence of parent-child interaction.

Child care workers also tend to have several limitations in relation to working with parents. One of the limiting factors, acutely perceived by many workers themselves, is the fact that child care workers tend to be relatively young and childless. This immediately raises doubts as to credibility in the eyes of parents and a realization that, in spite of professional expertise, they are lacking relevant personal experience.

A second limitation which has to be addressed in relation to the traditional child care role is the tendency of workers to over-identify with the child and to define themselves solely as advocates for the child. Child care workers are sometimes perceived, and often justifiably, as siding with the "innocent" child against the "hostile" or "ignorant" parent. Child care workers in general, not only those involved in parent education and support activities, need to ensure that in advocating for the child they do so in a manner congruent with a respect for the strengths and potentials of the parents and family as a whole.

A further aspect relating to parent group leadership pertains to the role of the leader. Parent groups vary in their emphasis on three major dimensions: knowledge, skills, and emotional support. Except for the relatively small number of groups emphasizing a high degree of knowledge dissemination, the most effective role for a group leader is as a facilitator, rather than an expert. As a facilitator, a child care worker can utilize skills in group dynamics and interpersonal communication to assist parents in sharing their experiential expertise relating to parenting concerns. The parents themselves can contribute important information on norms relating to child development and parenting practices in the community. The worker with particular child- and family-related experience and training can offer another useful perspective as a resource rather than as "the expert."

PROGRAM EFFECTIVENESS: A CAUTIONARY NOTE

Perhaps the major issue in the field of parent education and support is the evaluation of its effectiveness. Current enthusiasm for the various approaches tends to assume that all parent education and support efforts are unqualifiably good—the more the better! Two recent studies suggest that parent group approaches may not be benign and may in fact encourage some of the very behaviors they are seeking to reduce or eliminate.

Shain, Suurvali and Kilty (1980) report on an evaluation of a parenting skills program which was implemented to assess the impact of enhancing parents' communication skills about their children's alcohol use. It is important to note that this program utilized trained group leaders who implemented a series of ten two-hour sessions over a period of ten weeks which were based largely on Thomas Gordon's parent effectiveness training content supplemented by other sources.

The evaluation determined that if mom and dad smoked and drank it was *more* likely that their children would smoke and drink as communication improved. Further, in the evaluator's own words:

> There was some evidence... that PCP (Parent Communication Project) could be *divisive* [emphasis in original] in families, e.g., where mother came against the wishes of father.... This divisive ness was reflected in children's perceptions of parents behaviour— mothers becoming more accepting, fathers more rejecting. Clearly this sets up quite a bit of tension in the family. This effect was only formally observed in lower S.E.S. (socio-economic status) families but it was seen informally in middle-class families too where at-

tendance at the course by women reportedly had at least a temporarily disruptive effect on marital harmony. Sometimes, it was permanent. Several divorces or separate household arrangements may
have been stimulated by attendance at the course (Shain, quoted in
Anglin, 1984).

Another researcher, referring to a different parenting program, has also
noted that "it is possible that the support groups had a negative effect on
relationships with spouses" (Kagey, Vivace & Lutz, 1981). These observations ought to give us pause for reflection. With tens of thousands
of parents, the vast majority mothers attending on their own, all subjected to parent group experiences, it is incumbent on those offering programs to ensure that they "first do not harm." It may well be that some
current approaches are indeed doing more harm than good to family life.
However, few programs have even attempted to assess their effects in a
manner that would bring forth such data. It is essential that, in addition to
cost-benefit analyses, such data be sought out in future evaluation efforts.

It would appear that for both economic and theoretical reasons, the
coming decade will see continued high interest in the area of parent education and support. Several trends will likely be important in this regard,
including the continued questioning of professionalism, the retrenchment
of government services, and the weakening of the traditional economic
structures. In seeking to contribute to the support of children and
families, child care workers will need to draw upon the literature of numerous disciplines and become involved in advocacy at the macrosystem
level of society as well as in direct work with parents.

SUMMARY

This chapter has introduced the reader to one of the most promising
and challenging areas of child care work. The roles and methodologies
for child care workers have only begun to be sketched out, and much developmental and ground-breaking work has yet to be done. As we seek to
intervene in the lives of children, parents, and families, we need to develop our understanding of the changes taking place in family life, the
social ecology of human development, informal and formal helping, the
realities of parenting, and the strengths and limitations of parent education and support programs.

As a profession, child care is in a unique position to build on its considerable strengths and to shift its modes of operation to best suit the
needs and realities of parents. A first step in this direction will be the ac-

ceptance of a new vision of the child care profession and an unfailing commitment to the well-being of children and families.

NOTE

1. The Family Support Worker Program originally established under the auspices of the B.C. Ministry of Human Resources (now Social Services and Housing) was terminated in October 1983. Data on the program are presented here because of its innovative nature. For a detailed postmortem on the Family Support Worker Program, refer to Currie and Pishalski, 1983.

REFERENCES

Anglin, J. P. (1983a). *The 7% solution: The myth of the "normal," "typical" Canadian family*. Unpublished manuscript, School of Child Care, University of Victoria.

Anglin, J. P. (1983b). Setting the sights: An assessment of child care job functions and training needs in British Columbia. In C. Denholm, A. Pence & R. V. Ferguson (Eds.) *The scope of professional child care in British Columbia: Part I* (2d ed.), pp. 9–24. University of Victoria.

Anglin, J. P. (Ed.) (1984). *Proceedings of education and support for parenting: An ecological perspective on primary prevention*. Symposium held at the University of Victoria, British Columbia: Health and Welfare Canada.

Anglin, J. P. (1985). Developing education and support groups for parents of children in residential care. *Residential Care and Treatment, 3* (2), 15–27.

Brim, O. G., Jr. (1965). *Education for childrearing*. New York: The Free Press.

Bronfenbrenner, U. (1979). *The ecology of human development: Experiments by nature and design*. Cambridge, Massachusetts: Harvard University Press.

Canadian Mental Health Association (1982). *The primary prevention project instructors manual*. Toronto.

Caplan, G. (1974). Support systems. In G. Caplan (Ed.) *Support systems and community mental health.* New York: Basic Books.

Chess, S., Thomas, A. & Birch, H. G. (1976). *Your child is a person: A psychological approach to parenthood without guilt.* Middlesex, England: Penguin.

Coates, R. (1981). Community-based services for juvenile delinquents: Concepts and implications for practice. *Journal of Social Issues, 37,* 87–101.

Cochran, M. & Woolever, F. (Eds.). (1983). Beyond the deficit model: The empowerment of parents with information and informal supports. In I. E. Sigel & L. M. Laosa (Eds.) *Changing families.* New York: Plenum Press.

Currie, J. & Pishalski, F. (1983). *Loosening the fabric: The termination of the family support program in British Columbia.* Victoria, BC: Report of the Southern Vancouver Island Chapter of the British Columbia Association of Social Workers and The British Columbia Child Care Services Association.

Eichler, M. (1983). *Families in Canada today: Recent changes and their policy consequences.* Toronto: Gage.

Ferguson, R. V. & Anglin, J. P. (1985). The child care profession: A vision for the future. *Child Care Quarterly, 14* (2), 85–102.

Galinsky, E. (1981). *Between generations: The six stages of parenthood.* New York: Berkley Books.

Garbarino, J. (1983). Social support networks: Rx for the helping professions. In J. K. Whittaker & J. Garbarino (Eds.) *Social support networks: Informal helping in the human services* (pp. 3–28). New York: Aldine.

Grubb, W. N. & Lazerson, M. (1982). *Broken promises: How Americans fail their children.* New York: Basic Books.

Hobbs, N., Dokecki, P. R., Hoover-Dempsey, K. V., Thoroney, R. M., Shayne, M. W. & Weeks, K. H. (1984). *Strengthening families.* San Francisco: Jossey-Bass.

Kagey, J. R., Vivace, J. & Lutz, W. (1981). Mental health primary prevention: The role of parent mutual support groups. *American Journal of Public Health, 71* (2), 166–167.

Katz, A. H. & Bender, E. I. (1976). *The strength in us: Self-help groups in the modern world.* New York: New Viewpoints.

Littauer, C. (1980). Working with families of children in residential treatment. *Child Welfare, 59* (4), 225–234.

Mahoney, A. (1981). Family participation for juvenile offenders in deinstitutionalization programs. *Journal of Social Issues, 37,* 133–134.

Powell, D. (1984). Enhancing the effectiveness of parent education: An analysis of program assumptions. In L. Katz (Ed.) *Current topics in early childhood education, Vol. V* (pp. 121–139). Norwood, New Jersey: Ablex.

Rapoport, R., Rapoport, R. N. & Strelitz, Z. (1980). *Fathers, mothers and society: Perspectives on parenting.* New York: Vintage Books.

Schlossman, S. L. (1976). Before home start: Notes toward a history of parent education in America, 1897–1929. *Harvard Educational Review, 46* (3), 436–467.

Shain, M., Suurvali, H. & Kilty, H. L. (1980). *Final report on the parent communication project.* Toronto: Addiction Research Foundation.

Steere, G. H. (1964). *Changing values in child socialization: A study of United States child-rearing literature, 1865–1939.* Ann Arbor: University Microfilms.

Strong-Boag, V. (1982). Intruders in the nursery: Child-care professionals reshape the years one to five. In J. Parr (Ed.) *Childhood and family in Canadian history* (pp. 106–178). Toronto: McClelland and Stewart.

Webster, C. D., Somjen, L., Sloman, L., Bradley, S., Mooney, S. A. & Mack, J. E. (1979). The child care worker in the family: Some case examples and implications for the design of family-centered programs. *Child Care Quarterly, 8* (1), 5–18.

Weiss, H. (1983). Introduction. In *Programs to strengthen families: A resource guide.* Report of the Yale Bush Center in Child Development and Social Policy and the Family Resource Coalition.

Whittaker, J. K. (1983). Social support networks in child welfare. In J. K. Whittaker & J. Garbarino (Eds.) *Social support networks: Informal helping in the human services* (pp. 167–187). New York: Aldine.

Whittaker, J. K. & Garbarino, J. (1983). *Social support networks: Informal helping in the human services.* New York: Aldine.

10

The Future of Child Care in Canada

ROY FERGUSON, ALAN PENCE AND CAREY DENHOLM

The previous chapters in this book outlined selected segments of the umbrella model of child care presented in the introduction. The variety of functions and settings depicted in these chapters indicate the degree to which the child care field has developed from its early origins in day care and residential care. While the generic aspects of child care (the essence of practice) will remain the same, the field will continue to evolve. The following is an outline of some of the forces which will affect the future development of the child care field.

NEW DIRECTIONS

Canadian society is undergoing major and rapid transformations which are impinging upon the human services system and affecting the evolution of professional child care. These trends are universal, affecting all of North America (Naisbitt, 1984); they include shifts toward a greater emphasis on information and information technologies, longterm goals, decentralized structures, private sector involvement, networking structures, and multiple options.

These new directions in our society have major implications for child care professionals. For example, child care professionals will have to place a greater emphasis on new and increasingly sophisticated forms of research to meet the demand for more and better professional information. New books, journals, and professional newsletters will be required to disseminate the increased amount of information generated in the child care field. And child care professionals will need to balance interpersonal, clinical, and technical skills to function effectively within the new information-oriented society.

In adopting a longterm strategic planning perspective, child care professionals will need to reconceptualize their roles and functions and expand them in a manner which adapts to the changing societal trends. They must move beyond a shortterm, defensive, and conceptually rigid position and take a broad perspective of the roles, functions, and scope of professional child care.

The movement towards more decentralized human service delivery structures means that services for children and families will develop from the ground up rather than the top down, resulting in greater diversification and increased responsiveness to individual needs. The number of professional opportunities and choices will increase, and child care personnel will have a greater potential range of involvement in the delivery of human services.

Concomitant with the tendency of governments at all levels to "downsize" is the transfer of more government services to the private sector, as well as an increased emphasis on self-help mechanisms. As more services and programs develop at the community level, new roles and functions for child care professionals, particularly those with an entrepreneurial orientation, will imerge.

The quest for multiple options has created a society in which there exists unprecedented choice and diversity regarding material goods, entertainment, food, and music, as well as in family structures, roles, and employment. Similarly, within the human service professions, a variety of therapeutic approaches are being used by multidisciplinary teams who characteristically adopt a pragmatic and eclectic viewpoint when addressing the specific needs of their clients. Child care personnel can no longer rely only on intuition and clinical experience or apply a singular approach to all the situations they encounter. In the future, the skilled professional will possess a variety of skills and will apply them differentially according to the unique clinical needs of each client.

The above is a brief summary of some of the new directions evident in our society and some of their possible implications for the child care professional. We will now turn our attention to the process of adaptation necessary if child care professionals are to take advantage of the opportunities presented by these trends.

ADAPTATION: THE SHIFTING NATURE OF CHILD CARE

In order to adapt to the many trends evident throughout North American society, the child care workers must be prepared to demonstrate openness and flexibility while building upon those attributes which are unique and central to the field. The child care professional will need to resist the temptation to hold on to restricting (though often comfortable) roles and definitions in the face of shifting social and governmental perceptions and demands. The ability of the professional to adapt and change must not be restricted by a rigid definition. Child care will need to be conceptualized as a professional field with a broad scope, one which can expand its roles and functions in response to changing service needs and trends.

The Nature of Change

It is clear that we are in a time of enormous change within the human service field. The child care professional can feel threatened by this change and can deal with it by ignoring or denying it and becoming entrenched in old ways. On the other hand, change within the field and in society in general can be viewed as an opportunity for the child care professional to develop new roles and functions which may not have been possible before.

The Change Cycle

Change is a continuous and ongoing process: the nature, type, and magnitude of the change may vary, but the responses are quite similar. Change usually creates stress which, in turn, throws the individual, organization, or system into a state of disequilibrium. In response, one adapts to the changes, and a state of relative equilibrium returns, until the next major changes occur and the whole cycle repeats itself. This cyclical process is illustrated in the diagram on the next page (Figure 1).

The change cycle depicts a process where an adaptation is made to restore equilibrium in the system. However, if an adaptation is not made, the system remains in a state of disequilibrium which, if allowed to continue, can create more stress, resulting in still greater disequilibrium, and so on. The downward spiral which ensues can be a destructive process ultimately leading to the disintegration of the system.

When applying this concept to child care, it is clear that every effort must be made to adapt to the present changes in the field. The child care professional cannot afford simply to sit back and wait for this crisis to pass because, in view of the cyclical nature of the change process, other crises will undoubtedly follow. Adaptation is achieved through continual monitoring and assessment of the changing scene, seizing opportunities as they are presented.

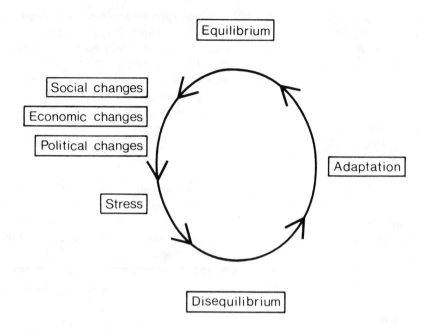

FIGURE 1. The Change Cycle

Considerations in the Adaptation Process

As the child care professional prepares for the challenges of the near future, he or she must adapt to the lack of rigidity within the structure of the child care field. Largely because of its newness, compared to many allied human service fields, child care has operated within a flexible organizational format. Child care professionals have also been able to observe the operation of other more established fields, identifying some of their structural problems, and avoiding similar errors. The resulting flexibility is one of the attributes of the child care field which will make it easier to meet the challenges of the future.

One of the primary adaptations is the need for diversification within the child care field. The scope of the field of child care must be expanded to meet changing societal trends. Every effort must be made to adopt an inclusive rather than exclusive attitude in defining the scope of the child care field. The similarities among child care professionals far exceed the differences, and the field of child care must be defined broadly, in order to include various child care professionals in residential care institutions, mental health clinics, schools, hospitals, day care centers, correctional institutions, infant development programs, and community-based programs. In Chapter One, we depicted this broad scope using an umbrella graphic in which each of the sections of the umbrella represents a different specialized area of service and the handle indicates the range of educational and training opportunities.

In order to be actively involved in the development of such a continuum of care for children and families, the child care field must also recognize the importance of a generalist orientation in its practitioners. It is interesting to observe that some of the more established human service professions now emphasize general practice after having focussed on increasing specialization for the past two or three decades. While there certainly is a need for specialists in all of the professional areas, the greater need now is for generalists who are capable of creating and operating within a broad continuum of services. In *Megatrends* (1984), Naisbitt warns that "we are moving from the specialist who is soon obsolete to the generalist who can adapt" (p. 32).

The child care field has avoided a high degree of specialization and, consequently, does not have to backtrack, as do some of the other professional fields trying to achieve a more generalized focus. Accordingly, child care workers will find adaptation easier.

It is clear that the practice of child care will continue to shift as the field adapts to the various social, political, and economic changes which impinge upon society. And just as change is a continuous process, so too is adaptation. An understanding of prevailing trends within society makes such shifts easier to anticipate, which facilitates the process of adaptation. It can be said that the health, well-being and future of the child care field will be based upon its ability to adapt.

AN EXPANDED SCOPE FOR CHILD CARE: THE IMPLICATIONS

A central theme throughout this book is the importance of developing an expanded scope of the child care field across the country. The first chapter outlined some of the prevailing trends existing in North America, ones which are having an impact upon the entire human service delivery system. It was suggested that instead of becoming entrenched in old ways and restricting definitions, the child care field should seize the opportunities provided by these trends and expand its roles and functions in response to the changing service needs. An inclusive rather than exclusive perspective was presented as necessary to define the scope of the child care field. The subsequent chapters focussed on some of the more typical settings and functions constituting the broad child care service continuum. It should be evident that, across the settings and activities described in these chapters, the similarities in child care function far exceed the differences.

As the child care field adapts to the prevailing societal trends, largely through diversification of function and scope, there are a number of implications to be considered.

Ecological Perspective

Throughout this discussion we have repeatedly observed the critical importance of the interplay of the child care practitioner and environmental context. Child care is, above all, a field concerned with the social ecology of human development. Increasingly, practitioners, researchers, and policy makers concerned with human development and care are adopting social ecological perspectives to help describe and explain more adequately the true complexities of their concerns. Recently Powell (1982) called for the adoption of such a perspective on the nature of child care. As described in capsule form by Bronfenbrenner:

> The ecology of human development involves the scientific study of the mutual accommodation betwen an active, growing human being and the changing human properties of the immediate settings in which the developing person lives, as this process is affected by relations between these settings, and by the larger contexts in which the settings are embedded (1979, p. 21).

It is our contention that a parallel perspective on the ecology of the child care field is also necessary to understand and promote its continued development. Our consideration of the following various elements asumes the adoption of such an ecological perspective.

Education and Training

In order to function within a wide scope of roles and functions the child care worker must receive broad-based professional training containing a core of generic skills. For example, the Conference-Research Sequence in Child Care Education (VanderVen et al., 1982) produced some guidelines for curriculum content which included areas such as human growth and development, program planning, group dynamics, communication, behavioral management, and so forth. This core of knowledge and skills could be applied to any setting in which a child care worker might be functioning and will facilitate a broader range of employment opportunities for persons with this generic professional preparation. Links to allied professions are also provided by this core curriculum.

Child care education and training programs will need to be designed carefully to maintain a good balance between the instruction of human and technical skills. As advances are made in the development of distance education packages and coursework for child care workers, attention must be given to the provision of good, well-supervised clinical practica which closely relate to these activities. Similarly, the student must also be able to explore and understand elements of self in the helping process. Distance education technology allows much of the training of child care professionals to be decentralized, but particular care must be given to the provision of those parts of the training process which do not lend themselves as readily to this format.

The basic education and training of child care professionals will be built around these core, generic skills, which form a foundation upon which the more specialized knowledge and skills required for a particular practice setting can be added as required. In order to keep pace with rapid changes in the field, the child care professional must be prepared for training which continues over an extended period of time. Accordingly, child care educators must work toward ensuring continuity between education and training activities which occur within service agencies, community colleges, and university undergraduate and graduate programs.

Career Ladders

In the past, child care services have been plagued with high staff turnover rates. This has usually been attributed to the existence of job-related stress in the worker, compounded by limited career ladders. Too often the pay and authority given to child care professionals were not commensurate with their responsibility. There tended to be an inherent avoidance of promotion within the field, as noted by Beker (1977): "If we continue to maintain, as many of us have, that promotions somehow taint the 'purity' of the child care worker, we will never attain professional stature" (p. 166).

An expanded scope for child care would immediately create more horizontal career ladders because there would be a greater array of employment opportunities. Child care professionals who were experiencing considerable stress, or those who simply felt the need for a change, could move horizontally to another area of child care practice and continue in their careers without disruption. Since there would be more areas of practice in an expanded scope, there would also be more vertical career ladders available.

Professional Stature

In order to meet the mandate created by a broader scope, child care must place greater emphasis on professionalism. It will be necessary to establish a somewhat delicate balance between this increased desire for professionalism while maintaining public accountability. We must avoid the pitfalls experienced by some of the more established disciplines where, in their zeal to professionalize, they sometimes lost sight of the needs of the persons for whom they existed. This self-serving appearance created in the general public a basic distrust of professionals, and this is reflected in George Bernard Shaw's statement that "every profession is a conspiracy against the layman." However, we can learn from the experience of our colleagues and work towards developing a style of professionalism which places the needs of the client before those of the profession.

Practice standards must be created to function as guidelines for professionals as they move out into a variety of new areas. While these collective standards need to be developed, they should not replace the individual standards already in existence.

In an effort to enhance professional stature, child care must create its own body of knowledge and professional literature and develop the ability to supervise its own practitioners. Child care must adopt a universal code of ethics in addition to sanctions for misconduct and must operate under the auspices of a professional association. These are some of the basic characteristics of any professional field.

To establish a higher professional profile, child care will need to be more involved in public policy. This has traditionally been an area in which child care professionals have not been very active, but political involvement is necessary when advocating for children and families. Responsible advocacy is an important function of the child care field, particularly in a time when human services are not considered a priority to many governments. Beker (1979) suggests that professionalism "is a reality that imposes special responsibilities on all of us" (p. 245). Our responsibility is to assist the evolution of professionalism in child care in a conscientious and thoughtful manner.

Professional Communication/Organization

As the scope of the profession expands, the need for effective communication mechanisms for child care professionals becomes greater. A method is required to connect professionals and provide them with a sense of the similarities in their functioning, despite the variety of settings in which they practice. They must be able to identify the common issues and concerns which are inherent throughout the many areas of child care practice. A broadened definition of the scope of child care will significantly increase the numbers of persons within the field, so that efficient co-ordination and communication must become central issues.

There will be need for small, decentralized organizational structures geared to regional issues and specific interests within different settings such as day care, residential care, hospital care, and so forth. At the same time, there must also be national and international mechanisms to function as an interface for this network of regional structures.

As the roles and functions of child care diversify, the need for information and support for individual practitioners and special interest groups will grow. As a result, professional networking becomes particularly important, and regional and central organizational structures can both facilitate this networking process.

Professional Influence

If the scope of child care is expanded and all the practitioners are effectively co-ordinated in communication and organizational networks as described, the power and social impact of this large, wide-ranging field will be greatly enhanced. Its increased size will contribute towards the establishment of a tremendous lobby power which can then be utilized by the central organizational structures when advocating for children. The child care field will have a larger role to play; rather than only responding to trends, it may, in fact, be capable of creating them.

In this chapter, we have emphasized the opportunities that are emerging from changes in human services and in the larger sociocultural context. It is certainly true that these changes also present dangers, not only for the child care field but also for children and families. The historical trend in society since the Second World War has been towards an increasing dependence upon formalized, bureaucratized, and professionalized forms of care and support. Our social and economic policies have served to erode the viability of family and community support networks. In this context, one which has reinforced our dependency and weakened our capacities to care for ourselves and others, a simple withdrawal of government programs and support in the name of "financial restraint" is both unrealistic and irresponsible.

Yet, these changes and trends have created some potential opportunities for the child care field. In order to adapt to the changes we are experiencing, child care must expand its scope while maintaining the concerns of children and families at the core of its professional identity. Roles, functions, and personal preferences must be adjusted in response to these opportunities in order that a continuum of care, which addresses the needs of children, families, and community life at all levels of society, can be established.

The current changes in society present the chance to construct within child care a new vision for the future. We must seize these opportunities yet bear in mind the observation of the French philosopher and writer, Paul Valery, who wrote, ''the problem with today is that the future isn't what it used to be.''

REFERENCES

Beker, J. (1977). On defining the child care profession. *Child Care Quarterly, 6,* 165–166.

Beker, J. (1979). Professional frontiers in child care: Unfinished business and new priorities. *Child Care Quarterly, 8,* 245–253.

Bronfenbrenner, U. (1979). *The ecology of human development: Experiments by nature and design.* Cambridge: Harvard University Press.

Naisbitt, J. (1984). *Megatrends.* New York: Warner Books.

Powell, D. R. (1982). The role of research in the development of the child care profession. *Child Care Quarterly, 11,* 4–11.

VanderVen, K., Mattingly, M. A. & Morris, M. G. (1982). Principles and guidelines for child care personnel preparation programs. *Child Care Quarterly, 11,* 242–249.

Authors

Left to right: Alan Pence, Carey Denholm, Roy Ferguson

Carey J. Denholm, Ph.D. (U. of Victoria)
Assistant Professor, School of Child Care,
University of Victoria, Victoria, B.C.

   Dr. Denholm currently teaches courses on group methods with children and adolescents, advanced practica and professional development. As his background has been in the Canadian and Australian education system, Dr. Denholm has concentrated on raising the profile of professional school-based child care through several key publications (*Canadian Trends in School Based Child Care* [1981], *The Scope of Professional Child Care in British Columbia* [1983]). Dr. Denholm's current research involves adolescents, stress, and the effects of hospitalization. He consults to various school systems and maintains a private practice with adolescents and families.

Roy V. Ferguson, Ph.D. (U. of Alberta)
Associate Professor, School of Child Care,
University of Victoria, Victoria, B.C.

   Dr. Ferguson began his career in Edmonton, first working at the Alberta Guidance Clinic and then on the Unit for Emotionally Disturbed

Children at the Glenrose Hospital. In 1973, he moved to Calgary where he established the Department of Psychology and the Preschool Language and Behaviour Program at Alberta Children's Hospital. While in Calgary he was Chairman of the Regional Children's Mental Health Committee and had cross appointments with both Psychology and Medicine at the University of Calgary.

Dr. Ferguson continued as Director of the Department of Psychology at the Alberta Children's Hospital until 1979, when he moved to Victoria to be the Director of the School of Child Care at the University of Victoria, until 1984. He was involved in the establishment of Child Life programs at Victoria General Hospital and Queen Alexandra Hospital for Children and provides consultation to the B.C. Ministry of Health.

Alan R. Pence, Ph.D. (Oregon)
Director and Associate Professor, School of Child Care,
University of Victoria, Victoria, B.C.

Dr. Pence's primary area of interest and work over the last fifteen years has been day care and working families. His day care work experience began with three years of frontline work with young children which was followed by several years of work as a staff trainer and program director. During his doctoral studies, Dr. Pence became interested and involved in various facets of research on children and families. He has employed historical and ecological/quasi-experimental approaches in day care research at community (Victoria) and national (Canadian) level studies. Dr. Pence is currently information co-ordinator for a National Day Care Research Network, which co-ordinates research with field and government interests across Canada.

James P. Anglin, M.S.W. (U.B.C.)
Assistant Professor, School of Child Care,
University of Victoria, Victoria, B.C.

Prior to joining the School of Child Care in 1979, Mr. Anglin worked in a mental health center, a therapeutic group home, at the Vanier Institute in Ottawa, and the Children's Services Division in Toronto. His current professional interests are the future of the child care profession, needs assessment for child care education and training, standards of practice, family support, and parent education. Publications include articles in the *Journal of Child Care, Child Care Quarterly, Apprentissage et So-cialization, Residential Group Care and Treatment,* and the *Journal of Children in Contemporary Society,* and chapters in various books on families and child care.

Dana Brynelsen
Provincial Advisor, Infant Development Programme,
Vancouver, B.C.

After teaching school in northern and coastal British Columbia, Ms. Brynelsen was initially employed to supervise the Vancouver-Richmond Infant Development Programme (I.D.P.) in 1973. As Provincial Advisor for Infant Development Programmes, she now assists communities in implementing and operating staff training programs and advises and supports I.D.P. staff. Ms. Brynelsen has provided consultation on the operation of I.D.P.'s throughout Canada and has spoken on the I.D.P. internationally. She also co-ordinates the Institute on Infant Development at the University of British Columbia. Her particular interests relate to parent-professional relationships; she is editor of a news journal for parents, circulated to 2,000 families in British Columbia.

Patricia M. Canning, Ph.D. (Windsor)
Associate Professor, Department of Child Study,
Mount Saint Vincent University,
Halifax, Nova Scotia

Dr. Canning's research and professional interests include child care policy, the development of child care services in developing countries and isolated communities in Canada, and the analysis of training needs for child care professionals. Recent projects include participating in the National Daycare Research Network's study of child care needs and formulating women's training programs in child development in Antigua and the Dominican Republic, as well as a study of the effects of early intervention programs on children and families in an isolated northern community.

Helen Cummings, R.N. Dip. Pub. Health
(U. of Alberta)
Supervisor, Calgary Early Intervention Program,
Calgary Health Services, Calgary, Alberta

Ms. Cummings has worked for ten years in community health nursing and for thirteen years in the rehabilitation field with mentally handicapped persons. She is presently involved in providing home-based support for families with developmentally delayed children from birth to 3½ years.

Gerry Fewster, Ph.D. (U. of Calgary)
Executive Director, William Roper Hull Home
and Director, Hull Institute, Calgary, Alberta.

Gerry Fewster is also Editor of the *Journal of Child Care* and Adjunct Professor of Educational Psychology at the University of Calgary. Over the years, he has worked in a variety of clinical, teaching, and administrative capacities, always with a fundamental commitment to the professional development of child care. He has presented at many national and international conferences and published in numerous professional texts and journals.

Peter Gabor, M.S.W. (McGill)
Associate Professor and Division Head,
Faculty of Social Welfare (Lethbridge Division),
University of Calgary, Lethbridge, Alberta

Mr. Gabor has been involved in the child care field for the past fifteen years. In that time he has had line, supervisory, management, and government funding responsibilities. Since 1982, he has been teaching and conducting research. Recent research projects include the implementation of the *Young Offenders Act*, communication skill acquisition by child care workers, and a study of perceptions held by young people receiving child welfare services.

Thom Garfat, M.A. (Lakehead)
Director of Treatment,
Youth Horizons Reception Centre, Montreal, Quebec

Mr. Garfat has taught at the School of Child Care, University of Victoria, and has been the Executive Director of the Pacific Centre for Human Development. He began his professional life as a frontline child care worker and is actively involved in child care in Canada and the United States as a speaker, trainer, and consultant. Mr. Garfat was the chairman of the first Canadian Child Care Workers Conference and continues to be actively involved in the planning of child care conferences at the national and international level.

Robert Glossop, Ph.D. (Birmingham)
Co-ordinator of Programs and Research,
The Vanier Institute of the Family, Ottawa, Ontario

For the past ten years Dr. Glossop has been employed as a sociologist and policy analyst by The Vanier Institute of the Family. It has been the integration and interpretation of family research in light of public policy issues to which he has devoted his energies on behalf of the Institute. Areas of research interest and publication have included: economics and family life; family policy; the integration of conceptual frameworks for family research; media and family interaction; and the design and delivery of family support services.

Carolyn A. Larsen, B.Sc.N. (U.B.C.)
Director, Child Life and School Services:
Montreal Children's Hospital,
Lecturer (part-time), Education Department,
Concordia University, Montreal, Quebec

Ms. Larsen has served as the director of the Child Life Service and co-ordinator of school teaching services at The Montreal Children's Hospital since 1966. She has had extensive teaching experience with early childhood education students and has been a clinical instructor of pediatric and psychiatric nursing. Ms. Larsen has been actively involved in the work of the Association for the Care of Children's Health, chairing its first conference in Canada in 1972, and serving as president and editorial board member. She is also completing an M.A. at McGill University.

Barbara Maslowsky, M.A. (Sheffield)
Staff Trainer, Probation Services,
Ministry of Community and Social Services,
Toronto, Ontario

Ms. Maslowsky's prior work experience includes being a classification officer in a penetentiary, a counselor in a corrections halfway house, a probation officer to juvenile offenders, and community education co-ordinator for the John Howard Society of Ontario. She is currently involved in the implementation of new legislation in Ontario, the *Child and Family Services Act* (proclaimed 1 November 1985).

R. Del Phillips, M.P.A. (U. of Victoria)
Investigator, Office of the Ombudsman,
Province of British Columbia, Victoria, B.C.

Mr. Phillips has managed institutions and programs for young offenders. In addition, he has been a sessional lecturer in the School of Child Care, University of Victoria, on topics related to young offenders. Mr. Phillips is responsible for analyzing complaints from young offenders in provincial institutions and preparing recommendations to ministry representatives. He is also the president of a large non-profit society providing community programs to children, youth, and families.

David Watkins, M.A. (Simon Fraser University)
Principal, Victoria High School, Victoria, B.C.

Mr. Watkins began his teaching career in the Kamloops School District; he later taught in Dawson Creek, Langley, and Victoria. He has remained a strong child care advocate and has made numerous presentations in support of child care within the school system.

Members of the Editorial Board
(LISTED ALPHABETICALLY)

Ted Dunlop, Ed.D. (Toronto)
Chairman, School of Continuous Learning, Georgian College of Applied Arts and Technology, Barrie, Ontario

Over the course of the past fifteen years, Dr. Dunlop has been involved as a child care practitioner, educator, and administrator in a variety of agencies, colleges, and universities in four provinces. At present, he is responsible for the development of all continuing education offerings at Georgian College, including child care and youth worker programs.

Mary Lynn Gokiert, Ph.D. (University of Alberta)
Program Head, Child Care Worker Program, Grant MacEwan Community College, Edmonton, Alberta

Prior to commencing as Program Head in 1982, Dr. Gokiert has had experience as a consultant psychologist to various school systems in the areas of student learning, parent and teacher consultation, and program development. This also involved the provision of and consultation to rural counseling services, including training of lay counselors and individual, child, marital and family counseling.

Dr. Gokiert has been a child care educator since 1976; her current interest is in individual and group counseling, child care methodology, and psychopathology of childhood including assessment and treatment.

Mark Greenwald, B.A. (Ohio State)
Co-ordinator, Special Care Counselling Programme, Vanier College, Montreal, Quebec

Mr. Greenwald is involved in working as an activity therapist, teacher, and counselor in a variety of mental health, education, and correctional settings. In his current work as a clinical instructor and supervisor he has become involved in the development of a model of supervision that can help child care supervisors understand, apply, and evaluate their own role and function. Mr. Greenwald is presently examining educational and clinical resources that would enable professionally trained workers to perform ''caring'' for all people with special needs and for all people across the life span.

Kristine L. Hansen, Ph.D. (Simon Fraser)
Assistant Professor and Chair, Department of Psychology, University of Winnipeg, Manitoba

Dr. Hansen is a developmental psychologist with research interests in children's social development. Prior to her academic training, she worked for several years as a child care worker with emotionally dis-

Youth and has written and spoken frequently on such issues as the *Young Offenders Act,* child sexual abuse, environmental health risks to children, the impact of national economic policies on families, fair play in organized children's sports, and youth employment. Most recently, he created the quarterly publication, *Youth Policy Today and the Canadian Youth Foundation.*

Christopher D. Webster, Ph.D. (Dalhousie)
Head, Psychology, Clarke Institute of Psychiatry and Professor of Psychiatry, Psychiatry and Criminology, University of Toronto, Ontario
   After several years as a Research Scientist at the Addiction Research Foundation in Toronto and as a Special Lecturer in Psychology within the University of Toronto, Dr. Webster moved to the Clarke Institute of Psychiatry in 1972. Within the Institute he acted as Research Co-ordinator of the Child and Family Study Centre working mainly with autistic children and their families. In 1975, he became Professor and Director of the Child Care Programme, at the University of Victoria. He returned in 1977 to the Clarke Institute of Psychiatry to take up an appointment as Research Scientist with the newly formed Metropolitan Toronto Forensic Service. Dr. Webster has written texts on autism and pre-trial clinical assessment and has co-edited books on mental disorder and criminal responsibility, the prediction of dangerousness, and clinical criminology.

Author Index

Subject Index